African Theatre
12

Published titles in the series:
African Theatre in Development
African Theatre: Playwrights & Politics
African Theatre: Women
African Theatre: Southern Africa
African Theatre: Soyinka: Blackout, Blowout & Beyond
African Theatre: Youth
African Theatre 7: Companies
African Theatre 8: Diasporas
African Theatre 9: Histories 1850–1950
African Theatre 10: Media & Performance
African Theatre 11: Festivals
African Theatre 12: Shakespeare in & out of Africa

Forthcoming:
African Theatre 13: Soyinka & Ngũgĩ

Articles not exceeding 5,000 words should be submitted preferably as an email attachment.

Style: Preferably use UK rather than US spellings. Italicise titles of books or plays. Use single inverted commas and double for quotes within quotes. Type notes at the end of the text on a separate sheet. Do not justify the right-hand margins.

References should follow the style of this volume (Surname date: page number) in text. All references should then be listed at the end of article in full:
Surname, name, date, *title of work* (place of publication: name of publisher)
Surname, name, date, 'title of article' in surname, initial (ed./eds) title of work
(place of publication: publisher).
or Surname, name, date, 'title of article', *Journal*, vol., no: page numbers.

Reviewers should provide full bibliographic details, including extent, ISBN and price.

Copyright: Please ensure, where appropriate, that clearance has been obtained from copyright holders of material used. Illustrations may also be submitted if appropriate and if accompanied by full captions and with reproduction rights clearly indicated. It is the responsibility of the contributors to clear all permissions.

All submissions should be accompanied by a brief biographical profile. The editors cannot undertake to return material submitted and contributors are advised to keep a copy of all material sent in case of loss in transit.

Editorial address
African Theatre, c/o Workshop Theatre, School of English,
University of Leeds, Leeds LS2 9JT, UK • j.e.plastow@leeds.ac.uk

Books for Review & Review articles
Professor Martin Banham, Reviews Editor, *African Theatre,*
Workshop Theatre, School of English, University of Leeds LS2 9JT, UK
martinbanham@btinternet.com

African Theatre 12
Shakespeare
in & out of Africa

Volume Editor
Jane Plastow

Reviews Editor
Martin Banham

JC JAMES CURREY

James Currey
is an imprint of Boydell and Brewer Ltd
PO Box 9, Woodbridge, Suffolk IP12 3DF (GB)

and of

Boydell & Brewer Inc.
668 Mt Hope Avenue, Rochester, NY 14620-2731 (US)
www.boydellandbrewer.com
www.jamescurrey.com

The publisher has no responsibility for the continued existence or accuracy of URLs for
external or third-party internet websites referred to in this book, and does not guarantee that
any content on such websites is, or will remain, accurate or appropriate.

British Library Cataloguing in Publication Data
available on request from the British Library

ISBN 978-1-84701-080-3 (James Currey paper)

Papers used by Boydell and Brewer are natural, recyclable products
made from wood grown in sustainable forests

Typeset in 10/11 pt Monotype Bembo by Long House, Cumbria, UK
Printed in Great Britain by CPI Group (UK) Ltd, Croydon, CR0 4YY

Contents

Notes on Contributors

Adesola Adeyemi holds a BA (Hons), MA and PhD from the Universities of Ibadan, Natal and Leeds respectively. His research interests are in postcolonial theatre and performance studies, particularly the works of Femi Osofisan, and in British theatre, especially the works of Kwame Kwei-Armah, Oladipo Agboluaje and Ade Solanke as they explore the politics of identity on the British stage. He also edits *Opon Ifa Review*, a journal of arts and literature, and teaches Drama at the Department of Communication and Creative Arts, University of Greenwich, London.

Ashish Beesoondial completed his MA in Theatre Making at the University of Leeds, UK, and is currently heading the Performing Arts Unit at the Mauritius Institute of Education. Apart from his involvement in theatre productions, his research interests extend to Theatre for Development and performance-based approaches in the teaching of languages and literature. He is also takes a keen interest in Creolistics and African Literature.

Eunice S. Ferreira is Assistant Professor of Theatre at Skidmore College, Saratoga Springs, New York where she seeks to combine scholarship with artistic vision and practice. Her dissertation, 'Theatre in Cape Verde: Resisting, Reclaiming, and Recreating National and Cultural Identity in Postcolonial Lusophone Africa', examines post-independence theatre in Cape Verde, West Africa from 1975 to 2005. Her scholarship focuses on the relationship of theatre to issues of language and cultural identity at the intersections of African, Lusophone and diasporic studies. She has produced, directed and choreographed plays ranging from Greek tragedy to musical comedy, with an interest in multicultural casting, translation and multilingual performance.

Colette Gordon is a Lecturer in the Department of English at the University of the Witwatersrand, following a lectureship at the University of Cape Town and fellowship at the Folger Shakespeare Library. Her articles on economic criticism, Shakespeare in South Africa, and contemporary performance have appeared in *Shakespeare, Cahiers Élizabéthains, Shakespeare in Southern Africa,* and *Borrowers and Lenders,* with work on Shakespeare and prison forthcoming. Her main project is a book-length study of the interaction between early modern credit culture and stage performance entitled *Shakespeare's Play of Credit.*

Christine Matzke teaches as Bayreuth University. She specialises an African theatre and literature, and has held posts at the Institute of Asian and African Studies, Humboldt-Universität zu Berlin, and at Goethe-Universität, Frankfurt am Main. Her research interests include theatre and cultural production in Eritrea, and post-colonial crime fiction. She recently co-edited *African Theatre 8: Diasporas.*

Juwon Ogungbe is a composer, singer, theatre music director and music educator. He has been commissioned by the Royal Shakespeare Company, Manchester Royal Exchange Theatre, LIFT, Collective Artistes, Badejo Arts, The Southbank Centre, Union Dance, BBC Radio Drama, amongst many others. He has also devised and led major projects for music in the community initiatives, with the British Council, Horniman Museum, the Victoria and Albert Museum, Sinfonia ViVa, Lontano, English Pocket Opera, Lewisham Education Arts Network and many others. Juwon has performed principal baritone roles in many operas, and given song recitals of a wide range of the western classical music repertoire.

Femi Osofisan, well-known Nigerian poet, playwright and dramatist, retired recently from the University of Ibadan, and is currently Visiting Research Professor at the Obafemi Awolowo University, Ile Ife. He is one of the co-editors of *African Theatre.*

Jane Plastow is Professor of African Theatre and director of the Leeds University Centre for African Theatre (LUCAS). She works predominantly on East African theatre as an applied theatre activist, theatre trainer, director and academic. She has previously edited *African Theatre 3: Women.*

Arne Pohlmeier is the German-born but Cameroon-raised director of Two Gents Productions. He is currently based in London, with strong interests in Shakespeare, African performance and collaboration. Pohlmeier has directed all the Two Gents shows since the company formed in 2007 and is currently developing further projects in Cameroon.

Kate Stafford is the founder and Artistic Director of Bilimankhwe Arts, an intercultural theatre company based in London. She trained at the Bristol Old Vic Theatre School and worked as an actor for 20 years before moving to Blantyre, Malawi, and embarking on a directing career. In 2003 she founded Nanzikambe Arts Development Organisation in Malawi and was Artistic Director there for three years, directing and producing more than 10 plays including a trilogy of African Shakespeares with Malawian actors.

Dev Virahsawmy has been working on Mauritian Creole, which he calls 'Morisien', the national language of Mauritius, since 1966. He writes exclusively in Morisien – a thousand poems, 24 plays, 20 short stories, 5 novellas, and a novel. He has translated seven Shakespeare plays into Morisien (*Julius Caesar, Much Ado About Nothing, Macbeth, Othello, Hamlet, King Lear, Twelfth Night*), and has also translated into Morisien *Joseph and his Amazing Technicolour Dreamcoat, Les Miserables, Godspell, The Little Prince of Antoine de St Exupery*, the *Bhagavad-Gita,* chapters from the Quran, the Bible, among other projects. Dev has been politically very active for about 20 years and currently devotes his time to the development and promotion of Morisien as the national language of his country.

Michael Walling is Artistic Director of Border Crossings and has directed most of the company's productions, including *Consumed, The Orientations Trilogy, The Dilemma of a Ghost* (co-produced with National Theatre of Ghana), *Twelfth Night* (African tour) and Dev Virahswamy's *Toufann.* Michael has also directed *Paul and Virgine* and *Macbeth* in Mauritius, *The Tempest* in India, and, in the USA, *A Midsummer Night's Dream, Romeo and Juliet* and *Two Gentlemen of Verona.* He was awarded a Drammy for Best Director with this last production. He is also director of the Origins Festival of First Nations. Michael is Visiting Professor at Rose Bruford College, and author of books and articles on intercultural performance.

Penelope Woods is a Research Associate with the Centre of Excellence for the History of Emotions, at the University of Western Australia. She is researching audience and emotion in early modern performance history as well as theatre spectatorship today, through collaborations with UK and Australian theatres. Penelope also works on cross-cultural performance and the international theatre tour both now and historically. Penelope is on the editorial board for *Parergon*, the journal of the Australian and New Zealand Association for Medieval and Early Modern Studies, and is a member of the Architectural Research Group at Shakespeare's Globe and the New Fortune Theatre Committee at the University of Western Australia.

Introduction

JANE PLASTOW

For Shakespeare, Africa was a place at the far end of imagination where men might grow into devils, freakish monstrosities or flawed and noble heroes, and the land was a space of wonder and magical beauty.[1] In the nineteenth century missionaries sought to use Shakespeare as part of the 'civilising mission' and as one of Ngugi wa Thiong'o's 'cultural bombs',[2] to teach English and inculcate an idea of the superiority of English culture. However, in the process, generations of Africans came to 'own' Shakespeare as part of their hybrid consciousness. Consequently Shakespeare was appropriated. His imagined spaces – 'fair Verona', and times – ancient Rome and Greece, could easily be reimagined as African. In postcolonial times many of Africa's most eminent playwrights, Dev Virahsawmy, Femi Osofisan and Tsegaye Gebre-Medhin among them, have taken Shakespeare's plays and made translations, adaptations and tradaptations for their own aesthetic and socio-political purposes.[3] A fair amount has been written about Shakespeare and Africa,[4] from the first production by presumably homesick sailors in Sierra Leone in 1607,[5] the school productions of colonial Anglophone Africa, to such seminal translations as those in the 1960s by Tanzania's first president, Julius Nyerere, of *Julius Caesar* and *The Merchant of Venice*,[6] to prove the linguistic sophistication of Kiswahili.

African Theatre: Shakespeare is interested in the relationship of Shakespeare to Africa in the early 21st century. The idea for the book originated in the Globe to Globe festival held in the New Globe Theatre in 2012 as part of the events of the Cultural Olympics commissioned to run alongside the sporting Games[7]. The Globe put on 37 Shakespeare productions, each from a different nation and a language from that country. Five of those productions were African. From Kenya came *The Merry Wives of Windsor* in Kiswahili; from Nigeria, *The Winter's Tale,* in classical Yoruba. Shakespeare's epic poem, *Venus and Adonis*, was adapted using six of South Africa's twelve official languages, while the world's newest nation, South Sudan, offered *Cymbeline* in Juba Arabic. The fifth production, *The Two Gentlemen of Verona* in Shona, represented Zimbabwe. Each play was put on for just two performances, a matinee and an evening show over two days, to generally large and multi-cultural audiences. They received enthusiastic reviews, albeit only from a minority of the more liberal press as more conservative newspapers generally failed to send reviewers.

At the core of this book are articles on four of the African Shakespeare offerings. The editors commissioned writers with a range of relationships to Shakespeare and Africa in order to enable readers to approach the productions from a variety of perspectives. There are two Shakespeare specialists writing on *Venus and Adonis* and *The Two Gentlemen of Verona* respectively, but while Colette Gordon is a South African writing with acute awareness of the complex issues relating to this particular *Venus and Adonis* being seen as in any way representative of South Africa. Penelope Woods writes as a researcher (at the time of writing a member of The Globe academic team), concerned primarily with issues of audience reception. We then commissioned an African and a European African theatre scholar to write about the Nigerian and South Sudan productions. Sola Adeyemi is a Nigerian actor, director and theatre academic who witnessed various stages of the production of *The Winter's Tale* in both Lagos and London and who explores differences in perception of audiences in each location. Christine Matzke wrote from Germany after visiting London to see the festival production, and had to undertake extensive background research for her chapter on *Cymbeline*, which is the first ever piece of scholarly writing on theatre from South Sudan.

Certain issues recur in these essays on single plays – questions of language, reception, understandings, Africanisation, patronage, translation and adaptation, and choice of plays and companies. However, we also wanted to ask writers to consider the implications of putting on these African Shakespeares in the old colonial capital at a moment when the postcolonial world was celebrating an ideal of Olympic togetherness. *African Theatre: Shakespeare* therefore opens with an essay by one of our series editors. Femi Osofisan is a leading Nigerian playwright with a love of Shakespeare and a rich history of writing theatrical adaptations and responses to a number of Western and Nigerian playwrights. Indeed our playscript for this issue is Osofisan's *Wẹsóo, Hamlet!* – a contemporary Nigerian take on an iconic Shakespeare play. Osofisan takes on board criticisms by other writers in *African Theatre: Shakespeare* regarding the way the Globe to Globe event was organised, with no provision made for helping the productions to tour in the countries they came from. Thus one might see the whole event as a piece of metropolitan vainglory, feeding London culture while ignoring African hunger. However, Osofisan also asks the reader to look at African cultural policies. Using the example of Nigeria, he examines how knowledge of Shakespeare has diminished, only kept alive through obligatory school examination curricula. He explains how and bemoans the fact that, following a model of colonial cultural philistinism, postcolonial African governments have allowed performance traditions, both indigenous and international, to whither with little or no state support. Discussion of the Festival concludes with a round table discussion by a number of African and European directors and playwrights who have all been involved in putting on Shakespeare in Africa. It was convened by Michael Walling, the director of Border Crossings. Juwon Ogungbe, Arne Pohlmeier (the director of *Two Gentlemen of Verona*), Kate Stafford and Dev Virahsawmy (the subject of one of our concluding articles by Ashish Besoondial), discuss with Michael Walling a series of questions about the aesthetics and politics of intercultural productions, and how Shakespeare is translated, adapted and received when put on in Africa and by African companies in European settings.

We were concerned that this book should not only focus on Shakespeare as produced for a London audience, but would also look at performances made in and for Africa. To this end, we commissioned two pieces from island nations, Cape Verde off the coast of western Africa, and Mauritius in the far east. Eunice Ferreira's article, 'Crioulo Shakespeareano and the Creolising of *King Lear*', examines the work of João Branco: a Portuguese man who sees himself as an adopted son of Cape Verde, and has set up both a theatre company and a theatre training school. Ferreira focuses on a recent production of *King Lear*, translated from a Portuguese version into the creole of the particular Cape Verde island of São Vicente. Ashish Besoonidal is also interested in creole but here in the Mauritian version. '"*Sa bezsominn Shakespeare la*": The Brave New World of Dev Virahsawmy' discusses the history of this radical playwright and political activist and how his plays embody political issues, through the use of popular creole. Further, Virahsawmy often borrows characters and situations from Shakespeare but takes them far from the original to debate contemporary concerns, such as abortion and euthanasia, as well as the larger issues of class and political oppression.

Few of the productions discussed in *African Theatre: Shakespeare* are simple translations, although all are in African languages. Language choice, as we see most acutely in the final two chapters of this volume, is an issue loaded with social significance. Creoles are the languages of the people, not of the ruling classes, so Branco and Virahsawmy are making strong statements of identity and allegiance in their choices of translation and adaptation. However, language is also interesting in relation to the Globe to Globe productions. The organisers wanted African languages: perhaps this looked simple from the outside, but which African languages would be chosen? *Venus and Adonis* became *UVenas no Adonisi* and used six South African vernaculars. The company putting on *Cymbeline* chose to speak Juba Arabic, sometimes described as a pidgin, although South Sudan has chosen English as its official language. Most bizarrely of all, the Shona production *Vakamona Vaviri Ve Zimbabwe* (*The Two Gentlemen of Verona*) was a translation of a version originally created in English by two Zimbabwean actors working in London.[8] It was only translated, again for London, for the festival, to represent Zimbabwe, although no funds could be found to take the work to the country where it could be understood.

Having chosen a language, the directors, playwrights and companies had to decide on a form and aesthetic for their production. Indeed, there have been previous attempts to create 'authentic' performances. Christine Matzke has written elsewhere about an amateur company of medical staff, all members of the Eritrean People's Liberation Front, who put on Shakespearean plays in the 1980s, during the national liberation war, in costumes improvised to reproduce Elizabethan dress.[9] In this volume we see translations, *UVenas no Adonisi, Cymbeline, Ìtàn Ògìnìntìn (The Winter's Tale)* and Branco's *King Lear* – although all have elements of adaptation and selection. Other pieces are more heavily adapted and Virahsawmy's plays sometimes use Shakespeare simply as a springboard for a wild, iconoclastic imagination. As Osofisan argues, most of these plays took the original story and re-imagined it in and for contemporary Africa. He raises interesting questions about whether something of Shakespeare's poetry and playwriting brilliance is in danger of being lost if all that is borrowed is a tale transformed to make an African point, about corruption, as in Virahsawmy; unity as in South Sudan's *Cymbeline*, or gender politics, in *UVenas no Adonisi*. The essays in this volume constantly ask questions about how companies can make Shakespeare meaningful for African audiences. They also ask who the chosen aesthetic is for. When I saw the Yoruba *Winter's Tale*, I, like many reviewers, was stunned by the fabulous masks, but Sola Adeyemi in his article on the production tells us that Nigerians thought the maskers poor and the masks possibly inappropriate to mainstream Yoruba culture. The implication is that this was just a pyrotechnical display for ignorant London folk. At the other extreme, Eunice Ferriera challenges the improvisational liberties given to the Fool in Branco's *King Lear*, questioning whether his antics were inappropriately populist: acting up to a home crowd.

African Theatre: Shakespeare asks many more questions than it answers, but the questions are fascinating, raising many issues about intercultural, multi-cultural and cross-cultural culture and performance which can be applied to other artistic endeavours. The book also points to possible trajectories for international Shakespeare in the 21st century which may be of interest to Shakespeare scholars previously unacquainted with how the poet has been adopted and adapted across the fifty-four nations of the African continent. This volume, via Shakespeare, offers just a glimpse into that continent of infinite cultural diversity.

NOTES

1 I think here of Caliban and Othello, and of the extraordinarily beautiful descriptions of the island in *The Tempest*.
2 Ngugi argues that:
> The biggest weapon wielded and actually daily unleashed by imperialism against [...] collective defiance is the cultural bomb. The effect of a cultural bomb is to annihilate a people's belief in their names, in their language, in their environment, in their heritage

of struggle, in their unity, in their capacities and ultimately in themselves. (*Decolonising the Mind*, p. 3)

3 Femi Osofisan, Nigeria's best known playwright after Wole Soyinka, is renowned for his adaptations of Western and African plays. He has adapted *Hamlet* (published in this volume as *Wẹ̀sóo, Hamlet!*), and *Love's Labour's Lost* (as *Love's Unlike Lading*). Dev Virahsawmy has produced radical tradaptations into Mauritanian creole based on works such as *Macbeth* (*Zeneral Macbeff*) and *The Tempest* (*Toufann*), amongst others. Tsegaye Gebre-Medhin, the pre-eminent Ethiopian playwright, translated both *Othello* and *Hamlet* into Amharic for the Ethiopian stage. The former was so popular it ran for three years in the 1980s.

4 See reviews below of the recent books *Shakespeare and the Coconuts* by Natasha Distiller and *Reading Revolution: Shakespeare on Robben Island*, by Ashwin Desai. Also 'Shakespeare and Africa' by Martin Banham, Jane Plastow and Roshni Mooneram, in *The Cambridge Companiion to Shakespeare on Stage*, *Shakespeare in South Africa: Stage productions During the Apartheid Era* by Rohan Quince and *Remembering 'The Tempest'* by Jane Wilkinson.

5 *Hamlet* was performed on a ship harboured off Sierra Leone in September 1607. This was the first known amateur production of the play.

6 For more on Nyerere's translations see Jane Plastow, (1996) *African Theatre and Politics: The Evolution of Theatre in Ethiopia, Tanzania, and Zimbabwe. A Comparative Study*, Amsterdam and Atlanta GA: Rodopi, Chapter 3.

7 For more information on the festival see the article from *The Guardian*: *World Shakespeare festival: around the Globe in 37 plays* http://www.guardian.co.uk/stage/2012/apr/20/world-shakespeare-festival-globe-theatre-rsc. The Globe festival brochure can be downloaded at http://globetoglobe.shakespearesglobe.com/schedule

8 All the plays put on were recorded and are available from The Globe.

9 Two Gents Productions was set up in London in 2007 with two Zimbabwean actors, Denton Chikura, Tonderai Munyevu, and a German director, Arne Pohlmeier. Their two-hander version of *The Two Gentlemen of Verona* was their first production.

10 See Christine Matzke (2004) 'Shakespeare and Surgery in the Eritrean Liberation Struggle: Performance Culture in Orota', *Journal of Eritrean Studies* (Asmara), 3.1, May: 26–40.

Shakespeare, Africa & the Globe Olympiad

FEMI OSOFISAN

The May 2012 Globe to Globe festival was energetically promoted. The organisers put out an announcement in which they proclaimed:

> ...the wild journeys of [Shakespeare's] plays, first travelled in English, soon multiplied into many fresh journeys, in a whole host of different tongues. We are bringing together artists from all over the globe, to enjoy speaking these plays in their own language, in our Globe, within the architecture Shakespeare wrote for...

In excited tones, they continued:

> Many of the world's greatest directors, over six hundred actors from all nations, and audiences from every corner of our polyglot community, will assemble to celebrate the stories, the characters and the relationships, which are etched into all of us. Shakespeare is the language which brings us together better than any other, and which reminds of our almost infinite difference, and of our strange and humbling commonality.

You could not but be infected by this enthusiasm as they concluded:

> A Globe beside the Thames is where many of these plays began their extraordinary journey. Another Globe beside the Thames is delighted to be bringing these plays, dressed in the clothes of many peoples, back home ... Please come and join us![1]

Of the 37 productions that came to the New Globe stage, five were from Africa – namely from the Anglophone, ex-British colonies of Nigeria, South Sudan, Zimbabwe, Kenya and South Africa. But the languages they spoke exceeded this total number of countries, because the South African contribution alone played in six out of its eleven official languages. Thus at that festival, spectators heard Yoruba, Juba Arabic, Shona, Swahili, and then Zulu, Xhosa, Sotho, Setswana and Afrikaans, in adaptations, respectively, of *The Winter's Tale* (*Ìtàn Ògìnìntìn* by the Renegade Theatre), Cymbeline (by the South Sudan Theatre Company), *Two Gentlemen of Verona* (*Vakamona*

1

Vaviri Ve Zimbabwe by Two Gents Theatre Productions), *The Merry Wives of Windsor* (*Heri Wanawake Wa Windsor* by the Bitter Pill Company), and the love poem *Venus and Adonis* (dramatised as *UVenas no Adonisi* by the Isango Ensemble).

This experiment at presenting a 'globalised Shakespeare' was, from all reports, a hugely successful venture. As was to be expected, it led to a grand multilingual and multicultural carnival of a kind that had never been witnessed before in London or elsewhere. Seats were nearly always sold out. Thousands of spectators who had either never been to the theatre before, or specifically to the Globe theatre, were attracted to see the shows, and spoke of the experience afterwards in near ecstatic terms.

The African contributions were not left out of this rapturous reception. *The Two Gentlemen*, for instance, was said to be 'a deft, dexterous and wickedly joyful production', but all of the plays were equally applauded. Reviewers in newspapers and on the Festival's website, as the articles in this issue recall, spoke of 'standing ovations' (Matzke), of 'irresistible performance', 'ecstatic evenings', and so on.

It is not hard to see why the performances generated such warm responses. In the first place, the actors were for the most part experienced and talented artists, working with no less talented directors. For some of them, the historic uniqueness of the occasion, the sheer euphoria of taking part in such an extraordinary event was like an inebriation: so intoxicating that it inspired them to spectacular performances. Actors from Nigeria, for instance, spoke of the unprecedented good fortune of coming to perform on a stage they had only read about in their classrooms and never dreamt nor imagined they would ever walk upon!

The structure of the Globe stage was an obvious advantage for the Africans as it was, ironically, not for some of the European companies, who found it strange and awkward. While the latter are more accustomed to performing in the enclosed proscenium spaces of the West End or the Barbican and similar conventional theatres, with their sophisticated technological gadgets, and with the audience separated somewhere in the dark, our African actors were very much at ease with the architecture of the new Globe theatre, which was built to recapture the original ambiance of the Elizabethan stage, with an open space and a thrust or apron stage, making no provision for any scenery or elaborate props, and, above all, where the bulk of the audience is fully visible, standing close to the actors on all sides.

This arrangement allowed the actors to have the kind of audience they would have at home, and this no doubt inspired them to give a better and livelier performance. Thus a mutual interactive rapport developed between the two – the actors directly talking to spectators and even involving them in the action, and the spectators in turn shouting back their responses, acclaiming or disputing statements, laughing aloud without inhibition at the jokes, singing the songs along with the actors, and so on. As Julie Sanders confessed in wonder: 'What this production also became a story of on the night for me, however, was one about audience participation of a very specific kind…'[2]

All this effervescence would not have been attained, I imagine, but for a factor which proved to be the greatest asset to these productions – which was the absolute flexibility that the companies were offered by the producers, to adapt the selected Shakespeare play according to their own desires and capabilities. For instance, by working in their own languages, the actors were able to dispense with the somewhat stilted diction of Shakespeare's English, and so to go ahead confidently to transform the Bard's characters and situations into their own familiar local ones. Naturally, this helped in no little way to enhance verisimilitude and to lend authenticity to the actions on stage.

By being relieved of the obligation to stick slavishly to the original play, the various companies could more credibly adapt the themes of the drama to the ongoing concerns of their own environments, as well as to the grammar of their own performance cultures. Again, Sanders confirms this: '[I]t became abundantly clear … that a number of the keynotes of conventional British theatre productions of this play would be joyously set aside, and, indeed, turned on their head.' Of *Ìtàn Ògìnìtìn*, she said '[It was] a show that reworked, rethought and intervened in Shakespeare's play in all kinds of exciting and memorable ways.' But her comments were just as valid for virtually all the productions, including those not from Africa, for all the companies took advantage of this liberty of interpretation. Some were so emboldened that they not only translated the storylines into their own preferred narrative idioms, but even went as far as to replace the original fables with their reworkings.

Thus it is no surprise that almost all the reviewers were dazzled by the incorporation of the resources of dance, music, circus, aerial skills, choreography and 'spectacular pyrotechnics', and so on — a composite mechanics of performance sometimes described as 'total theatre'. It is uncommon in British drama, particularly in Shakespeare productions, but a form with which those knowledgeable about African performance traditions would already be familiar.

In line with this reliance on traditional performance forms was the almost spontaneous adoption, and by virtually all the companies, of the story-telling format of our folk tales. This was obviously the most appropriate form for the barren, physical setting of the New Globe, and some of the productions exploited this to the full, even going as far as reenacting the call-and-response formula that African storytellers employ at the beginning of a performance to draw the attention of the audience. Even the 'stripped-down' method of the Two Gents' Theatre's version of *The Two Gentlemen* acknowledged, on the evidence of such plays as *Woza Albert!* and the work of Barry Simon, Mbongeni Ngema and Percy Mtwa to be a direct inspiration from the Township Market Theatre, in South Africa, can be interpreted, if properly studied, as only a sophisticated development of the one-man narrative performance of the *mvets*; the local story-tellers found in all our traditional cultures.

As expected, the flexibility even in the area of thematic interpretation would naturally inspire the theatre companies to slant their plays towards a familiar didacticism. Hence the Shakespeare play quite often became a parable about the sociopolitical tensions within their various home territories. The South Sudan script for instance, was overt propaganda for national unity. Aware of the problems of their new country as a 'multivalent, multivocal, polyphonic…even cacophonous' entity [Matzke], easily susceptible after years of struggle and civil war to fissiparous forces, the actors thoughtfully turned their production into a plea for unity based on compromise and mutual understanding. One of the actors, Francis Paulino, speaks eloquently about this:

> We are a country which has just come out from a long war. We are just starting from scratch. […] Maybe the issues for the government are security, housing, education. I am not saying these things are bad, but you need to remember that culture is one of the fundamental things. It is the one developing the country, and it is the one to help people. This idea of unity in diversity, it also needs to be there. …Back in [South] Sudan we have this issue of tribalism. […] How are we going to solve that? We are only going to solve it with culture. This is how we can unite.

Another actor, Solga expresses it in even more poetic words:

> This notion of performance as offering – as a gift given *first* to the absent and unfinished nation, and only *then* shared amongst the spectators in the global capital – framed the work ahead, and opened, for me, the stale corners of this messy play to fresh and compassionate readings.

This common approach of focusing on some collective problem to form the thematic kernel behind the appropriation of Shakespeare, also helped to turn what could have been a serious disadvantage into a positive asset for the companies in the area of actor recruitment and composition. As can be seen, except perhaps for the Two Gents Theatre Company, which was already an established group, almost all the others were *ad hoc* groups assembled for the occasion. Their names might be well known on account of previous productions, and of course this also applies to the names of the founders and/or artistic directors, but these facts were never an accurate guide to the performers in a particular project, owing to the constant turnover in the cast of actors. Mostly performers were recruited according to the needs of the moment.

It is not hard to see how this impermanence can have its problems, especially where the career of individual actors is concerned. In a situation where contracts are unstable or impermanent, one of the risks is the licence it seems to give to the director/producer to exploit the artistes, especially on projects where foreign exchange is involved. This is an issue raised for instance, in a discerning piece by Colette Gordon about the Isango

Ensemble from South Africa, where she reminds us of the litigation raised continually against Dornford May and Malefane by members of Isango, who allege that while international media, and company PR, celebrate Isango's productions from the township, a recurrent theme in the complaints from performers has been precisely that they *still* live in the townships, while Dornford May and Malefane, who travel to receive international awards (awards it is claimed the company were told would make them all rich), raise a family in the wealthy suburbs.

This is an aspect of these shows that is hardly ever discussed in reviews of the 'glowing performances'. Although Gordon states in fairness that it is very hard to assess either the truth, or the significance, of these claims, it is nevertheless a problem that we all know dogs all professional companies in which the actors are engaged on temporary contracts. On the side of producers, the advantages are of course obvious. Most importantly, for instance, it leaves the door open to the possibility of renewal and rejuvenation through fresh recruitment into the companies, while also helping to ensure discipline, for the actors, painfully aware of the rarity of such opportunities on our continent, are always careful to behave themselves and abide by company rules.

On this occasion in any case, the various groups were not just able to showcase talents that already existed, but also to cast widely among the available pool of actors in the country in order to reinforce their cast with the appropriate actors for specific parts. The preparations for Cymbeline are an illustration here:

> When news spread about the Globe to Globe festival, artists, scholars and activists from various backgrounds joined forces to form a new theatre troupe. ... It was not us who selected ourselves. People said, Derik is there, Abuk is there. Why don't you consult Taban as an advisor? ...Cast and creative team came from all walks of professional life (teachers, chefs, social and health care workers, TV producers, writers, etc.) and they hailed from all regional states of South Sudan...

The process employed by the Renegade Theatre, as Adeyemi reports was not substantially different:

> I was present as an observer on one of the audition days. There were tens of actors and actresses; the strategy was different from the usual practice of giving actors scenes to interpret: none of the actors /actresses was asked to read from the script; rather, their dexterity in speaking classical Yoruba and their understanding of the language were tested. The actors were also asked to demonstrate skills in singing and dancing and [were] questioned on their ability to either drum or interpret drumming language.

However, these same factors which worked so well for the enormous success of the companies and their productions in the UK, may ironically have been the reason for the poor response to the whole experiment in Africa itself. One would have expected that, with such a triumphant exposure on the international stage of African theatre practitioners and the glowing display of our cultural heritage to a global audience, the actors and directors involved in the project would return home to tumultuous applause, akin to the one received by the sportsmen and women at the Olympic Games. But surprisingly, their return passed almost unnoticed at home, and the entire event received scant mention by the press. What could have been the reasons for this?

To answer this question, we would have to consider a number of factors, but the first of these, I believe, must be sought in the very *raison d'être* of the festival itself. For the organisers, as we earlier pointed out, the target audience was primarily and exclusively the London one; not once did spectators in Africa or elsewhere even come into their orbit, except perhaps those who would come to the city as tourists.

> We are bringing together artists from all over the globe, to enjoy speaking these plays in their own language, in our Globe, within the architecture Shakespeare wrote for...

Hence, in selecting the troupes to feature at the festival, the languages spoken by the extant immigrant communities in London were the decisive criteria. The significance of the city as a vast cultural melting-pot, in which diverse communities speaking several different languages now reside and commingle, was to be marked jubilantly not in terms of its unusually opulent cosmopolitanism, but rather, in terms of its role as a site for the expression and exhibition of the English cultural hegemony in today's global market. And who better than Shakespeare to serve as a symbolic marker for this purpose? '[The] hidden agenda in the Globe to Globe season,' confirms Michael Walling during the panel discussion published in this issue, '[is that] a lot of this work is actually being made for western audiences, and not for Africa at all.' This notion of a shared 'global', but in fact very English, sensibility, already coded in their view in the plays of Shakespeare, made the Bard singularly suited for their insidious agenda of cultural colonisation.

It explains why the producers would be interested in promoting the productions on the London stage, but not afterwards in the participating countries themselves. On the same discussion panel, Arne Pohlmeier, direc-tor of the Shona version of *Two Gentlemen of Verona*, complains bitterly of his inability to find a sponsor to take the play to Zimbabwe, in spite of the large Shona population there, with a well demonstrated interest in the theatre.

From this we can go on to look at the kind of plays selected, and their prospective popularity in their home countries. As we said, the decision was to focus only on migrant settlers in London, and so to choose some Shakespeare plays already in translation in each mother tongue. But unfor-tunately the producers encountered unforeseen problems on this front because they discovered that for many of these languages, either the translations did not exist at all or were unsuitable for their purpose. They therefore found themselves obliged in many cases to commission new plays for the occasion, and often at rather short notice.

For instance, given that many of the countries are Anglophone, where English is the national *lingua franca*, the existing adaptations of Shakespeare tend to be in English (sprinkled of course with local phrases and expressions here and there), or in musical librettos. But these available scripts, such as Ahmed Yerima's *Otaelo*, for instance, or Wale Ogunyemi's *Aare Akogun* in the Nigerian repertory, were obviously not qualified by the rules of the game. It is obvious therefore that in such emergency situations the best could not be guaranteed, either in the standard of script, or even in the talent of performers.

The approach of the producers also entailed having to search for the right people to handle the productions, especially in countries where there was no reliable National Theatre, or an established union such as Equity in control of the profession. The problem was further compounded by the fact that there is a substantial dearth of information in London about the true situation of theatrical activity on the African continent. Even within the countries themselves such information is hard to obtain, and mostly what is available is strictly restricted to activities in the capital cities. Quite often therefore the most active groups are unknown abroad, performances that are popular, especially outside the capital cities, are unreported, and even published scripts do not circulate beyond limited circles. In such circumstances, the only available source of information for the London producer would be perhaps the embassies, who themselves are singularly uninformed on such matters, or some of the expatriates living in the countries, or the exiles based in the UK. None of these, sadly, could be expected to possess up-to-date information about the current theatrical situation in the home country.

This lapse must have been responsible no doubt for the choice of companies such as Two Gents, based in London, or Isango, with a known record of touring performances, rather than for example *Amakhosi*, known and established in Harare and Bulawayo, or any of the directors from South Africa, in spite of the strong tradition of dramatic activity in that country. It would also account for the choice of the Renegade Theatre, a relatively young and amateur company in Lagos, instead of more established practitioners, and of their own recourse to a hastily commissioned script from Ipadeola. None of the actors was comfortable with the work because the author chose a formal, archaic form of Yoruba rather than the current colloquial language. This *ad hoc* approach would also explain, I think, the decision by almost all the companies to play up the exotic elements in their productions, a choice that won them uproarious reactions in London, but which was invariably criticised by some of their more discerning countrymen in the audience.

Still, we must not overlook the fact that the tepid reception of, or indifference to, our artists' achievements in London might have been partly due to the usual indifference shown by our media to cultural events, except where such events are serving some political purpose. The current exception may be Nollywood; but such is the situation that, without persecution or harassment from the government, artists stand a slim chance of getting

the attention of the media. Politics and sports tend to dominate our life
so ubiquitously that all other matters are considered to be of secondary
importance, at least by our journalists. They would not be much interested
therefore in talking about the arrival of the artists from London.

All the same, even with this bleak proviso, a world event of such magni-
tude as the Globe to Globe in a metropolitan centre like London, in which
many countries and all the continents were involved, ought to have merited
more than a passing glance. If we are to find a more convincing reason for
the fact that there are so few standing companies in our countries, with scant
media interest, and practically no ready translations of Shakespeare in the
indigenous languages, then we have to probe into the wider context of the
current state of theatre itself on the continent today.

The truth is that, for almost two decades now, the theatre industry has
been more or less plunged into a state of crisis. In Nigeria for instance, where
perhaps the oldest and the most organised theatre industry – the *alarinjo*
theatre – has been flourishing since at least the early nineteenth century, live
performances have almost completely disappeared, sustained only by the
brave efforts of individuals such as Ogundokun and his Renegade Theatre
company. But even then their efforts to overcome the situation are only
spasmodic, and their impact is limited to Lagos, and to a clientele of die-
hard aficionados in an elite neighbourhood of the city.

Sad as it is to admit it, organised theatre, as opposed to informal amateur
performance, is no longer a popular activity in our countries. In its place has
grown the video film industry known universally as Nollywood, which has
now absorbed the energy of erstwhile stage actors and directors. Although
it cannot be said to be the cause of it, Nollywood has contributed in a
very large measure to the demise of the once-bubbling travelling theatre
companies.

One needs to understand here perhaps that the survival of the theatre has
always had to depend on these private initiatives. As far as official support
is concerned, the contribution of the state, from the central government
to the local council level, has always been at best merely tokenistic. This
neglect of the cultural sector has been rightly traced back to our colonial
history: whereas in the ancient times the palaces gave active patronage to
the arts, and richly sustained the work of poets and sculptors and so on, the
opposite was the case under British colonisation.

In the Anglophone territories especially, unlike their Francophone
counterparts, state support for the cultural sector was denied largely because
British colonial policy gave a strong backing to Christian missionaries, for
whom all indigenous culture was fetish and pagan, and so deserved to be
either erased or suppressed for the cause of 'civilisation'. Thus the British not
only left no enduring facilities in this area, but promoted instead an abiding
policy of neglect. Certainly it was this mind-set that our African politicians
who succeeded the British unfortunately inherited, and this has continued
till this very day, even into the sixth decade of Independence. Thus there

is nothing like an Arts Council or an Endowment Fund for the arts, and cultural policies, where they exist at all, are hardly ever implemented. A large and wealthy country like Nigeria has only one national theatre, based in Lagos, built in the euphoria of FESTAC 77[3] when the country was at the height of its oil boom. Since then, successive administrations have preferred to leave the structure in a decrepit state, mainly because the budgets approved yearly by the government for the cultural sector as a whole have always been scandalously meagre.

In those early years of independence, however, and in the wake of the oil boom, nobody seemed to mind this lack of government support. Even if offered, such support would most likely have been viewed by artists as an attempt to interfere with their freedom and to control their creativity. So dramatic activities have remained a private business, sufficiently buoyant and self-sustaining because of the enthusiastic support of the rapidly expanding population of the cities. None of the vital infrastructure required for the maintenance of a viable theatre industry was therefore demanded of the governments nor provided, and companies were content to ply their trade on temporary makeshift platforms erected in public squares, town halls, school fields or even hotel bars. Life was simple and uncomplicated; the companies could live comfortably on an evening's earnings at a time. But then the economy went bust almost overnight, and the oil boom turned into an oil doom, from which the country has still not recovered. In the ensuing recession, the currency was seriously devalued; the cost of living went up astronomically; and many lost their jobs. The nights became unsafe; and the theatres lost their audiences. It was in this precarious situation that video technology was discovered and grew to be a serendipitous lifeline for the theatre practitioners. They abandoned the risky roads and barely profitable live shows, and took to videography. Their films became so successful that they soon spread all over the continent, to the point that they can now be said to have conquered the entire black world, as they have spawned similar industries in other countries. It is against this prevailing scenario that we must appraise the lukewarm attitude to the plays in London. Theatre is no longer popular on the continent. Indeed it can be said that it still survives only because it is kept alive fortuitously in the syllabuses of schools.

Which brings us back to the issue of Shakespeare, for the question must then arise, with such an important role being played by schools in sustaining interest in the theatre, why would a grand Shakespeare festival not arouse a spontaneous outburst of interest on the continent? After all, as every educated person at least of my generation remembers, the plays of the Bard were central to the entire pedagogic system we were brought up with. In our day you could not pass through school without a pass in English, or English literature, a process that necessarily meant being inducted into the world of Shakespeare. At virtually every stage of that educational system, you were introduced to the works of the Bard, first through simplified editions and fictionalised versions, and then later, in the full awesomeness of his poetic drama. To be educated was to acquire the favour of entering into the magical splendours of his extraordinary mind and of accepting with awe his central, canonical status in the world of letters.

All Anglophone colonials then, in whatever area of specialisation, grew up with various lines from Shakespeare embedded in our heads, lines which we quoted with pride and delight at expedient moments, and which became as familiar as, if not even more familiar than, the proverbs and axioms of our indigenous languages. This habit of citation crossed the boundaries of professional qualifications. For instance, one of the most memorable of these occasions must be that moment when General Gowon, the former dictator of Nigeria, who had come to power through a bloody coup d'état, was attending an OAU summit in Kampala, and learnt abruptly that he himself had been overthrown in another coup at home. Gowon's reaction was a helpless sob of resignation, as familiar as it was instructive: 'All the world is a stage,' he quoted, 'And all the men and women merely players:/They have their exits and their entrances...' [from Shakespeare's *As You Like It*].

It is doubtful if any political leader in Africa today – indeed, any academic outside the field of literary studies – would be able to quote so tellingly from Shakespeare. This is not just because the standard of education has declined generally, but rather because, for better or for worse, Shakespeare no longer occupies such a central position in the acquirement of literacy, or even in the mastery of English itself. In the English departments, owing to the assault carried out some years ago upon the system by such figures as Ngugi wa Thiong'o and Henry Owuor-Anyumba at Makerere,[4] the offensive Eurocentric curriculum has undergone such significant alteration that priority has been directed to African authors, or authors from the black diaspora, and away from western authors. In the wake of this indigenisation programme, it should not surprise us that a festival in London on Shakespeare might generate interest among scholars perhaps, just because of its global dimensions, but not among the general populace, and certainly no longer because of the status of the playwright.

What conclusions could one reach from the whole experience? What, from such a historic event, could one say has been gained, or lost? From the perspective of those who participated in it – that is, the actors and directors and those who watched the shows – no-one can deny that it was an unforgettable experience, a life-time highlight that they will probably never have again. Certainly it will affect their future work, as Ogundokun for instance affirms in his interview on the festival blog. It will also inspire some of the troupes – the South Sudan Theatre Company is an example – to attempt to make an impact on the cultural and political future of their country. In like manner, it is quite logical to assume that the various ethnic communities in London who witnessed their groups perform and heard their languages spoken on such an imposing stage, will have gained some new confidence in their cultural identity, and acquired from the experience a more assured sense of their self-worth.

My doubts, however, concern the Bard himself, with regard to his standing within the African community. It remains doubtful if the festival has gone anywhere towards restoring his old status in our consciousness. Indeed for most of the artists, as it turned out, it was not Shakespeare as such that they performed, but rather the stories he inspired. What seems to have been celebrated was not the plays themselves so much as the incentive the plays offered the artists to exhibit their creativity and their own imaginative energies. This can be illustrated by one of the articles on the festival's webpage, where Sunnil Shanbag, the director of the Gujarati version of *All's Well That Ends Well* from Mumbai, has a discussion with Andrew Dickson, who had come to assess their rehearsal. Quite baldly he tells Dickson: 'You know, I'm not interested in a limited idea of Shakespeare.... We'll be performing *in the spirit of the play...*' [My emphasis]. It was this same spirit that guided the performances from Africa.

I think it is to be lamented that the works of a writer like Shakespeare have been evacuated from our syllabus, whatever our anxieties about the colonial experience. It was not for nothing after all that J. P. Clark, one of our pioneering poets, who is also fiercely Afro-centric, warmly recommended the works of the Bard as the ideal paradigm for African writers.[5] He did so because of the recognition everywhere in enlightened circles of their trans-national, universal and immortal value. Shakespeare's prescience, his profundity, and his comprehensive scope transcends the frontiers of any particular country or clime, such that, as Jan Kott[6] demonstrates, he remains forever our contemporary. Anywhere we come from, we can claim Shakespeare as our own; we can enter into his plays any time, and find ourselves at home. This is why his dramas are always available for adaptations. Not long ago, I myself used his *Hamlet* to explore the possibilities of a multi-cultural cast in the USA and, at the same time, to query the double-edged sword of multi-national investment in our economies in the developing world. I will therefore be in great sympathy with almost any initiative to promote Shakespeare on the continent: just not in the manner adopted by the Globe to Globe season.

My view is that if the magic of Shakespeare is to be resuscitated outside the UK, and at least in Africa, such experiments as the Globe to Globe will have to be re-imagined. I think they would only work if they were not aimed at the emigrant communities at the cosmopolitan centre in London or elsewhere in Europe, but instead at the populace resident in Africa itself; that is, when the target audience is shifted to Africa. Then the companies or troupes known to the local communities would be identified and recruited, and would perform to their home audiences. In that way, Shakespeare might regain his old influence here as a universal poet, forever relevant to all of us.

NOTES

1   Dominic Dromgoole – Artistic Director Tom Bird – Festival Director Globe to Globe is part of the World Shakespeare Festival for the London 2012 Festival.

2   Julie Sanders http://bloggingshakespeare.com/year-of-shakespeare-the-winters-tale

3   FESTAC 77 was the acronym for the Festival of Black Arts and Culture hosted by Nigeria in 1977 to celebrate the culture of all people of African descent worldwide. It was the second and has been the largest so far of such festivals, the first having been held in Dakar, Senegal, in 1966.

4   'On the Abolition of the English Department' (1968). [But perhaps this point should not be over-emphasised in the case of Eastern Africa. I have learnt, since writing this, that the curriculum in Makerere is still largely what it was, old-fashioned and Anglo-centric.]

5   See J.P. Clark (1970), *The Example of Shakespeare*, London: Longman.

6   See Jan Kott (1961), *Shakespeare Our Contemporary*. N.Y.: W. Norton & Company.

The Two Gentlemen of Zimbabwe & their Diaspora Audience at Shakespeare's Globe

PENELOPE WOODS

The trapdoor of the empty Globe stage lifted a fraction and Denton Chikura's head looked out, wide-eyed in wonder. Chikura flung the trapdoor open with a crash and the audience hushed in expectation. He gazed around in silent consternation at the visible Globe audience. Open-mouthed, he let out a high-pitched, aspirated 'Ah' of amazement. Slowly he began climbing out of the trapdoor, carrying something. He had one end of a large and battered blue trunk and as he manoeuvred it out of the trap, another head appeared and the other door of the trap banged open. Tonderai Munyevu clutched his heart in astonishment, seeing the assembled audience. The two black men, dressed somewhat incongruously in velvet breeches, hose and Elizabethan-style leather shoes, carried their luggage up onto the Globe stage, still looking around them in surprise. They took some steps backwards. As if unsure what to do next, they took an awkward but delighted bow. The audience cheered and clapped. They took another bow. The audience thundered applause.

Setting the trunk down, the Gents opened it and began to take out scraps of cloth. Shaking the travelling dust out of each, they lifted them out one by one and hung them carefully on a rope strung between two pillars at the back of the stage. There were thirteen items, including several scarves – one patterned, one diaphanous blue, one bright red – as well as a military beret, a yellow jerkin, a long silky white glove, a leash, a sash, and so on.

In my writing on audiences at Shakespeare's Globe I am accustomed to emphasise how unusual this theatre space and its auditorium are. This needs highlighting in order to clarify its significance for the different kind of audiences it produces. The 'standard' theatre auditorium in the UK is housed indoors – for obvious reasons of climate – and it still positions its audiences front-on to the stage in accordance with the development of theatre conventions dating back to the eighteenth century. The modern theatre in the UK is fitted with lighting rigs and sound systems, which serve an aesthetic function within the production, but are powerfully and coercively used to direct audience attention and to control audience behaviour. The houselights generally come down at the start of a production and audience members, habituated to this convention, go quiet and turn their attention obediently to the stage. The reconstructed Globe Theatre, however, disrupts almost all of these conventions.

Some of the 37 international Globe to Globe festival productions came from theatre traditions that are also, these days, predominantly indoors, front-on, and dependent on lighting for directing audience focus and behaviour. Some companies evidently found the transition to the open-air, almost-in-the-round, shared lighting of the Globe stage problematic and even uncomfortable,[1] whereas others found the radical difference of the playing conditions invigorating and even revelatory.[2] These complex responses were not always exclusive of one another.

However, some production companies were familiar with an audience which is visible and whose members play an active part in the performance. *Ìtàn Ògìnìntìn*, a translation of *The Winter's Tale* into Yoruba by Renegade Theatre from Nigeria, drew on a call and response tradition that its audience engaged in enthusiastically. Yohangza Theatre Company's performances of their long-running production of *A Midsummer Night's Dream* (in Korean) were played out to include the Globe audience, and we were handed neon bracelets to wear as if we were all part of a rave. Grupo Galpão's *Romeu e Julieta* in Brazilian Portuguese (which first played at the Globe in 1997) involved the visible audience, addressing us and even moving among us.

That the Globe Theatre space disrupts theatre and auditorium conventions in English theatre history has less significance in the context of the multiple theatrical conventions that negotiated the space, with multiple audience expectations at this international festival. However, that this theatre space foregrounds actor/audience interaction and makes the behaviour and response of audiences visible, thereby altering the ethical relationship between performer and audience, is highly significant for examining what happened in the audience at the international theatre festival. Hans-Thies Lehmann has identified a particular ethical potentiality that exists in the act of performance and its reception in the theatre. Describing this as 'an *aesthetic of responsibility* (or *response-ability)*'[3] Lehmann emphasises the significance of the audience role in responding and reciprocating. I have suggested that theatre architecture and audience conventions in the UK generally make the instantiation of this ethical relationship, this *aesthetic of responsibility*, unlikely. The Globe provides the conditions to make this possible, but not every company or every performance enables this exchange, which would 'move the mutual implication of actors and spectators in the theatrical production of images into the centre and thus make visible the broken thread between personal experience and perception'. Lehmann has described this as a 'politics of perception' and concludes that: 'Such an experience would be not only aesthetic but therein at the same time ethico-political.'[4] In this article I take testimonies from audiences about their experience of the Zimbabwean *Two Gentlemen of Verona* to evaluate the extent to which we might observe that an ethico-political exchange took place in the two performances by the Two Gents at Shakespeare's Globe.

Two Gents Theatre Productions are a three-man company who performed *Vakamona Vaviri Ve Zimbabwe*, a translation into Shona of *The Two Gentlemen of Verona*, at the Globe to Globe festival on 9 and 10 May 2012.[5] They were the smallest of all the companies to perform on the Globe's very large stage, with the two actors playing all fifteen characters between them. They brought their props with them in their only piece of set: a battered blue trunk. This trunk served as barber's stool, bath tub, taxi, bar, mixing deck, and . . . blue trunk, which underscored the peripatetic and playful ethos of their performance style, with its debt to Southern African 'township' theatre practice, on the one hand, and storytelling practices on the other. As Munyevu points out in an interview, this is a stripped-back theatre aesthetic that also resonates with European avant-garde theatre work and is very well received by audiences when the company tours to Poland and Germany. Differences between theatrical cultures are drawn on in the Gents work and aesthetic, but perhaps their work and touring practice also make cross-cultural similarities and overlaps apparent. Based in London, but comprising two actors from Zimbabwe and a director from Germany, via the US and Cameroon, Two Gents is a migrant theatre company whose work reflects this itinerant and diasporic experience of the world.[6]

Vakomana Vaviri Ve Zimbabwe opened in silence. Unlike other companies in the theatre festival who began with music or spectacle, in presenting themselves, their country, and their language, this production opened with its two actors carefully setting up their props in silence. Like most silences in theatres, this was not completely comfortable. An unframed silence runs against the grain of audience expectation. We are predisposed to expect to be given something to attend to, and a context in which to attend to it. This is particularly so at the start of a performance in other theatres, when the houselights come down on us and render us invisible to the actors, to each other, but perhaps also, to ourselves. Furthermore, we are not used to seeing the 'work' of the theatre being done before us at this point, since it is generally the technical staff who prepare and dress the scene before we arrive in the auditorium, and then operate scene changes so as not to intrude on our experience of the theatrical illusion.

In the self-conscious space of the Globe where all are visible to one another, people shuffled through this initial silence. They looked concerned, and perhaps wondered what was happening and when the play would start. The suspense, anticipation, or frustration built up. Rather than immersing us in a spectacle of bodies and an aesthetic of performance that was different, exotic or 'other', this silence was a gap for negotiation and approaching a quiet recognition of the cross-cultural event we were participating in, while becoming aware of its potential for disrupting theatrical conventions. Importantly, it gave us time to inhabit ourselves as visible audience members, recognising that we were visible to one another as well as to the performers, appreciating that our response affected them, and that we were accountable (response-able) within this cross-cultural exchange.

After three or four long minutes of silence, Chikura and Munyevu turned round and came down stage towards us. 'Two Gentlemen', Chikura said in English, in a resonant clear voice, 'both alike in dignity.' The audience burst into laughter. It was a relief to be talked to, to know that the play had begun and that we were all, probably, in the right place at the right time. It was a surprise to hear English when we were expecting Shona. It was also a surprise to hear a version of the opening of *Romeo and Juliet* when we were expecting *The Two Gentlemen of Verona*. Munyevu picked up where Chikura left off, swiftly reprising his line in Shona. Where Chikura had said 'in fair Verona where we lay our scene', Munyevu said something in Shona, emphasising, instead of 'Verona', the word '*Zimbabwe*'. Munyevu, we understood, even those of us who did not speak Shona, had repeated this line about where the scene was being set, in Shona, but corrected Chikura, indicating that this story would in fact be taking place in Zimbabwe.

The silence, the costumes, the multilingual introduction were skilful ways in which the boundaries that this complex site of performance instantiated were played with, tested and made visible. Chikura and Munyevu are Zimbabwean actors who live and work in London. As Chikura says, they live 'in between' Harare and London, feeling differently, but equally, at home in either city.[7] Shakespeare's Globe exists 'in-between' as well, between its existence as a working, profit-turning, 21st-century theatre, and its role as heritage site. As a reconstruction of the 400-year-old theatre for which Shakespeare wrote, it is imbued with a set of complex cultural and inescapably colonial values. Thus the translation of this play into Shona for an international theatre festival, and celebration of 'World Shakespeare', on this stage required other acts of appropriation and translation to be more than a cultural and linguistic 'exhibition'. The Gents harnessed the potential of the Globe theatre space to instantiate an ethical relationship between performer, play and audience in the terms of Lehmann's *aesthetics of responsibility*. As at other productions, the audiences were multicultural and multilingual. They were assembled at the matinee and evening performances with different hopes and desires for the performance, navigating each another's varying reactions and responses. The Gents made a feature of this multilingual and even heteroglossic condition of reception and the imbalances of understanding that defined the audience experience. Munyevu stopped the production at one point, and said in English: 'You don't understand do you?' There was a gale of laughter. He looked sardonically at the digital display boards at either side of the stage and said, 'Those aren't going to help you', to further laughter, and after a pause declared gleefully, 'and nor are we!' – and the Gents carried on in Shona. Bringing into focus the boundaries and asymmetries of language, understanding, expectation and values, made them available for reflection and response without attempting to 'solve' these problems. Increasingly, this is the condition of globalised living and global performance.

The Two Gents came into existence with work on a predominantly English-language production of *Two Gentlemen* in 2007. The play's director, Arne Pohlmeier, has suggested that the reason for choosing *Two Gentlemen* was simply that the company had two actors and the title consequently suggested itself. If this were the case, then the Gents stumbled fortuitously on a rich seam of analogies in this play about migration. Written in the early 1590s at a historical moment of burgeoning international trade links and touring acting companies, the play concerns the tribulations of two Renaissance Italian friends from the city-state of Verona who have their friendship tested by travel and amorous encounters. Valentine travels to Milan to make useful acquaintances and educate himself in the ways of the world. His childhood friend Proteus stays behind in Verona to woo his love, Julia. Antonio, Proteus' father, feels that his son 'cannot be a perfect man,/ Not being tried and tutored in the world' (1.3. 20-1) and sends Proteus to join his friend Valentine (thereby separating him from Julia, who nevertheless follows in disguise). Proteus, as his name suggests, turns out to be fickle and treacherous. On his arrival in Milan he falls in love with the Duke's daughter, Silvia, who is, however, already betrothed to his best friend. Proteus betrays Valentine, by revealing his plan to elope with Silvia to her father, who promptly banishes Valentine from Milan. When Silvia goes into the 'woods' to find Valentine, Proteus follows. Failing to woo her, he attempts a rape. Valentine happens to be watching and emerges to stop Proteus. Articulating the tension of domestic and global, Valentine declares: 'I must never trust thee more, / But count the world a stranger for thy sake. / The private wound is deepest.' (5.4.69-71) However, Proteus apologises and Valentine forgives his friend. As a sign of his forgiveness he 'gives' him Silvia. Proteus' true love, Julia, meanwhile, has also been watching, disguised as his male servant, Sebastian. She returns the ring that Proteus had given her on leaving Verona. When he realises who she is, he is overcome with remorse. The two friends agree to marry the 'right' women.

This early play by Shakespeare is not frequently performed. Its plot is erratic and fantastical. Its ending is violent, arbitrary, and difficult to reconcile in a 'comedy'. Its speech is predominantly dialogic, even though the play contains fifteen characters. A full-cast production can be static, and the set changes implied by scenes which switch from one city to another, to the woods, are generally exaggerated in modern design-led productions.[8] It is a play about asymmetric gender relations, patriarchy, and cultural values around global travel and migration; it examines the tensions that migration produces when the domestic conflicts with the global.

In writing about audience response to this production I have a few key sites of evidence. The first is my own experience of standing amongst the five hundred or so audience members for the performance. The second is the video footage of the production against which I can calibrate my sense that the laughter, for instance, following that first silence, was indeed a throaty burst of relief, rather than a smattering of polite laughter, or the hiccupping, rolling sound sparked by something very funny happening.[9] I also have taped interviews with the performers which offer up moments of cross-reference. Chikura for instance, comments on the staging choice of opening the show by coming up out of the trap, and his delight at the audience response. He describes the forging of this actor and audience relationship in those moments: 'we were encountering them and them us at the same time.'[10] Chikura, employs the language of 'encounter' as used by the philosopher Emmanuel Levinas, in his consideration of the particular ethical quality of the face-to-face encounter.[11] His use of a continuous past tense, 'we were encountering them', also points to the gap in the period of time and silence in which actor and audience forged a particular ethical relationship to one another.

Finally, I recorded conversations with audience members after the performance, specifically three conversations with three different groups of people who were present.[12] These conversations were set up to be a reasonably close approximation to a 'natural' conversation about a performance; they are unstructured and led predominantly by the features that the audience members wanted to discuss. I began these interactions by asking: 'What did you enjoy about the production?' or perhaps 'What was most memorable?' This was intended as an open-ended and natural way in which a show might be discussed among friends. Since each of these conversations took place in a group, the friends intermittently and spontaneously took over my role by interviewing each other.

No personal information was requested from the respondents in these conversations, so it is striking that the 'primary' respondent on each occasion began by identifying themself. Each chose to elucidate how they felt they were positioned in relationship to the performance, and to other audience members. This speaks to Lehmann's identification of a thread between personal experience and perception that must exist in order for the aesthetics of responsibility, and an ethico-political relationship to take place in the theatre. The first interview took place with a woman who described herself as 'Italian' and a 'friend' of the company. The second group of interviewees described themselves as 'three Zimbabweans'. The primary respondent in the final conversation described herself as 'an actor', and as 'half-Zimbabwean', although she was unable to understand the language of the play completely.

In my previous research with the audiences at the Globe, this initial act of identifying oneself was not entirely unusual.[13] Audience members in this theatre frequently identify and describe themselves as a preface to what they want to say about their experience of a production. At the Globe to Globe festival performances, this was more consistent and the descriptions were more frequently about national or linguistic alignments.[14] Nevertheless, this is a significant linguistic act that responds to a need to position oneself within an ethico-political relationship to the production. The subsequent conversation was then framed by the self-identification of the audience

Fig. 1. A 'word cloud', offering a visual and linguistic overview of the combined interviews with audience members following the matinee performance, Wednesday 9 May. The varying sizes of the words indicate how frequently they were used by interviewees.

member's relationship to the performance, other audience members, the theatre space, and other complexities of the performance event.

Three key features emerged in discussion with these audience members. The first was about language and understanding, the second about emotion (and music), and the third about performance skill, in particular the Gents' physicality and use of props. Whilst the issues of language and understanding represented a common concern in all the groups interviewed, it is also possible to see how the audience conversations reflected concerns that accorded with the ways each group of interviewees described and positioned themselves. The non-Shona, but also non-native English, speaker living in London and attending the production, who was also accustomed to the work of navigating meaning and understanding in multicultural contexts, talked most about language and understanding. The Zimbabweans who spoke of an 'affection' for the Gents and for Zimbabwe, articulated their experience in terms of its emotional ecology. The three actors were most concerned with the Gents' performance strategies and skill in telling the story with only two characters, and by using props.

The festival director, Tom Bird, took into consideration the diaspora language communities living in London and the UK when programming the festival. Most of the main non-English language groups in the UK were represented at the event: Polish, Urdu, Bengali, Guajarati, Arabic, French, Portuguese, Spanish, and Turkish. For the first time, in 2011, the National Census included a question about which language respondents considered to be their primary means of communication, and a fifth of Londoners, almost two million inhabitants, gave a language other than English in response. (These results were not available until after the festival.)

The census figures reveal that, after Somali, (85,918), Shona is the second most widely-spoken African language in England and Wales, (21,395)[15] The borough of Southwark, where the Globe Theatre is located, was one of three with the greatest proportion of the 3,000 Shona speakers in London.

There was a reasonable chance of attendance at the two performances by diaspora Shona-speaking audiences in the UK, besides the possibility of Shona-speaking audiences who may have travelled from abroad for the event. The first group of audience members who were interviewed felt that the reception of this performance had been particularly warm and responsive. They thought that the production had been 'very well-received'. The respondents also noted that there had been much shared 'understanding' of the production, although they initially suggested that the audience's linguistic comprehension was limited. However, reflecting on the level of understanding in this particular audience, respondents commented on the laughter that distinguished one community of audience members who had 'got' a joke in the play-text from those who did not understand the language in depth. One of the respondents also mentioned a member of the audience who replied out loud to the actors, saying 'Yes, that's true!' in English, although they had heard/understood the words in Shona.

In a post-performance interview, Munyevu described how one of the differences they noticed between audiences in the UK and in Zimbabwe was the greater responsiveness of audiences in the latter:

> In Zimbabwe people do get very involved with the story-line, so they do get upset with Proteus who is the character who does a lot of bad things; they do get upset and they whisper [. . .] 'you're *betraying* your friend!', 'you're a bad man', [...] they really get involved. And I think yesterday [Wednesday 9 May matinee] there was an element of that because we had some Shona people in the audience.

It is noteworthy that Munyevu goes on to say, ' I think the Globe audience anyway, likes to be involved.'[16] The audience interviewees felt there was a more responsive audience at the Globe than at other venues where the Gents had performed in the UK, and 'probably more of a diverse crew'; they thought there were 'a lot of Zimbabweans who [had] come'. Both Munyevu and the audience members make a similar conflation of the kind of interactive behaviour that might be expected from a Shona audience and the nature of audience participation and interaction found at Shakespeare's London Globe. Munyevu was speaking from his experience of the Gents' performances at the Harare International Festival of Arts, in 2009, but I suspect a similar reaction would come from audiences for Shona folk-tales, or *Ngano*, with their didactic or ethical narrative function clearly implicating the audience, through their inbuilt structures of call and response.[17] One audience respondent suggested, 'I think I like Shakespeare's Globe because it's not so strict.' This refers to the etiquette and conventions that prevent reciprocal exchange, and restrict audience involvement in London's traditional theatres.

My second interview took place with three women who had grown up in Zimbabwe, but said, '[W]hen we grew up, we weren't even given the option to learn Shona at school because we grew up in an incredibly racist white town.'[18] One respondent qualified this by saying: '...we grew up with the sound. And so listening to it, it is almost like listening to music in translation. And it just makes me think . . . I wish I'd learned.'

There is a musicality to language which is perhaps especially brought out in this multilingual context where the *sound* of language may be foregrounded because semantic comprehension is not necessarily available. But music itself was a significant feature of this production. The thirteenth item lifted out of the blue trunk was an *mbira* – a traditional musical instrument of the Shona people. It is a lamellophone, having between 22 and 28 metal 'tongues' attached at one end to a wooden back, which are played by depressing the free ends with the thumbs. The ethnomusicologist, Claire Jones, has described the *mbira* as 'emblematic of "culture" in Zimbabwe, virtually a national instrument.'[19] Scholarship on *mbira* music treats its historical and cultural significance alongside the beauty and complexity of the music itself; its socio-political function is bound up in its aesthetic. It is used in the telling of *Ngano*, at religious ceremonies, in protest and resistance songs, and in pop music. Munyevu describes the centrality of music to the production, saying that this choice represented a celebration of the 'songs of Zimbabwe'. The production is scored with Zimbabwean pop songs, reflecting 'urban, middle-class Zimbabwean life'. The use of the *mbira* also makes a connection with older and more traditional Shona performance practices.[20]

It is this music, the antithesis of the ruminative, ethical silence that opened this performance, that infuses the production. Chikura and Munyevu sing while Chikura plays the *mbira* throughout the play. The two joyful love scenes, for instance, are choreographed through music. Proteus and Julia fall in love as they sing a duet (2.2). At its climax, they kiss, and the ripple effect is expressed in the stunned hesitancy of Julia's singing after the kiss.[21] Valentine, on the other hand, stages a 'play-off' with Thurrio, his rival for Silvia's love (2.4). Valentine pretends to play exuberant Zimbabwean pop music through the beat box of the upturned blue trunk (Chikura sings this music himself), then Thurrio 'switches' the track to something pompous, old-fashioned and English (Munyevu sings an alternative English song). Valentine 'switches' it back, and Silvia enters singing enthusiastically along with Chikura, who pitches an octave higher. They dance delightedly and sexily, manifesting their joyous compatibility. These scenes need no linguistic translation for their musical telling of love and mutuality to be shared and understood.

Munyevu rejects any reductive 'political' reading of this production. (The Gents note that some audience members have sought to see the military beret worn by the Duke of Milan as a reference to Robert Mugabe and the Zimbabwean army, but they insist no such straightforward analogy was intended, or that it even works within the remit of the story). Rather,

Munyevu emphasises that the ethos of the production is a 'celebration of life, exuberance and clown-like joy'.[22] He remarks on the music as a touchstone of this ethos, also singling out the 'authentic' nature of the relationships fashioned between the characters in the play. Whilst the play is nominally about male friendship, the friends only have three scenes together: the first where they take a tender farewell of each other, the second in Milan where Valentine falls in love with Proteus' betrothed, and the last in an encounter in the woods, where they are reconciled.

Relationships between other characters the actors in the play are significantly more complex and nuanced. I am interested in how this production developed the interactions between the female characters and the relationships of service. The servant characters and the two gentlewomen, Julia and Silvia, have little power in this society. Their choices and life plans are almost always circumscribed by the choices made by either the eponymous Two Gentlemen, or the father figures, but their relationships are treated with notable care in this production.

As in *Romeo and Juliet* and *Much Ado About Nothing*, *Two Gentlemen* is a play that features several domestic servants. Domestic service is uncommon in the UK today and to many audience members it is an alien social arrangement. Consequently, service relationships can be treated theatrically as a historical oddity, or even as an exoticism, requiring no political or ethical consideration of their presentation. Modern productions can be lazy in their treatment of these highly significant and instrumental 'lower' characters, simply drawing on unimaginative and unethical clichés of servant practice. The Gents were unusually thoughtful in their treatment of these roles. Perhaps a cross-cultural interrogation of the play permits a new visibility of the service roles and the power asymmetries within the play and the society that it portrays.

After Proteus has taken his tender leave of Valentine, his servant 'Speed' enters (1.1). Valentine has asked him to deliver the first of many letters that crisscross the stage. (The Gents made a physical virtue of this potentially complex device. Each time a letter was sent and received, it was indicated by a character smacking the stage, and declaring '*tsamba*', which we learned was Shona for 'letter'). Valentine makes Speed sit down when he arrives, wraps him in a towel and begins to give him a shave. This is a lovely reversal of the conventional service relationship, which is never one way, especially in Shakespeare's plays, where they are nested within a nuanced and asymmetrical gift-exchange economy of loyalty and obligation. In the subsequent scene where Julia and her maid Lucetta discuss the former's suitors, Julia is having a bath (in the blue trunk) (1.2). Julia runs her own bath, whilst Lucetta sits on the side and gossips engagingly. (She is one of the most endearing and delightful characters in the production.) Julia gets out and dries herself, whilst Lucetta watches, gossiping. This thoughtfulness around the presentation of such service relationships was not commented on in interviews with audience members or with the Gents themselves, and certainly was overlooked in the only national review of the production in *The Guardian*.[23] In my view, this careful attention to the ethical dimensions of such interactions was a hallmark of the 'relationships' that Munyevu has described as central to the ethos of the production. In particular, Munyevu identifies the 'women' in the production, describing them as 'really true to women we know in Zimbabwe'.[24]

This discussion now focuses on the audience members who talked about the physicality of the production, and the use of props.[25] This last group of interviews was with actors in the audience who focused on the dexterity of the Gents' theatrical practice. They commented particularly on the performers' exceptional physicality and skill in switching so convincingly and clearly between so many characters, and how well developed the characters were. They commented on the simple, stylised use of props for creating characters with instant recognition. Silvia was signified by a white glove, the servant Speed by a yellow jerkin, Julia always wore a patterned scarf, and Lucetta, her servant, a red head scarf. These bits of fabric were so effectively imbued with character by the Gents that they could subsequently be swapped around: when required, an audience member could be draped in Julia's scarf, or Thurrio's sash, and effectively stand in for the character. Having established this performance language, the Gents identified moments in which to employ audience members as stand-ins, when their 'natural' audience behaviour would entertainingly read into the character. The blushing, awkward audience member singled out in the prologue to be Julia 'became' the blushing, awkward object of Munyevu's love. The frustrated, embarrassed audience member, collared with Thurrio's sash, turned into the frustrated, churlish suitor competing with the more charming and suave Valentine (3.4). The three hapless outlaws who set upon Valentine when he is banished to the woods (4.1) were drawn from the audience by Munyevu, who positioned them around the big blue trunk. He then acted as puppeteer to these volunteers. He waved their arms around in hopelessly unthreatening ways and ventriloquised their lines in a squeaking voice. They were both a delightful spectacle of audience awkwardness and yet the perfect evocation of the hapless, well-meaning outlaws who take Valentine to be their 'captain' rather than hijacking him. Notably, audience members were not invited to stand in for actors in the final scene, in which four characters are required to be present on stage.

Chikura commented on their difficulty in developing the final scene in which Silvia is raped:

> We found it really difficult to crack. [. . .] How, all of a sudden, in this comedy is there an attempted rape with this girl, bandied around at the end? [. . .] We found it really difficult to do this.[26]

Silvia was characterised throughout by a white glove (a rich, signifying device in the play, like the letter, since gloves 'act' as amorous tokens, go-betweens and the source of mishap and amorous confusion). As Proteus seized Silvia, in the person of Chikura, he wriggled out of the glove to return as Valentine, startling his friend in this moment of aggression, and Munyevu was left assaulting the glove. Silvia's sudden de-physicalisation, in an instant becoming a limp and helpless shred of fabric, was in itself poignant. The bathos of the play and this particular production, which deliberately played with the dynamic of absent/present characters in the logistics of a two-man production, was beautifully served by this tactic of suddenly deflated aggression. As with other decisions in the production, it demonstrated a lightness of touch that was provocative, dexterous and profound. With the resolution of the play, Chikura and Munyevu adopted the characters of Silvia and Julia, the female protagonists with their futures summarily settled, but about whose treatment and future happiness we might feel ambivalent. In the play text, these characters remain on stage but have no further lines to speak. The Gents effectively staged the silence of Silvia and Julia, requiring us once again to engage in an ethical, ruminative reflection on the play and negotiate our response to it. Kneeling downstage, the two women held each other close for several minutes.

The second set of respondents were clearly still caught up in the emotional plenitude of the end of the performance when they spoke to me. One of the respondents said:

> I think it was wonderful because .... although we couldn't understand very much of the... I think you could understand what the emotions were, and actually, even though it's such a silly story in many ways, at the ending when... well, it's almost tragic isn't it? At the end?[27]

'Emotion' transcended linguistic comprehension, giving a different access to both the nuance and the perceived profundity of the play. Engaged in the clear telling of troubled human relationships, and drawing on physicality and music, the Gents achieved moments of shared emotional clarity with the audience – Shona-speaking or not, Zimbabwean or not, familiar with the play or not. The respondent quoted above wove her personal experience into her perception of the play, in accordance with Lehmann's framework, but she also explored this as a shared ethical and personal response. She questioned her friends and sought out their experience of this moving ending. Her statement about how she responded to the production was also a question that sought a connection between audience members as well as between the actors and the audience. The points of greatest shared feeling and memorability revolved around the humour, music and joy of the performance, on the one hand, and, on the other, the sadness that infuses a society built on asymmetric power relations.

I have referred consistently to the 'ethos' of this production. This is a deliberate use of a complex Greek word that at one level signifies the local, the hearth or home, but expands to signify the values, customs or habits of the local or homely. It is from this root which the term 'ethics' derives. More generally, the term 'ethos' is used to refer to the 'character' of something. This resonates with issues of the global and the local in a World Shakespeare Festival, as well as with issues particular to this play. It also speaks to the prevalent and conflicting customs and conventions of theatre performance and reception that were brought out in this festival in the particular space of the Globe Theatre. Finally, it helps to designate the character of this complex production.

The Two Gents production at Shakespeare's Globe, within the context of this festival and audience, resulted in a particular moment of ethico-political performance. The production made visible the complex and conflicting boundaries of language, culture, heritage and ownership at work in this festival, the building itself, and the specific production. It worked in conjunction with the architectural conditions of the Globe Theatre to produce a self-conscious audience who reflected on their position in relationship to these claims and boundaries, but who also participated in the shared joys of love and friendship. This audience's act of responding both feelingly and ethically produced the *aesthetics of responsibility* as identified by Lehmann. It is apparent in the reflections of the audience members who felt able to respond (*response-able*), and who noted, and were invested in, other audience members' engagement and responses, in ways not often available in other theatres in the UK. It is also evident in audience members' acts of identifying and positioning themselves in relationship to the production. The production summoned them (and 'us' and 'me') to respond in their ('our', 'my') social, cultural and emotional being, through its creation of silences and its careful treatment of asymmetric relations. It also urged us to a new state of self-consciousness about our position in relationship to other members of the audience, and perhaps also to the wider world. The play's final line asserts: 'One feast, one house, one mutual happiness' (5.4.171). This assertion was challenged by the subsequent prolonged silence of the two women, holding each other in tender resignation. The mutuality of happiness, if it is to be found, will be found in our awareness of power imbalances in society and our place within them, and in the role we play in perpetuating or resisting these. This thoughtful, ethical and highly skilled theatre aesthetic made an important contribution within the cross-cultural multilingual festival of Globe to Globe. Its practice of probing, exposing and celebrating difference in ways that were simultaneously linguistic, emotional, musical, physical and design-led, speaks to a wider trend of performance in a multilingual globalised world. Its playful, footloose, fleet efficiency established a hyper-mobile, hyper-responsive, local and global production.

NOTES

1 The Italian company, I Termini, who performed *Giulio Cesare*, struggled to adapt what was evidently a black box or studio production for the open-air theatre with its visible audience. The company resisted the use of direct address or any acknowledgement of the presence of the Globe audience, while detailed features of the production involving UV

chalk and light-bulbs, for instance, were impossible to 'read' in the context of the open-air, ambient lighting of the Globe.

2 See interview with Oyun Atölyesi, the Turkish theatre company who performed *Antonius ile Kleopatra*, held at Shakespeare's Globe Library and Archives (henceforth SGLA), but also available online: http://bloggingshakespeare.com/year-of-shakespeare-antony-and-cleopatra [accessed 15 April 2013]. Haluk Bilginer, who played Antony, commented, 'Yesterday we did our first show here: what an eye-opener, what a beautiful experience. [. . .] It is completely different, of course. We have an Italian stage and typical, or classical, theatre set up [in Istanbul]. Here, you've got 360 degrees of audience almost, and it is a very warm atmosphere. It must be, if not the best theatre in the world, the best experience for an actor, for a theatre company, to perform [at the Globe]. It teaches you a lot about theatre. It teaches you a lot about performing, about theatre, about story-telling. We learned a lot.'

3 Hans Thies-Lehmann, (2006) *Postdramatic Theatre* (trans. by Karen Jürs-Munby. (London and New York: Routledge, pp. 185-6. (Emphasis in the original).

4 Lehmann, p. 185.

5 The translation of *Two Gentlemen* was done by Zimbabwean playwright and university lecturer, Noel Marerwa for the festival. Marerwa, who is based in Harare, has written several acclaimed plays that probe current cultural and social issues in Zimbabwe.

6 The play, *Magetsi*, written by Denton Chikura, and performed by the Gents, explicitly deals with experiences of migration and returning home to Zimbabwe. However, these experiences inform all of their productions in various ways.

7 Denton Chikura, Two Gentlemen of Verona Interview, 10 May 2012. Globe Education carried out interviews with all the companies who performed as part of Globe to Globe. The full interviews are held in the Globe Library and Archive. Highlights of the interviews carried out as part of the Globe to Globe Festival are additionally available on-line: https://soundcloud.com/globe-education [Last accessed 15 April 2013].

8 See for instance the production by the Royal Shakespeare Company, dir. David Thacker, 1991.

9 Recordings of the Globe to Globe performances are available at the Globe Library and Archive. A recording of the Thursday 10 May evening performance by the Two Gents is additionally available on-line at the time of writing: http://thespace.org/items/e000066w?t=cgmvw [Last accessed 15 April 2013].

10 Denton Chikura Interview.

11 Emmanuel Levinas (1979) *Totality and Infinity: An Essay on Exteriority*, trans. Alphonso Lingis. New York: Springer.

12 These audience conversations are available in the Globe to Globe Audience Archive at the Globe Library and Archive. They are also currently available online at the *Year of Shakespeare* website: http://bloggingshakespeare.com/year-of-shakespeare-the-two-gentlemen-of-verona [Last accessed 15 April 2013]. I shall henceforth refer to them as Audience Interview 1, 2 and 3.

13 Further conversational research with audience members at other theatres in the UK might help to establish whether this is a feature of Globe audiences, or whether audience members at other theatres engaging in a similar conversational framework would also feel the need to position or identify themselves in this way.

14 Further work on the Globe to Globe audiences is forthcoming.

15 *2011 census: Quick statistics for England and Wales, March 2011*, Office for National statistics, 30 January 2013, accessed online here: http://www.ons.gov.uk/ons/dcp171778_297002.pdf [10 April 2013].

16 Tonderai Munyevu, Two Gentlemen of Verona Interview, 10 May 2012, SGLA, and online at: https://soundcloud.com/globe-education.

17 The *Ngano* story-telling tradition is explicitly drawn on in the Gents' production of *Hamlet*, where the scene with the visiting players ((3.2) requires audience members to respond to the opening that Munyevu offers: '*Kwaivepo*' [once upon a time] with the standard response: '*dzepfunde*' [we are in agreement]. When this is performed for audiences who do not know the call and response terms, Munyevu appears to be astounded and exasperated

and then coaches the audience until they can get it right. For an account of this production see Colette Gordon (2011), '*Hamlet* in England. *Hamlet* in Exile: What's Hecuba to him, or *Kupenga* to them?' in *Shakespeare in Southern Africa*, 23, 'Banishment, Xenophobia, Home and Exile in Shakespeare and the Renaissance', 64–9.

18 Audience interview 2.

19 See Claire Jones (2008) 'Shona Women Mbira Players: Gender, Tradition and Nation in Zimbabwe', *Ethnomusicology Forum*, 17,1: 125–49.

20 Tonderai Munyevu Interview.

21 This kiss, between a man pretending to be a woman and another man, drew various responses from the audience. In an on-line review, Kiran Madzimbamuto-Ray commented: 'The shared kiss between Chikura as "Julia" and Munyevu's "Proteus" is a perfect example [of the confidence of the Two Gents with pushing audience expectations]'. Madzimbamuto-Ray describes this as 'drawing shocked gasps from the Zimbabwean audience.' See 'Shakespeare in Shona: Say it Proud', http://thinkafricapress.com/zimbabwe/shakespeare-shona-harare-bulawayo-globe-theatre-two-gentlemen-verona [accessed 15 April 2013].

22 Tonderai Munyevu Interview.

23 Alex Needham, 'The Two Gentlemen of Verona, Shakespeare's Globe, London', *The Guardian*, Monday 14 May 2012.

24 Tonderai Munyevu, Interview.

25 Audience Interview 3.

26 Denton Chikura interview.

27 Audience Interview 2.

WORKS CITED

Websites

Year of Shakespeare website: http://bloggingshakespeare.com/

Globe to Globe Interviews on-line, Globe Education, https://soundcloud.com/globe-education

Books & Articles

Jones, Claire (2008) 'Shona Women Mbira Players: Gender, Tradition and Nation in Zimbabwe', *Ethnomusicology Forum*, 17:1, 125–49.

Lehmann, Hans-Thies (2006) *Postdramatic Theatre* trans. by Karen Jürs-Munby, London and New York: Routledge.

Levinas, Emmanuel (1979) *Totality and Infinity: An Essay on Exteriority*, trans. Alphonso Lingis, New York: Springer.

Greenblatt, Stephen, Walter Greenblatt, Jean E. Howard, Katharine Eisaman Maus, eds (1997) *The Norton Shakespeare*, Oxford: Oxford University Press.

Madzimbamuto-Ray, Kiran (2012) Shakespeare in Shona: Say it Proud', http://thinkafrica press.com/zimbabwe/shakespeare-shona-harare-bulawayo-globe-theatre-two-gentlemen-verona

Needham, Alex (2012) 'The Two Gentlemen of Verona, Shakespeare's Globe, London', *The Guardian*, Monday 14 May .

Office for National Statistics (2011) *2011 Census: Quick Statistics for England and Wales, March 2011*. http://www.ons.gov.uk/ons/dcp171778_297002.pdf [accessed 30 January 2013].

Reviews

Madzimbamuto-Ray, Kiran, 'Shakespeare in Shona: Say it Proud', http://thinkafricapress. com/zimbabwe/shakespeare-shona-harare-bulawayo-globe-theatre-two-gentlemen-verona

Needham, Alex, 'The Two Gentlemen of Verona, Shakespeare's Globe, London', *The Guardian*, Monday 14 May 2012.

Shakespeare's African Nostos
Township nostalgia
& South African performance at sea

COLETTE GORDON

The opening act of the Globe to Globe festival, a South African adaptation of *Venus and Adonis*, the long narrative poem that first earned 'honey-tongued' Shakespeare his fame, exceeded in several respects the festival's exacting rubric of '37 plays, 37 languages'.[1] Created and performed by the Isango Ensemble, '*UVenas no Adonisi*', was at once an exemplar and an exception in the festival. As a dramatisation of a poem, *UVenas* lay somewhat outside the main programme. Isango's 'contribution' did not complete the festival lineup of plays (which lacked *Two Noble Kinsmen*) but rather emphasised the raggedness of this incomplete works after the RSC's well publicised Complete Works Festival in 2006-2007, an Olympic feat of programming.[2] And as the Ensemble performed in a total of six languages (a nod, though still an incomplete gesture, to South Africa's eleven official languages), their multilingual performance pushed the festival well beyond the tidy promise of 37 languages for 37 plays. But, while the performance undermined the illusion of completeness in the programming, its blending of English, Zulu, Xhosa, Sotho, Setswana and Afrikaans underscored the festival's investment in multilingualism, an essentially different logic. The decision (articulated in the tagline) to direct the festival's global search toward *language* rather than nation allowed the festival to promote itself (and London) as a polyglot, cosmopolitan site of translation and cultural interpenetration. From this perspective, the project aimed to be inclusive, rather than encyclopedic, avoiding setting up a Shakespeare themed 'cultural' (read ethnographic) expo in the mode of the now infamous world fairs.

Still, the '37 plays in 37 languages' were in effect 37 productions from 37 countries. Hence the alternative tagline, which presented the programme under a more chauvinist banner: 'Shakespeare's Coming Home'. While the festival's multilingual proposition – apparently inspired by linguistic diversity in London's multi-ethnic communities – drew attention to linguistic difference *in* the city, ethnographic fascination remained and coverage of the festival went back and forth between these two poles: the celebration of multilingual cosmopolitanism versus expectations of national pageantry

Fig 1 Uvenas no Adonisi *at Shakespeare's Globe to Globe festival in 2012.*
Performed by the Isango Ensemble in South African languages (Photograph by Ellie
Kurrtz. Copyright © Shakespeare's Globe)

Fig 2 Zamile Gantana as Cupid in Uvenas no Adonisi *at Shakespeare's Globe to*
Globe festival in 2012 (Reproduced by kind permission of Isango Ensemble)

and the appeal of ethnographic spectacle. Thus *The Arts Desk* ran a subhead 'The World Shakespeare Festival begins triumphantly with a poem in six languages from a South African township',[3] but quoted the alternative tagline as the first line of the article. There was evident slippage in this Olympic celebration of 'culture', between a festival of languages (defining and linking communities) and a festival of national practices, a festival of nations. In general, the interest in *place* (Shakespeare's travels among strange people in strange lands) trumped the multilingual multicultural project (affirming global communities).[4] In the case of the opening show, as the Arts Desk's framing suggests, it was a specific locus, the *township*, that claimed attention (over South Africa's linguistic pluralism or the general appeal of South African theatre).[5] How this particular locus shaped the available meanings of *UVenas* and the narrative of Shakespeare's homecoming in the festival more broadly is the question this chapter addresses.

Venus and her sisters

UVenas was a sound choice for the opening, not least because, operating over and above the production's six official South African languages, the company's primary performance language is music – alongside money, supposedly a 'universal' language.[6] Many companies in the festival incorporated music and dance in their plays; the Globe's Research Coordinator reports that use of music at the festival exceeded both the theatre's norms and those of the participating companies.[7] But the Isango ensemble, billed as 'the best known and most widely feted of the theatre practitioners' was already well known and popular among London audiences for its energetic, accessible, family friendly adaptations of classic works, using music as the primary vehicle. Sometimes billed as an opera company, (although director Dornford May describes his work as 'lyric theatre'), Isango are generally known for producing musicals.[8] While the somewhat cynical Christmas show *Ikrismas Kherol* (after Dickens' *A Christmas Carol*) and other literary adaptations in their repertoire may be accurately called musical theatre, this is a weak descriptor for *UVenas no Adonisi* and for much of Isango's work, which might be usefully thought of in terms of *opera comique*, an umbrella genre defined by its easy mixture of spoken dialogue and sung numbers.

The company's skilful repurposing of the genre has included Bizet's *Carmen* (*UCarmen EKhayelitsha* and Mozart's singspiel *The Magic Flute* (*Impempe Yomlingo*). The sense in which *Carmen* can be termed 'comedy' points to a handling of genre that is Shakespearean – or now mostly familiar from Shakespeare. While 'Shakespearean' is still used popularly to describe grand, tragic themes, and noble passions, *opera comique's* sense of the comic points to a mixing of modes we find across Shakespeare's dramatic output, a combining of high and low (characters, themes, styles) that allows the comic and serious to appear alongside each other.

The ensemble embraces this mixed register in both matter and musical style. The score, composed by musical director Mandisi Dyantyis and performed with a combination of vocals, marimbas (a mainstay since *Impempe*), and 'township percussion' (stamping, clapping, and beating on oil drums) ranges from intense dramatic solos with the colour of Handel and Purcell's chamber opera works to large choral soundscapes that layer elements from traditional isiXhosa choruses, and the whole is shot through with playful quotation of popular musical styles, including jazz and, typically, a Motown number. The story similarly embraces shifts in tone. The incongruities of Shakespeare's notably playful treatment of Ovid are taken even further in Isango's physicalisation of the narrative poem. In dramatising Shakespeare's material (Venus' unsuccessful wooing of the doomed mortal Adonis), the ensemble move freely between the prosaic and the poetic, quotidian and mythic, local and 'universal' – the utopian no-place of the masque. The goddess as personated by the company walks sometimes in the air, sometimes on the ground, as the tone shifts between high tragedy, light domestic comedy, and occasional farce.[9]

Along with many of the festival productions, particularly those billed as 'from Africa', *UVenas* approaches its Shakespearean material as an occasion for ensemble storytelling. The narrative poem is ideal for this purpose, being less dependent on character and, most importantly, containing a strong and interesting, narrative voice. Where other companies had to create or impose a narrative voice, Isango could source theirs directly, and the musical idiom made it easy to work directly with the Shakespearean text. In this way, long sections of Shakespeare's richly descriptive and highly wrought English verse made their appearance, delivered in catchy musical arrangements. Pacing and repetition made their sense more easily digestible and their performance as music lifted some of the pressure on language and comprehension and allowed the production to move forward even where the audience might struggle to parse the lines. With substantial descriptive sections and dialogue from the poem delivered in dramatic arias, Shakespeare's English made up the bulk of the production, breaking the festival's 'rule' of avoiding English.[10] Some sections were translated, but this was mainly relegated to refrains. African languages featured rather in a sequence of comic scenes in Zulu, Xhosa, Sotho, and Setswana, performed without surtitles, where Venus (in various guises) appeals to Adonis in prose, using spoken dialogue. Those demotic scenes, translating the quarrel into everyday vernacular, offered the opportunity for free improvised translation, more personal characterisation, and a locally inflected sense of comedy. With these sketches, which were all variations on a theme of seduction, the ensemble also fulfilled the promise of a multilingual showcase, without significantly compromising the production's overall intelligibility to a monolingual English audience.[11]

Isango's flexible adaptation of the narrative poem within the very loose framework of *opera comique* appears, unsurprisingly, more successful as a staging of Shakespeare's poem than Zachary Wadsworth's chamber opera, which at its 2005 première looked already like a museum piece.[12] The argument between Venus and Adonis makes for a long, stilted, and uneventful discourse when performed by a static choir with soloists. *UVenas* allows for some engrossing interaction between its eponymous characters, and powerful solo work (particularly from Pauline Malefane playing an abandoned Venus in the second half). Dyantyis' score, at times very spare, achieves moments of chamber opera intensity. But the bedrock of the production is the chorus and its most powerful feature is the flexible interpenetration of solo and chorus, individual and group, character and narrative. The expansion of the chorus' role (especially the women's) would be a practical choice for Isango, turning a likely chamber opera into a suitable piece for a small company that depends on ensemble work, and especially on the strengths of its female performers.[13] Isango also draws on its performers' individual linguistic backgrounds to constitute its multilingualism; sharing lines between the performers increases the company's multilingual reach. But here the company's response to practical exigencies shaped powerful effects.

The ensemble is made up of a roughly equal number of female and male performers, which in *UVenas no Adonisi* align themselves with Venus and Adonis respectively, forming two groups along gender lines. Instead of offering a single choral narrative voice, or even a split male and female chorus function (as Britten does in his *Lucretia*, based on Shakepeare's second narrative poem *The Rape of Lucrece,* an inversion of and dark companion piece to *Venus and Adonis*), the creation of two choral groups in *UVenas* conjures distinct but interwoven musical and social communities (sometimes in harmony, sometimes in playful tension).[14] Isango's use of 'traditional' gender arrangements updates the now lifeless trope of Mars and Venus: the male chorus figures the exclusive sodality of the hunt (the hunters and their prey), while the women present domestic group life and a more relational, gender-inclusive sense of community.

The gender division follows the traditional division of the choir, particularly prominent in African choirs with their emphasis on call and response, and play between the bass and high registers. With the singers here working as an ensemble, in free movement on the stage, this arrangement functions also something like the gender divisions of the classical ballet. In the classical *corps de ballet*, dancers tend to oscillate between their gender-assigned group identity and the pressure (increasing as the ballet progresses) to pair up in *pas de deux* around the central coupling of the principals. *UVenas* makes a playful concession to this very Western form of hierarchical hetero-pageantry in the scene where Adonis' mount abandons him to chase after a passing mare. The rendering of this sequence constituted one of the productions high points. In a moment of beautifully orchestrated surprise, the men's pounding, and seemingly inexorable unison drumming, under the proud standard of Adonis' charger (a great frame puppet perhaps reminding the audience of the London hit *Warhorse* with its South African puppets), was slyly undermined by the gentle, playful marimba-led musical insinuations of the women parading their own hobbyhorse. As the singing on both sides modulated and fused into a giddy canter, men and women linked arms and coupled up in parody of the courtly dance: part ballet, part barn dance, part polite bacchanal. As they pranced off, the audience heard neighing echoes, perhaps a mock at Kenneth Branagh's panettone *Much Ado* with its ample hey-nonny-nonnying and pastoral tripping. In this scene, the conflict in *UVenas* was played out on the level of style rather than argument: a clash of musical idioms, addressing different sources of audience pleasure. The scene engaged, quite directly – and subversively – the London audience's investment in 'the power of… stamping feet' and warriors 'in full cry', the problem that I examine in the next section.[15]

At once dramatically effective and visually striking, the use of a large gender-divided chorus made an impression on audiences and reviewers. Scenes like this one were particularly effective in underscoring the gender tension. But *UVenas* involves a further and more complex division of voices, where the chorus does considerably more than echo or amplify the tension between the principals. Within the production, the male ensemble offered a complete picture of Adonis' (Mhlekazi Mosiea's) masculine world, taking the roles of hunter and quarry in the ritual dance, while Katlego Mmusi and Luvo Rasemeni gave a figure and personality to the emblematic figures of death and the boar.[16] The relation between chorus and titular characters became more complicated with Venus's presentation. In the first half of the production, the role was shared: a succession of singers from the women's group took up the mantle of Venus (literally a length of cloth that, when worn on the body, would invest a performer with the personality of the Goddess).[17] The audience thus watched a succession of Venuses worship, taunt, implore harass, and cajole Adonis, in different moods and idioms. In their spoken scenes, the performers taking the Goddess' part were given space to shape their appeals to Adonis. In most of these workshopped segments, the language and arguments that resulted were only loosely modelled on Shakespeare's. A translator preparing the script for surtitling (this production featured no surtitles) might find it difficult to link what is there back to the text of Shakespeare's poem.[18] But the adoption of a new voice for each stage of Adonis' seduction translated – in physical if not linguistic terms – the essential rhetorical movement that is at the core of Shakespeare's poem.

Rhetorical argument, not narrative, powers Shakespeare's long 'narrative poems', which above all dramatise the processes of persuasion. Antithesis: the war of white and red, chastity and passion, cold and hot, innocence and experience, and (in a notable inversion of regular roles) male and female, structures description in the poem. However, description takes a back seat to persuasion. Shakespeare's second narrative poem, *The Rape of Lucrece*, despite its violent theme, is full of instances of persuasion: the rapist Tarquin debates first with himself, then with his victim, and leaves her after the act to argue herself to death. The Venus of his *Venus and Adonis* is a tireless debater.

Although Adonis maintains a stony silence for most of the poem's onslaught, the boy does make some answer to the Goddess' bombardment, and then with devastating effect. Like Lucrece, Venus continues to debate with herself even after her interlocutor's departure, right up to the discovery of his death. *Venus and Adonis* is a poem of failure, of constant deflation; it is the failure of Venus's arguments that drives and structures the poem, forcing her to find fresh matter. Isango's dramatisation captures this essential movement, where each new face of Venus may mark the end of a line of argument. But the production's engagement with the poem's functional grammar, along with its more subtle and sophisticated effects, was downplayed or simply missed in discussion of *UVenas*. Treating *UVenas* as a musical spectacle, with a focus on colour, sound, and the impact and appositeness of 'tribal' African elements, at most critics noted the obvious antithesis between male and female, a (tribal) war of the sexes.

'In full cry': press reception

Despite the ensemble's standing in London, the reviewer for *The Standard* declared herself impressed by their 'wonderfully confident rendition'[19] of the Shakespearean material. *The Independent*'s correspondent, who noted that 'South Africa's contribution is a home-made adaptation of Venus and Adonis', reasoning that '[n]o other races can chant, dance and sing like Zulus and Xhosa in full cry' concluded (on what must have seemed to the author a high note) that 'the power of their stamping feet will make even the Globe shake.' The article, by Ivan Fallon, appeared in two versions. The second ran under the header 'Poetry in Motion as South Africans Tackle Shakespeare', suggesting 1) that South Africa struggles with poetry/Shakespeare, and 2) that poetry is in this case substituted by physical energy 'the power of their stamping feet'.[20]

The familiar strain of ethnic essentialism that runs through the popular press response is too common to be concerned with unpacking here; likewise the patronising framing of this 'homemade' 'contribution' to what sounds more like a nineteenth century expo than an exploration of multiculturalism – and in the case of *The Independent* that ugliest of the expo's inventions, the 'human zoo'. But here the observation of 'tribal' performance was not limited to the popular press. Peter Kirwan identified the South African production as 'celebratory of its diverse heritages', while 'aware of its future', the revealed kernel of a 'tribal story, a myth of essential human practices', in which tribal stands, oddly, for universal. This rhetorical move seems to attempt to match, in the contrast, the universalism of a tribal past with the universalism of a global present. Kirwan is a committed reviewer whose positioning as an academic theatre critic and the ambitious one-man blogger of the RSC *Complete Works* has seen him called upon several times to engage in public reflection around responsible reviewing practices. His review for *Year of Shakespeare* sketches a narrative of homecoming both for Shakespeare (who has in some sense always been in Africa?) and for South Africa, here trading in its 'traditional' past for a bright 'global' future. Of course the country is continually trading *in* its 'tribal' traditions to please an international media market. This reality indicates a rather dim future for South African theatre and a rather rosy imagining of the global market, one that the festival perhaps encourages.[21] More generally, the attempt to trace a narrative of homecoming in Isango's work for the festival exacts a toll on both language and logic in this review.

Lisa Cagnacci – whose assessment for *Shakespeare in Southern Africa* ascribes what is interesting in this production to Brecht (another strained narrative of homecoming) – suggests that 'Dornford-May creates the world of this production as a gender-divided space in which women and men are represented as separate tribes.'[22] The reversion here to the (common) description of tribal culture, displaced onto gender in this instance, obscures both the role of community in the ensemble's deft working of chorus and solo roles and the sophistication of its effects.[23] Venus's ensemble presentation was similarly confused by attempts to describe the production in terms of its tribal colour, in the *Evening Standard's* review, which speaks of 'chief Venus' (Malefane) and her 'sisters'. This characterisation, which does a poor job of explaining the role sharing, does manage to invoke and yoke together tribal hierarchy and a romanticised vision of African equality, setting the ranked hierarchy of the 'chief' and her attendants alongside the imagined African family of Venus and her 'sisters'.[24] Ivan Fallon for *The Independent* does somewhat better with the facts, noting: '[i]n fact there are seven Venuses to one (very athletic) Adonis, each representing different phases of the goddess's seduction process and becoming more and more irresistible as the musical develops to the point where one has to question Adonis's sexuality. How else can mortal flesh hold out?'[25] With similar salacious relish, Fiona Mountford assured the readers of the *Evening Standard* that '[n]o translation is required to understand what deliciously expressive chief Venus Malefane and her sisters want from the unwilling youth', pointing to the poem's universalism, but also to the substitution of enthusiastic bodies for a missing poetry.[26]

Despite the problems of an eclectic libretto, part extempore, presented in multiple languages, audiences familiar with Shakespeare's narrative poem *could* follow the developments in the poem, quite nearly, when they realised that each new face of Venus marks a key defeat in the poem and a corresponding shift in strategy that maps to the major movements of Shakespeare's poem. Venus' several changes represent not an escalation of erotic energy, the mounting of an irresistible sexual power (the defining erotic energy of the African Venus), but her repeated defeat in the face of Adonis' reasoned resolve. Director Dornford May, who suggested the project as an alternative when the company was offered *King John*, has had a long familiarity with the poem.[27] The structure created in *UVenas*, while allowing the performers some broad freedom of interpretation within a 'workshopping approach', still observes (and amplifies) the poem's highly rhetorical structure as well as its Ovidian echoes.[28] The translation effected here is not only between Shakespeare's original and the African context: the director's studied design also translates for a contemporary British audience the relationship between rhetoric and action that is now the most difficult and unfamiliar aspect of the poem. It is perhaps the director's greatest success in this production that his creative presence has been so overlooked. Press and academics have opted to ignore or downplay *UVenas'* more sophisticated handling of its source material, letting their attention be held by glimpses of 'tribal' life and the display of natural township talent.

This is a familiar mode of response. For critics working to convey to an armchair audience the excitement and immediacy of rehearsal and performance in the high stakes atmosphere of the 'world stage' premiere, their focus on the energy and spirit of the performers has seemed only natural. But after several years, this has established itself as a cliché. Citing numerous instances in coverage of *Impempe*, which *The Telegraph* labelled 'An Explosion of Joy from the Townships of South Africa', Sheila and J.Q. Davies have suggested that the trope of natural, spontaneous African performance – the 'happy native' now on a truly global postcolonial tour – may have blinded critics to the production's 'more challenging aspects and truly innovative moments'.[29] The case does not need to be made again for *UVenas*, which showed the same emphasis with similar effect – although Paul Taylor's comment for *The Independent* is a remarkable demonstration:

> *No company on Earth takes more joy in performing* or communicates that joy more *infectiously* to the souls of an audience than Cape Town's award-winning Isango Ensemble… the Isango Ensemble *delights* in darting around an emotional range that extends from warmly winning comic cheek to the kind of *full-throated fervor* [sic] that touches sublimity.[30] [My italics]

This can stand as a footnote to Davies and Davies' assessment of how the company is positioned by critics. But it is worth also noting the peculiar function that this image of the performers fulfills for audiences for international theatre. The trope of joyful performance serves this audience particularly well in shielding it from awareness either of the performers' exploitation or – and this is perhaps more interesting – their own. In choosing to return again and again to tropes of Isango's 'infectious' 'enthusiasm' and 'joyful energy', reviewers choose to attribute their own enthusiasm and pleasure to the company's pleasure in performance, rather than its *manipulation* of the audience's pleasure, which is after all the mainstay of theatre. It is interesting that, after several years, critics continue (naïvely?) to ascribe the effect of productions like *UVenas* to the performer's naïve raw emotional states, rather than their capacity to work a crowd. Taken against this background of critical consensus, Cagnacci's reading of the play as a working out of Elizabethan theatre through a tradition of Brechtian theatre appears unusual, but ultimately not surprising. This interpretation evidently works to secure the authenticity of the play's Elizabethanism via the authenticity of Brechtian meditation, lost in the UK, but (as in a romance) carried to South Africa, where it grew up and blossomed in the protest theatre of the 1970s. Thus a piece termed 'distinctively South African in its theatrical vocabulary', that this author insists 'could only have come from the imagination of a South African company', is taken to represent 'a piece of highbrow lyric passed via Brecht to the heart of a Cape Town rehearsal room and then delivered back to the stage for which Shakespeare wrote his most populist plays'. To one familiar with Isango's context and with South African protest theatre (better represented at the festival in the techniques of the two-hander Shona *Two Gentlemen of Zimbabwe* than in the visual and musical South African elements of *UVenas*) the tracing of direct descent through Brecht must seem an outlandish, and rather fanciful, account of origins.[31] But it makes sense as the creation of artistic genealogy to shape a narrative of homecoming, clearly (if obliquely) serving the story of Shakespeare's homecoming. In the scenario that Cagnacci pictures, Brecht and Shakespeare travel to Africa on the same ticket. What results is doubly authentic: authentically Elizabethan via Brecht's privileged engagement, authentically South African in accessing the real (historical) South African theatre, influenced by Brecht. This lends pedigree to the origins of a piece of 'international' theatre, assembled for an international festival and the international circuit.

No doubt it would be unfair to point out that it is the British director, Mark Dornford May (not Shakespeare, or Brecht) who has gone to South Africa and 'come home' to the London theatre with his ensemble. That is unfair to the director (emphatically invested in his South African identity),[32] but a fair caution to commentators who would like to picture William (and Bertold) going on a voyage of inspiration in Africa, while they wink at the show's actual conditions of production. It is hard to see why one would choose to read this production in terms of Brecht via Cape Town, except to secure a narrative of voyage and homecoming. In this story, Elizabethan stage practice travels to South Africa with Brecht and returns – on a Shakespeare ticket – to London. Such a narrative however displaces any proper concern with the history of theatre, Shakespeare, or opera in South Africa. Isango's contribution to the festival probably has more to say about theatre, and particularly opera in South Africa, than about either Brecht or Shakespeare in South Africa – a shortfall in discussion that this discussion will try to address.

Back to the township

Across the festival, finally, the trope of 'Shakespeare's coming home' gained more traction than the performance of linguistic community. Within this nationalist rubric, there existed a significant (and problematic) level of rhetorical construction around productions billed as coming 'from Africa'. Among those 'African' productions, *UVenas no Adonisi* was framed, also and importantly as a production 'from a township'. It was given particular prominence as an apex of the Shakespearean *nostos*, the far shore that Shakespeare reaches in Cagnacci's vision, and in many others.[33]

When the festival producer Tom Bird approached the Isango Ensemble, they engaged a company well known on the London and international circuit that could already boast a developed multilingual practice. But Isango frame their work as 'bringing the rich indigenous culture of [South Africa's] black population to bear on classics from the Western theatrical canon' (instead of promoting a 'rainbow nation' aesthetic) and achieve this, 'often finding a new context for the stories within a township setting'.[34] The township was highly visible at the festival, both in the production's *mise en scène* and in the framing of the company. Each served to establish for the audience the connection between the black South African performers and 'the township'. This framing entails particular stress on the background of the performers, the crafting of a rags to riches narrative in which Dornford May is credited primarily as mentor and coach. His 'paternal guidance', to quote Fallon's patronising term, has 'transformed a company of novices' into 'professional performers who can more than acquit themselves on the world stage.'[35]

The representation of township life brought to the Globe was less literal than in Dornford May's first South African venture, *UCarmen EKhayelitsha*, and in other adaptations from the company. These have tended to be explicit – even emphatic – about their location, the successful translation to the South African township setting being seen as a saleable mark of the company's quality. Responsive to its immediate and particular context (the Globe), *UVenas* fashioned a more abstract, masque-like sense of location, not identified with any particular time or place. But the township was referenced in the production's visual design and its use of 'found' elements. The more fantastical mixing of materials and historical styles had been rehearsed in *Impempe*. Presenting the production's iconic diva image, Malefane had played Mozart's Queen of the Night in a hoop skirt of cutoffs and feathers that *The Guardian* assumed to be an 'Elizabethan gown'.[36] The vague African Renaissance-Baroque style had then already been successfully deployed as a bridge between the real and the fantastical. But the costuming for *UVenas* appeared particularly fitting among the Globe Theatre's gaudy faux marble columns and crudely painted mythical wall scenes. Combining Elizabethan swagger and aristocratic fancy with the meanest materials, the look of Isango at the Globe neatly matched both the upstart pretensions of the original theatre and the modern violations of time and place entailed at the touristy Bankside replica.

For *UVenas*, Isango presented an eclectic reclamation aesthetic fitted to the improvisatory quality of the township's informal built environment that gestured at once to and away from the Globe stage. The thrust or apron stage, extending beyond the proscenium arch, imposed its form over any rendering of place, as it did for all of the companies in the festival – most of them, like Isango, accustomed to playing to audiences in small black box venues on the international circuit. The detailed local effects that the ensemble have achieved in such theatres – transporting audiences to the bleak plots, corrugated iron alleyways, and lamp–lit shack interiors that are stock images of the township – would have less impact on the Globe's uniformly lit, painted platform. Hence the company's rehearsal space, a reclaimed hall in downtown Cape Town, was set up to prepare the performers with markings to indicate the thrust stage, the musician's balcony, the pit, and columns, including daubed walls and gilded ceilings.

UVenas no Adonisi's self-described 'carnival' aesthetic aimed to strike a balance between the vivid evocation of township life and the creation of vivid and viable spectacle in the Globe's space.[37] The performer's bodies were the most visible site of this intermarriage. The costume designer, avoiding the cliché of brightly coloured African dress, had focused on texture, creating rich effects with fabrics in dusky, muted shades. For the women, short peplums to hip-length stood out over long full skirts, achieving the distinctive Elizabethan silhouette. The dress was set off by long fingerless gloves and loosely arranged ruffs, somewhat like traditional bead collars. The men's costumes, made of a mix of fabrics, combat print, hessian and a kind of rough mail, playfully echoed the women's. Here, the addition of overskirts suggested the padded round hose of Shakespeare's day. Where the women's faces were adorned with stipples of Xhosa face paint, the men's were daubed with war-paint, and they carried the standard–issue rough blankets that circulate in South African schools, prisons, and poorhouses. In the painted Globe, these rough materials, in slight variation across the costumes, took on a kind of richness and solidity, in a carefully calculated effect. A distinctive feature of the improvised physical environment of the township – oil barrels –were turned to use as drums, alongside marimbas, to generate a range of effects from the natural to the supernatural. (In Cape Town the drums were also used to represent the Globe theatre's great oak columns and were painted a brilliant, 'cheap and cheerful' turquoise.) Speaking to *The Independent*, Dyantyis explained: 'We try to limit our props and musical instruments to the kind of things you can find in a township', adding, 'Mark [Donford May] often says if you can't find it there, you can't use it.'[38] The strategy was undoubtedly successful on the Globe stage. But this last addition begs the question: why the restriction? It has often been noted that *Impempe* and *IKrismas Kherol* made use of video projection, flames, and lights through the trapdoor.

The use of limited props calls to mind a distinctive form of theatre associated with the townships: the small scale Apartheid era protest theatre that has taken the designation 'township theatre'. In this case it was better represented by Two Gents Productions' supple two-hander, *Vaviri Vakomana Vaviri Ve Zimbabwe*. This 'Zimbabwean' company (in fact based in London[39]) make deft use of no more than their two actor's bodies, voices, and a trunk containing minimal props (a glove, hat, scarves) to present the action and all the characters of Shakespeare's *The Two Gentlemen of Verona*. This is a feat of storytelling facilitated by the techniques of township theatre, which achieved its greatest expression in South Africa in the 1980s. Township theatre was organised not so much to reference the South African township as a location, as to function (creatively) within its supposed limits. At that time the use of a minimal cast and limited props was initiated as a *response* – not a gesture – to the restricted and oppressive conditions of black cultural life and expression under Apartheid. This theatre practice, focused on flexible storytelling, through narratives developed in workshops, and with minimal resources, made theatre (at least theoretically) accessible to black South Africans in the townships, both as audiences and as theatre makers. This was achieved without the aid of white theatre makers – although the well-known examples that gained international audiences later, were (like Two Gents Productions) typically collaborations between black performers and white directors.[40] These highly portable productions travelled, as did their proponents and techniques. Largely through direct contact with South African practitioners, township theatre came to exert a substantial influence on the development of post-independence Zimbabwean theatre; but it was also taken up in more privileged theatre cultures that found its flexible techniques useful for their purposes, such as the international theatre circuit in which Two Gents operate.

Township theatre made a theatrical virtue of necessity at a specific historical moment. As Two Gents demonstrates, that has added substantially to the idiom of contemporary 'global' theatre. Isango has a different relationship to the South African township, based essentially in the authenticity of its performers, where the township exists (and must exist) as the source and guarantee of that authenticity. 'The township' in this sense does not simply exist. The company is obliged continually to perform its authenticity, and thus the township, for its audiences on the international theatre circuit.

The construction of the township as a source of authenticity necessarily involves a degree of distortion, not just in the selective representations onstage, but in the way the company constitutes itself in relation to an image of the township. It is worth noting that the one thing the black opera company will in all likelihood not represent is the current status of opera in the townships and in South Africa. In communities located in the informal settlements around Cape Town, there exists a vibrant culture of choral singing, especially around church choirs. Isango highlights this tradition. There is also opera – although one would not get this impression reading the press or PR that the company generates. The University of Cape Town's Opera School has been sourcing talent from disadvantaged communities since before 1994. In Khayelitsha, which Isango claims as its home, a large number of aspirant singers either study at the opera school or work to be admitted to its programmes. The Cape Town Opera is the country's only permanent year-round company and a product of the reforming of the arts council and opera school after 1999. It has worked alongside the opera school in developing talent in Khayelitsha and other disadvantaged communities, and in providing opportunities for aspirant singers.

Isango's appeal on the international circuit as a black South African opera company (still associated with the hugely successful *UCarmen EKhayelitsha*) works in a similar way to that of international Shakespeare. With a pleasantly reassuring sense of surprise it inspires the thought that opera/Shakespeare/ whatever instance of high culture might emerge and thrive *even here*. It is the hope that lies behind *Time Out*'s framing of *Impempe*: '[y]et Khayelitsha, where unemployment and poverty seem insuperable, is the wellspring of a production of The Magic Flute'.[41] Readers are to marvel here at the fact that opera can emerge and thrive (spontaneously, in the metaphor of the wellspring), *even here* in South Africa, and among the country's most underprivileged. This is akin to the rhetorical force of 'Shakespeare's Coming Home' in Globe to Globe's international showcase, as we wonder at (yet happily accept) the evidence that a widely travelled Shakespeare is able to inspire, and take inspiration, so far from 'home': England.

Yet *UVenas no Adonisi* combines two forms (opera and Shakespearean theatre) that occupy very different places in South Africa's cultural life. This 'even here' model assumes that opera is as foreign to South Africans as Shakespearean performance. But while Shakespearean performance in South Africa remains typically the preserve of ingrained (and continuing) historical privilege, stagnation, and mediocrity, opera exists as a site of growth, transformation, and/aspiration.[42] Narratives of Isango's redemptive work in the townships proceed on the assumption that mainstream South Africa opera (if it exists at all) remains an unrepresentative white institution. Journalists routinely laud Isango's 'all black' productions, without questioning what this represents. Cape Town Opera is predominantly black, although this dominance is established by the large number of black singers in the chorus and principal roles are still routinely given to white singers. In national terms, the notion that the Cape Town Opera is the blackest opera company in the world is secondary to the fact that the opera is unusually representative and racially inclusive.[43]

For a short time Opera Africa (a Durban-based opera company formed in response to the withdrawal of funding for opera on the dissolving of the regional Performing Arts Councils after 1994) had the distinction of being 'the first 100 percent community black owned and managed opera company', although the company did not survive. The first 'all-black South African opera' was not Isango's *Impempe*, but Opera Africa's 1995 *Zauberflöte*. The closure of Opera Africa points to real material difficulties in South African performing arts. In general, audiences for opera remain relatively small, white, and affluent, but opera has undergone a massive transformation.

The media gives a flattened sense of South Africa's cultural landscape. This reportage fits with the narrative of Isango's redemptive work, and proceeds on the assumption that Isango operates in a cultural vacuum with regard to opera, thus ignoring the existence (and preexistence) of organisations and individuals promoting opera in the townships, as well as other similar projects.[44] The journalist who refers readers to the ensemble's 'full-throated singing chops [,] honed in the South African townships' choral tradition' foregrounds one truth: the vital role of township choirs. Yet he conceals another: the numbers of singers in the townships aspiring to, and receiving, classical training.[45] The worlds of *amakwaya* and opera are not as separate as this account might suppose. Choir leaders typically identify and train singers who go on to pursue classical studies. For example, a journalist who interviewed Dornford May in 2008, on the production of *Impempe* declared of the cast (many of whom now appear in the cast of *UVenas no Adonisi*), '[n]one of the three dozen participants was conventionally trained in the European manner, but each brought to the stage heaps of *natural* talent, honed in the South African choral tradition.' Leaving aside the tropes of raw skill, this was untrue of the company in 2008 and it is untrue now. The cast biographies prepared for the festival obscure the fact that many members had received earlier training through the UCT opera school.[46]

The director has made only (very) odd admissions of other contexts and networks that shape the 'natural talent' of his performers. In an interview in 2008 around the UK transfer of *Impempe* and *IKrismas Kherol*, Dornford May confided: 'three of the five new people have just finished at UCT music department. I said, "When did Mozart live?" No idea. "What was his first name?" No idea.'[47] These questions presumably reveal more about the director's relationship to the University than that of his performers, although it may be that they are taken out of context. A more rounded view emerges in an interview with David Lan, director of the Young Vic Theatre, where *Impempe* and *IKrismas Kherol* had their London season. Talking to *The Independent*, Lan noted that some members were 'university-trained, while others have had most of their experience in church choirs'. As if anticipating essentialist emphasis of the press on the 'raw' African talent from the townships, Lan insisted: "It's false, I believe, to think of talent as bedded into the DNA, as a force that will realise itself come what may. Talent is a relationship – with a parent, a friend, a teacher..." He pointed out that the careers of four of the strongest singers in the company could be attributed to a local choir leader, Nolufefe Mtshabe. The question was then posed, '[b]ut where are all the other teachers, companies, schools, and well-wishers needed to create the hundreds of thousands of relationships to activate the tremendous creativity there could be?' This stands not as a denial of the networks that exist (as emerges, unfortunately, in Isango's press), but as a call for further activity and investment, and for greater cooperation and collaboration between various cultural players.[48]

The decision to bring Isango to the Young Vic in 2008 was explicitly framed in terms of London's multiculturalism, invoking a notion of community that displaces geography and nation. As Lan explained: "[l]iving as we do in a world city, intimately and powerfully connected in one way or another to virtually every other community, we feel that to make shows for London we have to engage, in our own tiny way, with 'others' in 'other places'."[49] Lan's statement points to the fact that Dromgoole and Bird's project, while striking in its scope, was not radically new. To a large degree, the festival offered a stage for international theatre work and a multicultural project already happening in London. Thus in the festival's 'African' showcase, the productions from South Sudan and Nigeria weighed in against work by UK-based organisations that were positioned to produce African theatre for the international theatre market. These include the London-based company, Two Gents Productions, who produce their Zimbabwean work primarily within and for the London diaspora and festival circuit; and the UK company Bitter Pill (linked to Africa by its Zimbabwean-born British director), which brought Kenya's contribution to the festival through the process of workshops at the Harare festival and at The Oval House Theatre, Two Gents' London base. Bitter Pill moved directly from this work to a Zimbabwean project, *The Harare Files*, drawing acting talent from Two Gents. It is difficult to say on which side Dornford May's ensemble falls, as it is based in South Africa (Cape Town), but performs almost exclusively for international audiences. Overall, the representation of 'Africa' on the Globe to Globe stage clearly demonstrated that the grand Olympic festival project was as much involved with supporting existing projects of international theatre as bringing national theatres to London audiences.

Conclusion

There was something problematic in the framing of the greater part of the festival's productions 'from Africa' – although Lan's reflections on Isango's 2007 season suggest that this may be rooted in the festival's multicultural project (37 plays in 37 languages) as much as its nationalistic claim, 'Shakespeare's Coming Home' (after a successful global circumnavigation). The Isango Ensemble's association with the South African township is a particular case. The company's work clearly – indeed explicitly – depends on a reification of the township as the authentic locus of (black) South African life. As I have shown, this construction suppresses an acknowledgement of growth and change in the township that does not serve a vision of Isango's unique contribution (e.g. the development of opera in the townships existing and preexisting outside of the company). Given the pace of change – Khayelitsha is the largest and the fastest growing of South Africa's townships – this image appears outdated if not nostalgic. The word suggests here not the pain of historical memory (intimately part of the 'township' as an Apartheid legacy), but a sentimentalising and simplification of community, poverty and aspiration in South Africa's rapidly growing informal settlements.

Further, exploitation of the image of the township is uncomfortably linked to questions about the exploitation of performers. If the township has been a central trope in discussions of the ensemble's work, it has loomed equally large in actor's complaints against the company. Jasper Rees' breezy explanation that

> The Isango Ensemble from Cape Town has had a name change or two over the past decade, but it is essentially the same company which won an Olivier Award for its West End reinvention of The Magic Flute in 2008, and is even better known for its ravishing township-flavoured account of The Mysteries… obscures the company's fractured history since 2001, where every change of name has been accompanied by discord, litigation, the closing of doors, accusations of exploitation, suspicions of financial misconduct, and the surfacing of deep unhappiness, including sporadic protests and media campaigns against Dornford May from those he has employed.[50]

While the international media, and company PR celebrate Isango's productions from the township,[51] a recurrent theme in the complaints from performers has been precisely that they *still* live in the townships, while Dornford May and Malefane, who travel to receive international awards (it is claimed that the company were told these would make them all rich), raise a family in the wealthy suburbs.[52] It is very hard to assess either the truth or the significance of these claims. There is something Dickensian in the types that emerge: Dornford May as the scheming profiting exploiter, and his wife the iron-fisted madam forcing the singers to buy food from her family's catering company. The South African press has fanned the flames of controversy and incarnations of the project have ended in ashes to rise again. The tale of the death of Adonis, kept painfully alive in the flower that Venus plucks (a bitter Ovidian consolation), is apt material for the company. Retracing the unhappy legacy of Isango, here relegated mainly to footnotes, may act as a corrective to the blindness and forgetfulness of the British media. However, it allows one little room to talk or think about the value of the work being done by the company. As in *Venus and Adonis*, the company presents a history of repeated failures, in which great effort is spent, and no one emerges satisfied or unhurt. The story conveys the deep disappointment of Isango's performers, but presumably also the disappointed dreams of Dornford May and his one-time supporters. Sponsors Dick Enthoven and Eric Abraham (who expressed regret that the company had never performed in Khayelitsha) equally become unsympathetic, compromised figures in their engagement with the project, although they must once have felt and been motivated by something like the excitement Lan found in the company. It is possible that the ensemble needs less, not more, skepticism to realise any of its dreams. At the same time, audiences and reviewers might be more sceptical about their imaginative investment in the township. While the South African township is far from disappearing, the thought that Dornford May's project may in some sense *need* 'the township' as a centre of talent, vitality, and regeneration, to function as an image of redemptive poverty is, and should be, a troubling one.

NOTES

1 The festival was launched by a multilingual reading of the sonnets, a kind of opening ceremony presenting 154 sonnets in 'more than 25 languages'. But *UVenas no Adonisi* the dramatization of Shakespeare's long poem, was billed as the opening performance.

2 The Complete Works Festival successfully sold 2006-7 as Shakespeare's year, while the British cultural Olympiad, charged with mounting a full year of cultural display (2011-12), lacked such audience salience.

3 Jasper Rees, 'Globe to Globe: Venus and Adonis, Shakespeare's Globe', *The Arts Desk* 21/04/012 <http://www.theartsdesk.com/theatre/globe-globe-venus-and-adonis-shakespeares-globe> accessed 01/01/01.

4 In an interview with Globe Research, festival producer Tom Bird highlighted nationalism as the major aspect to emerge from the festival project, noting that "a sense of nationalism was ever present in the festival despite working against it", where participating companies were briefed to focus on *language* (translations). Amy Kenny, 'The Globe Olympic experience', panel presentation at The Year of Shakespeare London Workshop, London, 12 June 2012.

5 South African theatre makers have been well supported by tours in the UK, where their work frequently finds support. See 'War Horse and SA-UK Theatre Dynamics', *Financial Mail* (9/08/12).

6 In 2009 an awkward article in *The Independent* seeking to explain the appeal of 'African Theatre' in London repeatedly pointed to music's force in narrative-driven African theatre. Andrew Johnson, 'Out of Africa; Award-winning African plays find a new home in British theatres', *The Independent on Sunday* (05/07/09).

7 Amy Kenny, 'The Globe Olympic experience', panel presentation at The Year of Shakespeare London Workshop, London, 12 June 2012.

8 Dornford May explains: 'there is music, but it's not a musical... I do think people have become tired of formulaic music in theatre.' Johnson (05/07/09).

9 The production played up the more obvious elements of Greek myth. A bearded and portly Zamile Gantana performed a walk-on as Cupid, in rave bunny wings and a vest bearing the silver moniker 'Cupid'.

10 The speech is mainly between Venus and Adonis, but their long speeches shade into monologue, aiding the transposition to opera.

11 This can be compared with *Impempe*, which foregrounded musical and linguistic translation in its handling of Mozart's score and libretto.

12 Wadsworth was only 23 when he wrote his one act opera. A better point of comparison is Benjamin Britten's *Lucretia*. Other operatic treatments (John Blow's *Venus and Adonis* c.1683, Henri Desmaret's 1697 and Hans Werner Henze's 1997 chamber operas) have worked directly with the Ovidian material.

13 This goes beyond maintaining a star vehicle for Malefane (e.g. appearing as a female Scrooge in *iKrismas Kherol*). *The Mysteries* featured a female God, Jesus, and Satan.

14 Britten's opera makes use of a male and female chorus presented by two individuals.

15 See endnote 20.

16 The introduction of grim-visaged Death as the Goddess' rival in the second half allowed the warlike boar - a dancer in the dance of the hunt - to take on more affirming qualities of energy, virility, participation, though at the same time it shifted the production away from the *erotic* rivalry suggested in the poem.

17 In a more material, domestic context, the bedsheet also represented the snares of love.

18 South African audience members I have spoken with remarked the poor quality of dialogue produced for audiences who do not speak Nguni or Sotho-Twsana languages, suggesting that the actors' improvised speech sometimes verges on nonsense.

19 Fiona Mountford, *Evening Standard* (23/04/2012).

20 *The Independent* (18/04/12) <http://www.independent.co.uk/arts-entertainment/theatre-dance/reviews/venus-and-adonis-performed-by-isango-ensemble-directed-by-mark-dornfordmay-7647648.html; http://www.independent.co.uk/arts-entertainment/theatre-dance/features/poetry-in-motion-as-south-africans-tackle-shakespeare-7654699.html> accessed 01/01/01.

21 See Colette Gordon, 'Around the Globe and Back Again', *Year of Shakespeare* (14/06/12) <http://bloggingshakespeare.com/year-of-shakespeare-around-the-globe-and-back-again> accessed 01/01/01.

22 'A South African Aesthetic at Shakespeare's Globe', *Shakespeare in Southern Africa* 24 (2012): 64-6 (65).

23 The term 'community' appears nowhere in these discussions of 'tribes' and 'tribal' division.

24 The reviewer does pick up on the queenly position that Malefane takes in the company, as its musical director, female principal, and wife of the director (The *London Evening Standard* refers to Malefane and Dornford May as the 'Isangos'). From Carmen, to the Queen of the Night to Scrooge imagined as a ruthless female mine owner, the prepossessing soprano's onstage persona as the tough businesswomen matches her powerful role in the company. A series of dramatic diva (literally goddess) roles have perhaps fed (and unfairly) presentations of Malefane as a cold exploiter in the South Africa press.

25 Fallon, *Independent*

26 *Evening Standard*, 23/04/2012. See also director Jane Moriarty writing for the festival's blog ...'No matter whether or not we understood what was being said, there was absolutely no doubt as to what Venus had on her mind...' <http://blog.shakespearesglobe.com/venus-and-adonis-as-reviewed-by-the-young-directors/> accessed 14/01/01.

27 Conversation with director (16/04/2012)

28 Adonis' transformation into a flower in Ovid's account in *Metamorphoses* is the most obvious.

29 Davies and Davies, '"So take this Magic Flute and Blow. It will Protect Us As We Go": *Impempe Yomlingo* (2007-11) and South Africa's Ongoing Transition', *Opera Quarterly* (15/06/12), 1-18 (13)

30 'World-Class Show Kicks off a Bardic Global Gathering', *The Independent* 27/04/12, my italics

31 On the influence of township theatre in *Two Gents* and Zimbabwean theatre, see section below.

32 Dornford May was accepted into the Sotho clan in 2007. In the same year he told an interviewer 'I should have been born in Africa...I feel right at home here and am very passionate about this country...' Peter Tromp, 'From Film to Theatre', *Cape Times* (01/10/07).

33 Here the township takes its place among other spaces of abjection and exception that are popular sites of Shakespearean intervention: sites of incarceration, violent conflict, and trauma.

34 'Cape Crusaders', *Time Out* interview <http://www.timeout.com/london/classical-music/article/3377/cape-crusaders-isango-ensemble> accessed 01/10/10. Although the 'rainbow' nation is here rejected in favour of 'black theatre', Dornford May speaks proudly of his 'rainbow family'. Tim Whewell, 'From South Africa's townships to the opera house', *BBC Newsnight* (06/07/10) <news.bbc.co.uk/2/hi/programmes/newsnight/8739017.stm> accessed 01/02/2013.

35 Fallon, *Independent*.

36 Justin Cartwright, 'District Six Revisited: South Africa's New Fugard Theatre', *The Guardian* (03/04/10).

37 Company website <http://www.isangoensemble.org.za/shows/venus-adonis/> accessed 01/03/2013.

38 Fallon, *Independent*.

39 See Colette Gordon, '*Hamlet* in England, *Hamlet* in Exile' in *Shakespeare in Southern Africa* 23 Banishment, Xenophobia, Home and Exile in Shakespeare and the Renaissance (2011), 64-9.

40 Isango draws on its members' skills and cultural archive, as do Two Gents, through workshopping. It is reported that songs were composed in 15 days by performers workshopping in pairs. <http://blog.shakespearesglobe.com/venus-and-adonis-as-reviewed-by-the-young-directors/> accessed 03/03/2013.

41 'Cape Crusaders'

42 Gordon, 'Critical Conditions: Reviewing Shakespeare in South Africa', in *Cahiers Élisabéthains 40th Anniversary Special Issue* (2012), 117-26.

43 Jerg Koeningsdorf, 'Corrugated iron huts, Goethe, Apartheid', *Süddeutsche Zeitung*, 04/07/08.

44 A relevant example is the Umculo / Cape Festival's 2012 production of Henry Purcell's *The Fairy Queen* in collaboration with the National Youth Orchestra of South Africa.

45 Jasper Rees, 'The Magic Flute: Mozart in an African Groove' *The Telegraph* (03/02/2008) <http://www.telegraph.co.uk/culture/theatre/drama/3671148/The-Magic-Flute-Mozart-in-an-African-groove.html> accessed 12/11/2012.

46 Mhlekazi Whawha Moisea, who sings the role of Adonis was trained at the South African College of Music. Zamile Gantana studied at the University of Cape Town's Opera School, and Puleng Jackals and Mandisi Dyantyis (the musical director who has been a lynchpin of the company) both studied at UCT, Dyantyis was trained in jazz before he set his considerable talents to transcribing Mozart's *Magic Flute* in sol fa for voice and marimba and producing original scores for the company.

47 Rees, 'The Magic Flute: Mozart in an African Groove'.

48 David Lan, *The Independent* (15/11/07)

49 *Ibid.*

50 That history goes back to 2000 and the establishment of Dornford May's original South African performance group, *Dimpho Di Kopane*. This fell apart in 2006, when performers, disappointed at receiving no money from the international awards garnered by *UCarmen EKhayelitsha*, communicated their frustration to the media and Dornford May and Malefane resigned from the company (underwritten by millionaire Dick Enthoven) while inquiries were being made into their finances. Soon reformed under the name 'Isango Portobello', with generous sole sponsorship from South African born British producer Eric Abraham, the group lost its Portobello tag, along with their purpose-built permanent performance venue when, after only 9 months, Abraham had the company evicted from the Fugard, following poor box office takings and, again, concern over 'financial irregularities'. At this point, Abraham was a victim of highly publicised protest action from the company, but earlier in that year Dornford May and Malefane had been again accused of exploitative practices by performers in a media and facebook campaign that came to a head with the publication of an open letter that accused the pair of exploiting black artists, stealing their money and ideas, silencing dissent, and punitively cancelling their contracts. The letter published 14 April 2011 on Artslink.co.za was removed, following legal action by Dornford-May and Malefane. David Thomas, *Cape Times* (24/11/10); Philani Nombembe and Grace Johnson, u-Carmen director 'exploiter', *Sunday Times* (17/04/11).

51 The dominant thread on twitter, with many retweets, was 'Shakespeare's sexiest poem as done by a theatre company from South Africa's townships - should sizzle' bbckirstylangKirsty. <http://t.co/6CwcooU4>.

52 Performers from the troupe wrote to the *Mail and Guardian*: 'the whole DDK thing was a big fat lie and fake' and said Dornford-May is 'a fat Englishman [who] made a lot of money out of exploiting their backs black all over the world'. 'Huge amounts of money were spent to fly and put up English artists in hotels in South Africa', while the cast were sent back to their homes in the township. 'Where is Mark? In townships? No, hiding somewhere in his expensive house'. Brent Meersman, 'A real-life drama at the Fugard', *Mail & Guardian* (17/12/10).

Ìtàn Ògìnìntìn, The Winter's Tale
Shakespeare meets Yoruba gods

ADESOLA ADEYEMI

The production of *Ìtàn Ògìnìntìn*[1] for the Globe to Globe Shakespeare festival in the summer of 2012 generated much debate about the nature and reception of modern Nigerian performance culture. *Ìtàn Ògìnìntìn*, a re-reading of *The Winter's Tale* in Yoruba, was written by Chief Ayantade Ipadeola, a traditional drummer and performance artist. Reactions and reviews of the production were hugely varied for both the Nigerian and Globe Theatre performances. While some critics praised a dynamic interpretation of an iconic Shakespeare play that blurred the boundaries of drama, music and dance, and crafted an ecstatic and uplifting evening of African performance (Sanders 2012; Olive 2013), others considered questions about faithfulness to the original text and the subversion of Yoruba myths and performance culture (Sanusi 2012). The range of criticisms of this play raised an awareness of modern theatrical performances in Nigeria, especially among the theatre-going British public whose familiarity with such performances is often limited to Nollywood films and intercultural plays written by Nigerian–British writers such as Oladipo Agboluaje and Bola Agbaje. It is important to mention at the outset that shortly before this play was presented at The Globe, there had been a renewed interest in the drama of Nigerian–British writers. A few weeks before *Ìtàn Ògìnìntìn*, there were productions of three plays in London: Bola Agbaje's *Belong* (Jerwood Theatre Upstairs, Royal Court Theatre, London; 26 April–26 May 2012), *Pandora's Box* by Ade Solanke (Arcola Theatre, London; 9–26 May 2012), and Janice Okoh's *Egusi Soup* at Soho Theatre (23 May–9 June 2012).

Other recent productions from Nigeria in mainstream theatres have been restricted to works by major playwrights such as Wole Soyinka (*Death and the King's Horseman*, National Theatre 2009), Femi Osofisan (*Women of Owu*, 2004), and Zulu Sofola (*Wedlock of the Gods*, Cochrane Theatre 2010) as well as the works of Oladipo Agboluaje at various venues in the UK (*The Estate*, 2006; *The Christ of Coldharbour Lane*, 2007; *The Hounding of David Oluwale*, which is an adaptation of Kester Aspden's book *Nationality: Wog*, 2009; and *Iya Ile* (*The First Wife*, 2009). All these productions, in spite of their cultural source being Nigerian, are written and presented in English. The limited exposure to Nigerian theatre in a language other than English among the British public made the production of Ìtàn Ògìnìntìn a particularly interesting point of study.

To understand the nature of the interest created by the production and the dynamics of the reception in Nigeria and among the Globe audience as well as within the Nigerian community in England, a contextual analysis of Yoruba culture, myths and gods, and theatre practice in Nigeria is necessary.

Yoruba culture, myths and gods – an overview

Dramatic performances among the Yoruba people of southwest Nigeria commonly utilise elements of myths and rituals. They also use extra-linguistic codes such as dance forms, drumming, songs, poetry and poetic chants, and mime, in a representational mode. Most Yoruba performers, especially since the early twentieth century, have generously employed these codes, creating performances that blend traditional performance cultures with practices derived from Western theatre. These dramatists combine elements of Alarinjo tradition (see below) that dates back to the eighteenth century with elements translated from other dramatic performances.

The Yoruba people are a nation who all claim a common nodal ancestry from Oduduwa, the founder of the Yoruba nation. They share the same language, history, traditions, customs, and religion, and perform these shared characteristics as a way of life. Apart from Nigeria, Benin République, and Togo in Africa, the Yoruba are located in large concentration in the diasporic spaces of the Caribbean islands, Cuba, Peru, Brazil, and the United States of America as a result of the legacy of the trans-Atlantic slave trade.

The historic Yoruba state was divided into twenty-five complex, centralised kingdoms, which were further sub-divided into city-states and dependencies (Johnson 1901; Akintoye 2010) Of these cities, Ile-Ife[2] (Ife) is universally recognised as the most ritually important, and the place from which all Yoruba people claim ancestry. The kingdoms include Oyo and Ire, which feature as the settings in Ìtàn Ògìnìntìn. Other motifs that bind the Yoruba people include an acknowledgement of the pantheon of gods and deities, belief in predestination and reverence for the ancestors, particularly through their earthly representatives, the Ifa[3] priest (babalawo), and their symbolic presence in the Egungun[4] masquerade; (symbolic in the sense that male members of the Egungun cult don the masks to represent the ancestors). The gods and deities are also important to the Yoruba way of life. First among these gods are those whom the Supreme Being sent to create the world and they include Ogun, god of creativity and destruction, and of human relationships. When the gods were descending from heaven to the world, they encountered an impenetrable forest and it was Ogun who cleared the way for the other gods to pass. This 'bridging' action (Soyinka 1976) placed Ogun high among the gods. The ritual associated with his worship is one of the most diverse among the Yoruba people and it has provided material for many dramatic enactments, both in the popular tradition and in the western-influenced theatre of modern Nigerian dramatists. Next to the gods are deified kings and warriors whose achievements were honoured by their subjects, such as Sango, the fourth king of Oyo kingdom, who is worshipped as the god of thunder and lightning because of his anger and inclination for retribution; and his river-goddess wife, Oya.

Yoruba performance culture

Modern Yoruba performance culture, fashioned after the Alarinjo tradition, incorporates many elements from the various folk performances, ceremonies and festivals of the Yoruba people such as funeral and wedding ceremonies, and festivals associated with the worship and veneration of gods and goddesses. The elements include dances, songs, chanting, costuming and role play. Alarinjo performance consisted of dances, acrobatic displays, masked performances and poetic chants by itinerant performers. The first written accounts of the Alarinjo are in the travel journals of Hugh Clapperton and Richard Lander who stayed for seven weeks in 1826 at Katunga (Old Oyo, Oyo Ile), the capital of Oyo kingdom. The king had invited his guests to see a performance of an itinerant troupe that Wednesday evening in February 1826. The performance that Clapperton and Lander watched was already a tradition, having started in the late sixteenth century.[5] Thus, a secular Yoruba traditional performance culture that is decidedly different from the ritual performances associated with Ogun or Sango festivals emerged and proliferated until the early twentieth century, when the modern Alarinjo tradition was established in 1944 by Hubert Adedeji Ogunde (1916-1990), a retired teacher and policeman. Kola Ogunmola (1925-1973) followed, creating his own troupe in 1948, while Duro Ladipo (1931-1978) became a writer/actor/manager not long afterwards. These three became the reference point of the modern Yoruba Travelling Theatre, the new Alarinjo theatre.

Ogunde inaugurated the African Music Research Party and incorporated the performance structure of Alarinjo in his plays. He unmasked his performers and introduced dialogue and realism to the theatre. He also changed the presentation style from arena to a western style proscenium arch, and structured his theatre to reflect the reality of his society by focusing on 'the tragedy, the hopes, dreams, triumphs of his time and age' (Ogunbiyi 1981: 23). He brought back the term 'travelling' into Yoruba performance culture by organising extensive tours outside his base in Lagos, the former capital city of Nigeria. The Yoruba Travelling Theatre that arose out of the Ogunde initiatives has been described by Jeyifo as 'one of the most vigorous, widely popular and thriving theatre traditions in modern Africa'

(1984: 1), creating the basis for Yoruba modern performance culture. In qualifying the Yoruba Travelling Theatre as a popular cultural form, Jeyifo notes two features that are fundamental to its relevance:

1. The Travelling Theatre troupes have extensively and consciously drawn upon, and exploited traditional Yoruba folklore, performing arts and poetry, and the resources and properties of the Yoruba language. Furthermore, there is now a pervasive, articulated feeling that this Travelling Theatre movement is a contemporary expression of the collective identity of Yoruba society and as such should sustain and transmit the perceived traditional values of the Yoruba people.
2. There is a marked tendency among some of the troupes and individuals towards 'conscious' art and experimentation and the refinement of the technical and artistic equipment of the medium. (1984: 5)

The dramatic composition of the Yoruba Travelling Theatre is different from the norms applicable to the literary drama of the Western tradition. Even when the story is straightforward and based on historical material or popular myth, the dramas are largely improvised. This is because plays are constructed and structured with the capabilities of the members of the troupe in mind, and roles are 'carried' from one play into another so much that the actors 'become' their roles. For instance, Duro Ladipo was popularly known as and called Sango after playing the role in *Oba Koso*, (1961) an operatic Yoruba dance-drama.

Structurally, the dramas, especially from aspect of spectacle, are divided into the standard introduction-exposition-resolution plotting sequence. But no matter how simple the plot of a drama, it is always enriched with songs, dance, proverbs, folklore and eulogistic poems like *oríkì* (praise names), *ìwì* (egungun poetry), *ìjálá*, (hunters' poetry) and *ewì* (poetry). All these elements feature in *Ìtàn Ògìnìntìn*, performed on two days in May 2012 – a matinee on Thursday, 25th and an evening performance on Friday, 26th – at the Globe Theatre in London.

Ìtàn Ògìnìntìn: modern Alarinjo theatre

William Shakespeare's *The Winter's Tale* is a psychologically intense romantic comedy. Set in Sicily and Bohemia, its theme is the conflict between King Leontes of Sicilia and his childhood friend King Polixenes of Bohemia over Hermione, his wife, whom he suspects of having an affair with Polixenes. In anger, Leontes asks his consul to poison Polixenes. Camillo instead reveals the plan to Polixenes, who leaves the kingdom. In *Ìtàn Ògìnìntìn*, Leontes and Polixenes become two of the best-known characters in the Yoruba pantheon of gods: Sango, the god of thunder, and his sometime-rival, Ogun, the god of destruction and creativity. The source of the conflict between the two gods in Yoruba mythology is Oya, Sango's wife. Oya was first married to Ogun before leaving him to become queen in Sango's palace. However, Ayantade Ipadeola's re-reading has several new twists that present a fresh interpretation of the relationship between these gods while also subverting the original context and content of Shakespeare's play.

In Shakespeare's drama, Hermione gives birth to Perdita, whom Leontes orders to be killed on suspicion that the child is the product of a secret affair between Polixenes and Hermione. Hermione dies of grief at losing her child, however, rather than committing murder, the servant dumps the child in the forest, to be rescued and raised by Bohemian shepherds. Instead of being chronologically faithful to Shakespeare's narrative, Ipadeola created an 'opening glee' in the Alarinjo tradition at the beginning of the show. While Shakespeare's play opens in the antechamber of Leontes' palace, Ipadeola transported his audience directly to Act Three where a set of actors mime rowing a boat on a long sea journey, transporting the exhausted and hungry Antigonus and Oluola (Perdita) to Ogun's kingdom. The writer increased the remit of his creative license by eliminating perhaps the most famous line in Shakespeare's play – 'Exit, pursued by bear!' – replacing the scene with a reporting of Antigonus' mugging by robbers. Ayantade then introduces a metaphor, Igba (Time), as the Spirit of Story to fast-forward the narrative by sixteen years, from the discovery of baby Oluola by Darandaran (Old Shepherd) to her courtship rituals with Folawewo (Florizel), son of Ogun (Polixenes).At the same time he provides a lengthy flashback (45 minutes) to explain the passage of those sixteen years, a disjunction that takes us back to the first two Acts of *The Winter's Tale*.

Ogun, being a king, refuses to bless the union of his son to Oluola, who has been brought up as a commoner with no royal pretensions or even knowledge of her past. In desperation, and on Adeagbo's (Camillo's) advice, Folawewo elopes with Oluola to the court of Sango (Leontes). Here, Ayantade reveals the source of the conflict between Sango and Ogun to be the friendship between Oya, Sango's wife, and his friend Ogun, with Sango suspecting that Oya's pregnancy (and Oluola, the result of that pregnancy) was due to Ogun. After Sango's order to kill Oluola – an instruction 'modified' and 'converted' to banishment by Antigonus – Oya becomes fatally ill. Sango has no way of confirming this death as, in traditional Yoruba culture, a king is prevented from seeing corpses by virtue of his status as the representative of the ancestors and gods on earth. However, in bringing Yoruba myths into the play, unlike the original script where Hermione is turned into a statue, Oya translates the event into the world of the ancestors.

Very good friends, who used to exchange royal visits, then become estranged for sixteen years, until Ogun follows his son to Sango's court to bring him home and persuade him not to marry a commoner. At the court, the two friends resume their antagonism, until Adeagbo confesses the whole story, whereupon the two kings agree to the marriage between Folawewo and Oluola. At the wedding, Oya's statue is wheeled in on a pedestal, from which she descends to bless the marriage of her daughter with Ogun's son before returning to the world of the ancestors.

Ìtàn Ògìnìntìn: script and audition

Ìtàn Ògìnìntìn is written in classical Oyo Yoruba, a form of Yoruba comparable to Shakespearean English in structure and syntax, and as different from modern colloquial Yoruba as Elizabethan English is from contemporary colloquial English. This poses a great challenge for the actors, as was evident during the cast audition in Lagos, in September 2011. The audition was conducted by Wole Oguntokun, director of Renegade Theatre, advised by Bayo Oduneye, erstwhile director of the National Troupe of Nigeria and retired Arts Fellow of the University of Ibadan. Oguntokun, a lawyer, playwright and amateur theatre entrepreneur, started Renegade Theatre in Lagos, Nigeria in September 1998, with the production of *Who's Afraid of Wole Soyinka?*; a satire on the Nigerian military cabal then in power.

I was present as an observer on one of the audition days. There were tens of actors and actresses; the strategy was different from the usual practice of giving actors scenes to interpret: none of the actors or actresses was asked to read from the script; rather, their dexterity in speaking classical Yoruba and their understanding of the language were tested. The actors were also asked to demonstrate skills in singing and dancing and were questioned on their ability to either drum or interpret drumming language. A number of the actors, in my view and after speaking to some of them about their experience, found speaking or reading classical Yoruba very difficult. This is a form of Yoruba that is hardly spoken and even less understood by many present-day Yoruba speakers, especially those people who live in Lagos and who speak a variant of the language termed 'Lagos Yoruba', a mixture of Yoruba, pidgin English and standard English. None of the actors queried the choice of classical Yoruba; in fact, Jude Udueni, a graduate of Theatre Arts from the University of Ibadan whose oeuvre ranges from stage to television and film, told me that he would like there to be many more plays in Nigerian languages, based on familiar motifs and addressing local issues, to improve the development of cultural performances and promote less reliance on Western modes of theatrical practice. His comments point to the growing direction of theatre practice in Nigeria, where artists have gradually become insular in their approach to the practice of theatre. There are certain exceptions however, such as Patrick-Jude Oteh, who uses his Jos Repertory Theatre to produce an annual season of diverse drama from different regions of the world. The Jos Festival of Theatre has produced Peter Luke's *Hadrian The Seventh* (2003) Jean Anouilh's *Antigone* (2007), as well as August Wilson's *Jitney*, Tennessee Williams' *Cat on a Hot Tin Roof*, and Vaclav Havel's *Audience* in 2013. With such productions, the company's outlook is broadly liberal, more so than the productions of Renegade Theatre, for instance. Udueni's remarks are possibly borne out of the current limited cultural exchanges with other countries, lack of adequate professional training in theatre arts, and the shortage of books and journals. There are regular reality television shows and musicals, as well as other popular programmes – sports, comedies and music videos – from the USA and Europe on Nigerian television. However, critical materials, which can aid training and development, and influence complementary developments of local theatre are becoming increasingly difficult to acquire in the country.

During the 1980s, the military government of General Ibrahim Babangida (1985-1993) obtained some loans from the International Monetary Fund (IMF) and imposed austerity measures on the Nigerian economy. This was one of the circumstances that led to the migration of many academics and professionals from the country. Subsequently many qualified Nigerians emigrated, standards of education and services collapsed, and the education system and society in general became more insular and less exposed to contemporary developments, especially from the West. This insularity – or rather the sense of it – created a situation where theatre artists especially began to produce plays based on traditional performances. This also led to the growth of the local film industry, popularly referred to as Nollywood. Themes, resources and materials are locally sourced and developed and gradually, external influences have become minimal in the performances. While this has been largely beneficial to the creation of a vibrant local performance industry, it has also created an environment where critical reception is seldom constructive or knowledgeable in its critique of Nigerian performance relative to what goes on in the rest of the world. Instead, criticisms are sometimes based on how a performer's previous production was received. If it was popularly acclaimed, it then becomes the landmark by which that performer's other work is judged. Essentially, the yardstick becomes the known and familiar, irrespective of the standard of the present offering.

Further, theatre exchanges between Nigeria and Britain, and between Nigeria and other countries, have been reduced in recent decades, partly due to economic factors and partly due to a spate of actor defections. Many Nigerian theatre practitioners, such as Hubert Ogunde, Duro Ladipo, Wole Soyinka, and Bode Sowande, brought their troupes to perform on the British stage up until late 1990s; and through the facilitation of the British Council, many British troupes have also toured Nigeria. Many performers see travelling to Britain as a strategy to advance their professional development by finding ways to extend their tours. As a corollary, many theatre producers are wary of bringing Nigerian troupes to the United Kingdom because of the professional and economic cost.

At the audition for *Ìtàn Ògìnìntìn*, Oguntokun explained that his intention was to create a performance that, in spite of the rich Yoruba dialogue, would be understood by the audience. He wanted a production that would be dependent on the traditions of Alarinjo performance, where emphasis would be placed on extra-linguistic codes. But, more importantly, he wanted a production that would redeem the image of Nigerian actors as professionals who return home at the end of their international engagements.

Regarding the script, Oguntokun said in an interview with me: "There won't be a word of English spoken but the audience will get the message as it is meant to be understood [i.e. by suiting the correct actions to the words], and that is why we want people who can understand, speak and render proper Yoruba" (Adeyemi 2012). He confirmed that he had to use actors who may not be "the best" or the most versatile, but who could adopt the proper Yoruba expressions in a way that "will tell stories of the conflict between the two legendary Yoruba kings through Mr Shakespeare" (Adeyemi 2012). Indeed, the only non-Yoruba word, though rendered as Yoruba, was 'mile', in the song, 'Ogun Adubi'[6] – *ibon oyinbo rin maili mefa* ('the white man's bullet travels six miles') – sung to demonstrate the importance of Sango. The addition of this particular song to the production is mystifying; the conflict revolves around the kingdoms of Oyo in northern Yoruba, and Ire in the east. The inclusion of a folk song composed for a 20th-century British punitive expedition in western Yorubaland provides another disjunction to the play, as does the introduction of the Igunnuko masquerade (see below).

Ìtàn Ògìnìntìn: performance

Despite the 'strange' setting of the Globe stage and the Yard, where some of the scenes were staged, both areas which can prove daunting to many professionals, only two or three of the seventeen performers displayed any sign of being lost in the vastness of the stage and in their encounter with the close-pressing Globe audience. Some of the actors in this production were Adunni Orobiyi (Nefretiti), a professional singer and traditional poetry chanter who, as Igba (Time), sang with 'measured rendition' (Sanusi, 2012), and Olasunkanmi Adebayo, who displayed a 'crowd-winning comic performance' as Adeagbo (Camillo) (Sanders, 2012). Wale Adebayo (Sango) demonstrated a strong stage presence in the mode of a Yoruba Travelling Theatre stock character. Having played the role of Sango in other productions, his acting was not only believable, but also his expressions conveyed meanings that rendered the sub-titling screen on the stage redundant. His animated energy contrasted with the measured calmness and aloof nobility of Oya, his wife. The compelling depiction of this role elicited some comments from the matinee audience, who were mainly students from local schools, with a few Yoruba speakers and some regular Globe audience members. For instance, a student commented that, 'with this guy, you don't even have to speak the language.'

One of the most remarkable performances came from Adekunle Smart

Adejumo who, as the clown, morphed the role of Esu, the Yoruba trickster god, with that of Autolycus, to enliven his scenes with tricks and jokes that endeared him to the audience, even when his character was shown as mischievous and devilish. Most members of the audience – not only Nigerians – enjoyed his escapades and free dances. Nevertheless, this performance was trumped by the introduction of Igunnuko at the wedding of Ogun's son to Oluola.

The Igunnuko mask and its masking society is a ritual tradition introduced to Yoruba by Nupe[7] immigrants. The performance is usually staged during the funeral rites of a deceased elder (Drewal 1992: 45). It is also practised amongst the Egun-Yoruba who occupy the south-eastern region of present-day Yorubaland, between Nigeria and the Benin Republic. The Igunnuko is a form of spirit masquerade and the mask can grow in height to about eight metres or shrink to less than a metre as part of its performance. The costume is always colourful. Igunnuko is however not only performed at funerals, but performances can also be arranged to honour an important member of the society. Without knowledge of the relevance of Igunnuko at the wedding ceremony, the performance at the Globe still provided a memorable spectacle with the logic-defying body-bending and swaying movements of the masks, all of which added to the dramatic resonance of the play. The Igunnuko performance possibly elicited stronger reactions from the Globe audience than any other aspect of the production. As the two masques came on stage, there was general applause from the 1,500 ethnically diverse audience members in the galleries and in the yard. As they danced, the applause increased in some areas but was reduced or muted in others, especially where apparently Nigerian (Yoruba) people stood or were seated, (judging by their traditional dress and the way they chorused the songs). Mark Hamilton, a performance lecturer at Regent's College, London, commented on the colourful costumes and the movements, which reminded him of *kutiyattam* performances in the theatre temples of Kerala, India. In contrast, Peter Badejo, a Yoruba dance artist, remarked that the idea of Igunnuko was commendable as it shows an unusual cultural aspect of the Yoruba people. However he thought that its performance was flawed by poor manipulation of the form and the inability of the artists to demonstrate adequate skills to reduce the height of the masks as they entered the court, or to interpret the language of the drums. Most Nigerians in the Globe were happy to see a traditional Yoruba mask performance and to hear classical Yoruba spoken on London stage, and were less concerned about virtuosity in the use of materials. Yinka Ige and Tunde Euba, two Nigerian artists who have been living in London for more than ten years, echoed this sentiment. For them, this was a rare treat. However, some other members of the audience who were knowledgeable about traditional music and performance questioned aspects of the drumming and singing, especially the popular Fuji[8] beats, which neither had any bearing on the plot nor contributed to the advancement of the story. A non-Nigerian member of the audience with an obvious measure of critical understanding of the theatre was asked about her impression of the presentation and the performance. She said: 'I read the play before coming to see it, but what I have seen is different from Shakespeare. It's like a totally different play, but I enjoyed the singing and drumming.'

The audience, most of whom did not speak or understand Yoruba, were able to enjoy the performance by following the textual streaming, or surtitles, of the play on giant screens in the theatre, in a style that Femi Osofisan introduced in Nigeria with his 'Midnight' series of plays, especially *Midnight Hotel*, in the 1980s. Although this was unnecessary for the performance in Nigeria, held just before the company travelled to London, the Lagos audience found the play tedious and wordy, as the Nigerian *Sunday Guardian* editor, Jahman Anikulapo, informed me in subsequent correspondence. After we had watched the Globe performance together, he remarked that it was much improved, and had a much more 'discerning' reception than the Lagos Muson Hall performance. His use of the word 'discerning' revealed the state of theatre and performance culture in Nigeria. In an elaboration, his views relating to the expectations and theatrical knowledge of the Lagos audience are similar to my experience with audience members whose expectations and knowledge of theatre have been moulded by Nollywood[9] films. Most films in that tradition have simple storylines with conflicts that offer the victory of good over evil, and plots where the audience can easily predict the resolution.

Despite this perception, the audience at the plays' preview in Lagos had a different expectation; mostly because they were composed of regular patrons of Renegade Theatre and are familiar with Wole Oguntokun's style of production, which tends to focus on creating debates around political issues and individuals, in plays such as *Who's Afraid of Wole Soyinka?* (1998). Nonetheless, some of the audience members found *Ìtàn Ògìnìntìn* disjointed, with no obvious direction and with a lack of coherent storyline. The most puzzling was the ordering, or re-ordering, of Shakespeare's plot, which begins the play in the third Act and structures the bulk of the play as a flashback. Additionally, *The Winter's Tale* was not as familiar to the audience as other Shakespeare plays, such as *Macbeth* or *Julius Caesar*, and a few of the patrons found the drama unfamiliar and unclear, especially in the stage adaptation. However, the general consensus, as advanced by Ayo Arigbabu, an architect and a writer, was that the performance was presented with humour and enthusiasm, and was infused with accomplished dancing and clarity of dialogue.

Adding to the spectacle of the performance was the adoption of the performance styles of the Yoruba Travelling Theatre tradition, with its richness of improvisation and spontaneous ensemble acting that thrives well on audience participation. This mode of performance also worked admirably with the Globe audience and with the theatre's 'apron stage', which lends itself to actor-audience interaction. While this was one of the strengths of the production in London, it was an area that raised concern among the theatre audiences in Nigeria. Oluwafiropo Ewenla, the president of PEN Nigeria and one of the audience members in Lagos, commented on the production in an electronic forum, maintained as part of the development of Nigerian theatre,[10] stating that 'the performance displayed a lacklustre quality that begs for audience participation to force entertainment.' Perhaps this was due to the familiarity of the audience with a more professional performance of the codes – Igunnuko dance, popular songs, awareness of Adunni Nefretiti's capability as a singer and chanter, among other elements. This was the kind of information and knowledge that was probably not available to the Globe audience members, who were able to respond to the drama in isolation.

The general reception of the play in Lagos was more muted and not as passionate as the response given to the Globe production. This was probably due to the limited number of audience members who watched the preview in Lagos. The small attendance was caused by a number of factors, the most obvious being the venue. MUSON[11] Centre in Onikan, Lagos, is a popular performance venue but not easily accessible to Renegade Theatre's regular patrons who would have preferred the company's former home at the Terra Kulture Studios, a more informal performance venue on Victoria Island, Lagos, and a cheaper alternative to the MUSON Centre. It was also the company's home between 2007 and 2011. The circumstances of the company's exit from the Terra Kulture centre and the breakdown in cultural collaboration are not clear, and the move back[12] to MUSON Centre is even more mysterious.

The reviews of the Globe production were far more positive, and Julie Sanders, writing in her weblog, 'Blogging Shakespeare' heaped encomiums on the second and final performance, with a generous dose of superlatives. She even went so far as to write that the absent Wole Soyinka, a patron of the theatre troupe, 'was one of the proud guests of honour' (Sanders 2012). Writing in *The Guardian* newspaper (UK), Jon Gambrell (2012) remarked that '…this isn't the William Shakespeare you know. Instead, this is an African reboot of "The Winter's Tale".' And Aderinsola Ajao commented on *Naija.com*: 'Despite its performance in Yoruba, *Itan Oginintin* loses none of its original tragicomic appeal. It becomes yet another enchanting theatre piece rooted in Shakespeare but malleable to global cultures. Oguntokun and his entire crew succeed at this, making *Itan Oginintin* a definite classic, as memorable as any well-mounted performance of Shakespeare in English.'

Despite, or in spite of the controversies generated by this production, the theatre and the cultural exchanges it fosters between countries and people remain important in understanding the intercultural setting in which we operate. *Ìtàn Ògìnìntìn*, in manipulating the story-telling culture of the Yoruba to relate it to the creativity of Shakespeare and to reintroduce Yoruba myths to the wider world, has produced a scintillating theatrical offering that will reverberate in the tunnel of theatrical exchanges between

Nigerian and Britain for some time to come. Nevertheless, more than a year after the Globe production, Ìtàn Ògìnìntìn has not been revived for the general Nigerian public. This situation fuels some of the debates surrounding the production, with the play's most vocal critics giving the reason for lack of Nigerian production, after the London performance and the attendant publicity, as a tactic by the producer to evade criticism for his misrepresentation of Yoruba culture. This is a contentious point, as I found the production representative of certain Yoruba cultures notwithstanding its hodgepodge of ideas, stories and performance cultures. My view of the play is that it is a performance structured to entertain in a way that marries the pedigree of Shakespeare with the tradition of Yoruba performance culture. The performers' emphasis seemed focused on providing entertainment without obvious recognition of the cultural values of the play – values that could have augmented the understanding of Yoruba culture among the audience. Shakespeare's plays are not mere vehicles for entertainment; they also provide insights into the Elizabethan worldview, even as they sometimes locate history through the playwright's perspective. Ìtàn Ògìnìntìn could have performed a similar role for the Yoruba worldview.

NOTES

1   Ògìnnìntìn is used to refer to the wet, morning cold that follows a night rain in Yoruba. Ìtàn Ògìnìntìn is the closest that the playwright comes to 'winter's tale' in Yoruba. Note the difference in spelling; the first spelling is classical orthographical Yoruba.

2   Ile-Ife is considered to have been the first point of call for Oduduwa when he founded his nation. The name means 'where the day dawns', or 'where expansion [of land] begins'.

3   Ifa is important to the life of the Yoruba people. Traditionally, all ceremonies and ritual performances involve the consultation of Ifa through divination, employing Opèlè, a string with eight half seeds, or through the use of sixteen special palm kernels. The different patterns that these seeds form dictate the type of divination cast for the person seeking the assistance of Ifa. For more information, see Daramola, Olu and Adebayo Jeje, (1975), Awon Asa ati Orisa Ile Yorùbá (Ibadan: Onibonoje Press and Book Industries Ltd) and Adeoye, C. L, (1979) Asà àti Ise Yorùbá (Oxford University Press).

4   Egungun refers to all types of masquerades or masked performances associated with ancestral worship or veneration in Yorubaland.

5   For a detailed account of this performance as rendered by the adventurers, see Hugh Clapperton (1829), Journal of a Second Expedition into the Interior of Africa, London, 53–56; and Richard Lander (1830), Records of Clapperton's Last Expedition to Africa, London, Vol. 1, 115–21.

6   The Ogun Adubi (Adubi War) – 11 June – 31 July 1918 – is more officially known as 'Adubi Resistance of Tax Imposition and British Forced Labour Policy and the Natives'. It was one of a number of punitive expeditions in the British colony of Nigeria against insurrections protesting unfair taxation. This particular 'war' was waged against the people of Owu, Abeokuta, Nigeria. The folk song was made popular by Fela Anikulapo-Kuti as 'Gbagada Gbogodo' (Album: Open and Close, 1971) and Tunji Oyelana ('Ogun Adubi', 1972).

7   The Nupe people currently occupy Nigeria's Middle Belt. They are one of Nigeria's more than 250 ethnic groups.

8   Fuji is a Nigerian musical genre which developed in the 1980s from the improvisation of

Were music performed to wake Muslims for breakfast during the Ramadan fasting season.
9 Nollywood is Nigeria's feature film (video) industry.
10 The DapoAdelugba70 Forum is a closed discussion group maintained on Google server. Discussions are related to the development of Nigerian Theatre and theatre in Nigeria, with a bias towards reviving the culture of professional theatre practice in Nigeria. It is named after a professor of Theatre Arts who embodies professionalism in the arts, and who is one of the foremost theatre scholars in Nigeria.
11 The Music Society of Nigeria (MUSON) Centre was established in 1983 for the production and promotion of classical music. The centre is used nowadays for the production of various types of performances.
12 Renegade Theatre produced its plays at MUSON Centre between 1998 and 2007, after leaving its original home at the University of Lagos Arts Theatre.

REFERENCES

Adeyemi, Sola (2012). 'Wole Oguntokun: Interview', *Ambassador's Newsletter*, Vol 2, January, London: Shakespeare's Globe, p.4
Ajao, Aderinsola. *Itan Oginintin: Retelling Shakespeare's Winter's Tale*. http://ynaija.com/magazine/itan-oginintin-retelling-shakespeares-winters-tale/ Accessed 2 April 2013.
Akintoye, Stephen. (2010). *A History of the Yoruba People*. Dakar: Amalion Publishing.
Drewal, Margaret Thompson (1992). *Yoruba Ritual: Performers, Play, Agency*. Indiana CO: Indiana University Press.
Fiebach, Joachim. (1996). 'Cultural Identities, Interculturalism and Theatre: On the Popular Yoruba Travelling Theatre'. *Theatre Research International*, 21, 1: Spring, 52–58.
Gambrell, Jon (2012). 'Itan Oginintin: The Winter's Tale's African Reboot'. *The HuffingtonPost*. http://www.guardian.co.uk/world/feedarticle/10258572 (Published 25 May 2012; accessed 22 February 2013)
Jeyifo, Biodun (1984). *The Yorùbá Popular Travelling Theatre of Nigeria*, Lagos: Nigeria Magazine.
Johnson, Samuel (1901). The *History of the Yorubas from the Earliest Times to the Beginning of the British Protectorate*, Lagos: Church Missionary Society.
Ogunbiyi, Yemi (ed.). (1981). *Drama and Theatre in Nigeria: A Critical Source Book*, Lagos: Nigeria Magazine.
Sanders, Julie (2012). 'Year of Shakespeare: The Winter's Tale'. Blogging Shakespeare. http://bloggingshakespeare.com/year-of-shakespeare-the-winters-tale (Accessed 30 May 2012)
Sanusi, Lookman [with Sola Adeyemi] (2012). 'Itan Oginnintin At The Shakespeare Globe… Much More Desired From Nigeria', *The Guardian* (newspaper), Nigeria. http://www.ngrguardiannews.com/index.php?option=com_content&view=article&id=88719:itan-oginnintin-at-the-shakespeare-globe-much-more-desired-from-nigeria&catid=180:arts&Itemid=707 (Accessed 11 June 2012)
Soyinka, Wole (1976). *Myth, Literature and the African World*, Cambridge: Cambridge University Press.

Performing the Nation at the London Globe – Notes on a Southern Sudanese *Cymbeline*

'We will be like other people in other places'

CHRISTINE MATZKE

In a world where everything seems to have already been seen and staged, a deceptively straightforward production of one of Shakespeare's later and lesser known plays caused quite a stir at the London 'Globe to Globe festival: Shakespeare in 37 languages', itself part of the nationwide Cultural Olympiad, the cultural events running alongside the Games in 2012. The South Sudan Theatre Company's *Cymbeline*, performed in Juba Arabic, had critics and audience in raptures: 'standing ovations' (Bloomekatz 2012); a 'historic [...] performance' (Mayen 2012); plus a four- (out of five-) star review by *The Guardian* which declared that the actors 'played with this much heart, even Shakespeare's most rambling romance becomes irresistible' (Trueman 2012).

Irresistible the performance certainly was but as Kim Solga perceptively points out, it was evident that the appeal of the company was 'most over-determined by its circumstances' (2012).[1] Here was a theatre company that represented the world's newest nation-state, South Sudan; a country which had emerged out of two lengthy, violent civil wars (1955-1972, 1983-2005), a complex six-year peace process after the Comprehensive Peace Agreement of 2005, and a virtually unanimous vote for independence in January 2011. This had led to secession from Sudan on 9 July 2011. While the official transformation process from the region 'Southern Sudan' to the Republic of South Sudan seemed to have been concluded, the process of nation-building was still in its infancy, with larger problems such as border demarcation, control over oil fields, and internal conflicts posing a major if not critical challenge.[2] With all these issues on their plate, a British Council blogger observed 'everyone was wondering, where did poor ravaged South Sudan find actresses and actors of such a calibre?' (Calderbank 2012).

While I was not surprised at the company's high performance standards, having witnessed South Sudanese refugees practising songs and dances in Eritrea, I too was primarily lured to London because of the company's background, and not by the Bard. Creative production from South Sudan was relatively hard to come by internationally. There had been the odd novel and collection of poetry and a comparatively constant stream of recent documentaries and auto-/biographies, largely of so-called 'Lost Boys', the generation of children displaced in the second civil war (1983–2005), separated from their families and often orphaned. (One of the latest dealt with the now American athlete Lopez Lomong who was to compete in the London Olympics).[3] Regarding theatre, I was aware of a full-length play *about*, rather than *by*, 'The Lost Boys of Sudan' (by American playwright Lonnie Carter, produced by the Children's Theater Company, Minneapolis in 2010 [Carter 2010]), and a much earlier Sudanese drama by Khalid Almubarak Mustafa, *The Reth* (1978), about a theatrical ritual on the occasion of the death of the king of the Shilluk, one of the principal ethnolinguistic groups in South Sudan (Mustafa 2004: 78). If anything, it was anthropological material that was available, most of it rather old and presumably outdated given the lengthy disruptions of community life due to the wars.[4]

There was another factor that made me book my passage to London. Taban lo Liyong had been actively involved in the selection of *Cymbeline*, hence my hope that he would join the performers on tour. Poet, academic and essayist, his often polemic and idiosyncratic writings had been formative for the emergence of East African literature in English in the 1960s; they had also been decisive for my becoming a student of African literature and theatre.[5] Known as a Ugandan writer, Taban is of South Sudanese origin and when the University of Juba relocated to the South after the Comprehensive Peace Agreement in 2005, he had left his post at the University of Venda, South Africa, to go to Juba.

Taban did not come to London but I was amply compensated by eventually meeting the key players of the creative team: the translator and co-director Joseph Abuk and his colleague, co-director Derik Uya Alfred, and some of the actors. As the demand for press interviews was high, finding a slot in their busy schedule proved difficult. My idea of spending a little time with the company was impossible to arrange, and my first interview was rescheduled when I was already at the appointed time and place. I felt a strong need to talk to people involved in the production, even if the allotted time was short. I had greatly enjoyed the matinee world premiere of their *Cymbeline* on 2 May 2012, a much more informal and less frequented event than the evening show the following day, which dignitaries and people from the British culture industry attended.[6] Regardless of my enjoyment, I had only been able to access a fraction of the production's theatrical signs. With limited scenery, except for the occasional set-piece such as Innogen's [*sic*] bed, meaning was largely conveyed through the sheer physicality of the performance and, to a lesser extent, the reaction of the small but vocal contingent of South Sudanese expatriates in the audience. The words were meaningless to the majority of the audience; for most of us Shakespeare's poetic skills were lost in translation. I did not understand Juba Arabic, and the surtitle synopses were crude and frequently did not match the action on stage.[7] Occasionally, elliptical utterances in English were thrown in: 'Oh my love' (Posthumus to Innogen), 'One kiss only' (Jackimo watching the sleeping Innogen) or 'This woman very crazy' (Cymbeline on the late Queen) – but they were deliberately exaggerated and played for laughs rather than comprehension. Often they were directed at the groundlings or galleries, not to fellow actors. Comedy became the defining factor of the production, an aspect to which I will return below. While the show seemed to catch the spirit of early modern theatre for contemporary times – with playful mythic, historical and comic characters, music, cross-dressing and vivid stage fights – any academic discussion of whether the play was 'Roman', 'Italian', 'Scottish' or 'Welsh' (Maley 2008: 120), a 'fairy tale' (Sharpe and Wright 2011: 186), 'romance', 'history play' or 'tragicomic pastoral' (Landry 1982: 68) was made redundant by the events on stage. For Joseph Abuk it was essentially a 'human tale' (nterview 4 May 2012) presented, as Matt Trueman put it, as a 'dressing-up box tomfoolery, sending itself up wherever possible' (2012).

Yet, despite the general carefree spirit of the production, there was a serious undertone to the play which was indeed linked to the emergence of the world's newest nation. During the opening scene, Francis Paulino Lugali, the actor playing the Doctor and Posthumus ('Postumus' in the programme), announced the play as an 'offering' to South Sudan (cf. Solga 2012). This was greeted with applause and delighted roars from the audience. Unlike the various editions of the text, the play was not introduced by two Gentlemen but by the entire cast, turning the opening scene into a vivid story-telling session represented by all members of the company and, by extension, the nation. Trueman notes that 'Cymbeline's final cry of peace is followed by an eruption of the national anthem' (2012); the beginning of the anthem was also heard at the end of the trailer produced for the show. Nation and nation-building were generally prominent in the publicity material. The programme flyer for *Cymbeline*, for example, announced that 'Culture must play a key role in *forging a national identity* [my italics], and the British Council is delighted that this company will perform at Shakespeare's Globe as their first international performance' (Programme 2012). On the festival's homepage Dominic Dromgoole, the new Globe's Artistic Director, and Festival Director Tom Bird moreover declared that:

> Shakespeare is the language which brings us together better than any other, and which reminds of our almost infinite difference, and of our strange and humbling commonality. And above all there are the plays themselves, plays which have travelled far and wide, and which on their travels have midwifed new theatre cultures, spread light and laughter, and helped nations, new and old, to define themselves. (Dromgoole & Bird 2012)

While Britain was 'performing itself very much in relation to Shakespeare' during the Games (Yvette Hutchison, University of Warwick panel, 7 May 2012), others were invited to join by celebrating, performing and 'imagining' their nations (Anderson 1994) through the 'universality' of the Bard. In the glaring absence of their own national Olympic team,[8] this seemed all the more important for South Sudan. In other words, Shakespeare became indeed the midwife to the international presentation of South Sudanese culture(s) (though not to the birth of a 'new' theatre culture), with South Sudan inscribing itself as a 'Global Player' on the stage of cosmopolitan London. '...when we return to the South', Joseph Abuk told *Al Arabiya News*, 'we will be like other people in other places. [...] We met 37 countries and participated with them. They considered us their equal. This will be a great thing for South Sudan' (Mayen 2012).

In these notes on the South Sudan Theatre Company's *Cymbeline*, I will work towards a preliminary reading of the London performance against the context of both country and company. Largely based on my attendance at the matinee performance on 2 May 2012, a recording of the full production,[9] my interviews with the co-directors and two actors, Francis Paulino Lugali and Esther Liberato Bagirasas, as well as a recorded panel discussion with company members at Warwick University,[10] I will mainly focus on how the South Sudanese nation was performed through Shakespeare.[11] After a theoretical introduction to the concept of 'national imaginaries', I will move to the politics of context – particularly the emergence of the SSTC in relation to (South) Sudanese theatre history – and then discuss selected aspects of artistic style and form in this production of *Cymbeline*. Given the dearth of relevant material at present, it goes without saying that my findings cannot be anything but preliminary and contingent.

From 'imagining the nation' to 'national imaginaries': the example of *Cymbeline*

In her ground-breaking study on Swahili music and cultural politics in Tanzania, Kelly M. Askew proposes the term 'national imaginaries' as a substitute for Benedict Anderson's much-quoted 'imagined communities' or 'imagined nations' (Askew 2002: 273) as these terms 'betray a finality not reflected in real life' (273). She argues that earlier theories of nation and nationalism (e.g. Gellner 1983, Anderson 1994 [1983], Hobsbawm and Ranger 2012 [1983]) often glossed over the 'dialogic nature of nationalism' (Askew 2002: 279) by assuming 'congruence between the political and national and often the cultural unit' (Askew 2002: 9). They thus failed to see 'nation' as a state construction in constant negotiation with a frequently heterogeneous citizenry. In the old unified and now in the two Sudans, national subjects have always been ethno-linguistically complex and culturally diverse, with over sixty ethnicities recorded for South Sudan alone.[12] Instead of situating the power to imagine community and 'invent traditions' (Hobsbawm 2012: 1-14) exclusively with political and intellectual elites in a top-down flow to a seemingly homogenous body of citizens, Askew proposes to conceptualise nationalism 'as a series of continually negotiated relationships between people who share occupancy in a defined geographic, political, or ideological space' (Askew 2002: 12). In South Sudan, as recent research has shown (Frahm 2012), this includes not only people living within the nation's physical boundaries, but also transnational individuals of South Sudanese heritage and/or diaspora communities in Europe, Australia and North America. While they usually join these negotiations via online media, participation can also happen in and through performance. In the case of the London *Cymbeline* contributors to this exchange even included non-South Sudanese members of the audience who were gathered in the same theatrical space. Askew thus defines 'national imaginaries' as 'multiple and often contradictory layers and fragments of ideology that underlie continually shifting conceptions of any given nation' (Askew 2002: 273). If we follow her argument, then the national imaginary of South Sudan can be understood as 'a living, breathing entity that rejects codification, universalism, and essentialism. It is multivalent, multivocal, polyphonic – perhaps even cacophonous' (Askew 2002: 273).

Interestingly, Askew notes similar dynamics for performance *per se*. Performance cannot be seen as a one-way practice owned by artists and transmitted to an audience, but as 'a process actively engaged in by everyone in attendance' (Askew 2020: 23). If we combine performance and the idea of national imaginaries in our thinking, then interesting dynamics emerge. At the Globe the spectators consisted largely of British and international viewers but, importantly, also of UK-based South Sudanese (and possibly Sudanese) expatriates along with representatives of the British culture industry and the government of South Sudan. During the performance of *Cymbeline*, all of them became 'spect-actors', not necessarily in the Boalian sense, but as 'contributors' and 'participant-witnesses' (as opposed to the more anthropological 'participant-observer') to a South Sudanese national imaginary.[13] The spectators acknowledged and responded to what was presented in performance. By doing so, they took part in the SSTC's 'imagining' of their nation through one of Shakespeare's later plays. If we consider performance not as reflective, but as constitutive of the idea of a nation (Askew 2002: 23), then the London *Cymbeline* can be understood as actively participating in the creation and projection of the new Republic of South Sudan.

While my rendering of Askew's argument necessarily remains reductive and incomplete, I wish to draw attention to the prominence she gives to performance as part of a country's national imaginaries. Performance practices are of importance not only because they play a leading cultural role in many regions of Africa, including South Sudan,[14] but also because performance is always momentary and passing. As an act susceptible to 'modification, unrehearsed action, unanticipated response, and the contingencies of everyday life' (Askew 2002: 5), performance doubly embodies the transience of the act of imagining the nation. Through the perpetual reenactments it requires and the continuous negotiation of meaning between artists and audience, performance ultimately fails to produce a comprehensive representation of the nation (Askew 2002: 23-4). Instead it can carry the contradictions inherent in ideas of a particular nation, and can both reinforce and counter official narratives. This I believe to have been the case with the Globe to Globe *Cymbeline*. While the production clearly served as an authorised cultural signboard for South Sudan – with the Minister of Culture, the Hon. Dr Cirino Hiteng Ofuho, attending – there was much in both process and final product that challenged the idea of a stable, unified nation.

There was no indication, for example, that the government had financially supported the project; most funding seemed to have come from the troupe's international founding patrons and individual donations.[15] During their week in London, there were hints that the company was indeed underfunded as they had to move to a less expensive hotel. Company members also worried whether the government would be supporting their work on returning home (cf. Bloomekatz 2012), and whether they would be able perform before local audiences in Juba and elsewhere. Unlike the three recently manufactured state symbols – the South Sudanese Flag, the Coat of Arms, and the National Anthem in which Joseph Abuk, as chairperson of the technical committee, had played a crucial part (Martell 2011) – the production of *Cymbeline* was not permanently inscribed into the official national narrative. It only came to life with each audience and in each performance. Spectators were invited to 'track a national identity in the making', as the SSTC website put it, not a finished product.

After this brief theoretical introduction, I will now shift my research narrative to an overview of performance culture in South Sudan, followed by a discussion of the production process and aspects of *Cymbeline* in performance.

The South Sudan Theatre Company: a thumbnail theatre history

I have already suggested that the Globe's claim of Shakespeare having 'midwifed new theatre cultures' does not quite hold in the case of South Sudan. While the country is certainly 'new' as a nation-state and while the Globe to Globe festival undoubtedly spawned the South Sudan Theatre Company (SSTC) as an artistic body, South Sudanese theatre practices have deep roots in various strands of performance culture, including Shakespeare and other dramatic literatures. In the old Sudan, these performance cultures were usually divided into an Arab-Islamic component, particularly modern Arab theatre and drama, and the so-called 'indigenous African traditions' (Mustafa 2000: 223) which were thought to relate to 'non-Islamic', largely communal events (Mustafa 2004: 77), including music and dance. Before I am tempted to go straight into recollecting some sort of 'South Sudanese theatre history', another word of caution is in order. In a recent article on Sudanese popular music, Ahmad Sikainga identifies two issues which complicate the writing of historical narratives of theatre for both Sudans. For one, there is a general 'dominance of political analysis and a comparative absence of social and cultural history' (Sikainga 2011: 145) which makes it difficult to collate data on theatre in any form. Secondly, he views the common binary of an 'Arab Muslim north versus an African and Christian or non-Muslim south' (145) as limiting and reductive. Nonetheless, the North-South rift remains a much-cited argument and was also invoked by company members in conversation. The imagined split is usually attributed to a mix of centuries of slave trading and other forms of North-South exploitation plus a divisive British colonial policy and various post-colonial interventions.[16] Such narratives however do not take into account 'the merging of a great diversity of indigenous and external influences' (Sikainga 2011: 145) in cultural production. The few available sources suggest that Sudan and South Sudan have never been monolithic cultural entities but that people and cultural influences moved around and beyond the borders of the old Sudan. There were no rigid boundaries: rather, there was considerable cultural diversity within 'North' and 'South' which was inspired by both local and external artistic practices.[17] In the 20th and early 21st centuries, a great number of South Sudanese were displaced during the civil wars. Some moved north, particularly to Greater Khartoum, others were forced to live as refugees in neighbouring countries, such as Egypt, Uganda, Kenya or Ethiopia. These migratory movements, even if largely involuntary, all had an impact on (South) Sudanese performance cultures. Other influences can be traced back to Turco-Egyptian and Anglo-Egyptian regimes, to Christian (often Italian) missionaries, and to West African immigrants on Hajj to Mecca. British and Egyptian influences on the old Sudan are probably the most systematically recorded, even if far from being complete. Sikainga, for example, notes the introduction of military bands and brass instruments under foreign rule, with particular 'ethnic' musical forms – such as the Binga, Banda or Shilluk Marches – emerging in the British army (Sikainga 2011: 148). European acting styles were fused with local performance forms, leading to the emergence of phenomena such as 'Mono Drama' (a blend of mime, story-telling and music) performed by the first modern South Sudanese actor and former British conscript, Amuna Cabase, after World War II.[18] Arabic dramatic literature, on the other hand, came with teachers from Egypt, Lebanon and Syria (Mustafa 2000: 224). More important for the given context was the introduction and production of Shakespeare and other European-style drama at Gordon Memorial College, later the University of Khartoum, founded on behalf of Lord Kitchener in 1902. With the opening of the Bakht Ar Ruda Teacher Training Institute in 1934, the teaching of Shakespeare and other dramatists spread further (Mustafa 2004: 80). While I cannot necessarily claim similar developments for Southern Sudan under British rule – education being largely in the hands of Christian missionaries with the explicit task 'to teach practical skills' (James 2011: 48) – Shakespeare somehow also made it to the South, if only through people who had received education in the North or elsewhere.[19] Taban lo Lyiong, Joseph Abuk and Derik Uya Alfred could serve as examples, as does the current Minister of Culture, Youth and Sports, Dr Cirino Hiteng. With degrees from universities in Kenya and the United Kingdom, Hiteng supported the South Sudan Theatre Company's application to the Globe,[20] and by doing so contributed quite decisively to the creation of a South Sudanese national imaginary. As Ros Wynne-Jones (2012) of *The Independent* records:

> '[…] the proposal we got from SSTC was the single most compelling and irresistible,' says Tom Bird, director of Globe to Globe.'It was six months before independence, and was written by the man who would go on to become the country's first minister for culture. He wrote that he used to lie in the Bush under the stars reading Shakespeare plays to avoid thinking about the killing that would happen the next day. No other proposal was like it.'

While Bird's account pays tribute to the astonishing if violent history of the Republic of South Sudan, it also highlights Hiteng's clever evocation of the liberation struggle on which South Sudanese collective identity is still largely built. Ole Frahm, in an article on the construction of national identity in South Sudanese online media, asserts that 'South Sudanese collective action and collective identity have historically been primarily reactive' (Frahm 2012: 22) against an outer foe, largely the North. 'Thus, confronting and fighting a common enemy has been more important in defining the South Sudanese nation than have internal dynamics of unifying around a positive common denominator (shared ancestry, language, destiny, etc.)' (23-24). The image of reading Shakespeare on the battlefield clearly evokes that history, but it also invokes a romanticised image of valiant liberation fighters with a learned appreciation of world culture. I have come across similar liberation war nostalgia in Eritrea where such images have become part of the nation's master narratives and 'cultural memory'.[21] Similar developments can be assumed in South Sudan; the above account at least strongly suggests that the London *Cymbeline* is being appropriated for such purposes.

Interestingly enough, most members of the South Sudanese Theatre Company seem to have had little connection to the fighting forces of the liberation war; at least they did not serve as reference points in the narrative of the newly established theatre company. Instead, it was the idea of 'unifying around a positive common denominator', i.e. the performance which brought the company together. As Francis Paulino put it:

> We are a country which has just come out from a long war. We are just starting from scratch. […] Maybe the issues for the government are security, housing, education. I am not saying these things are bad, but you need to remember that

culture is one of the fundamental things. It is the one developing the country, and it is the one to help people. This idea of unity in diversity, it also needs to be there. How can we solve our problems? Back in [South] Sudan we have this issue of tribalism. [...] How are we going to solve that? We are only going to solve it with culture. This is how we can unite. (4 May 2012)

Similar sentiments were voiced by the two co-directors, Joseph Abuk and Derik Uya Alfred. Their narrative, though not in opposition to Hiteng's, clearly had a different emphasis. First and foremost it was directed inward ('unity'), not to the outside world ('fighting the North', 'performing in London'). Unity also played an important role in the establishment of the SSTC, their choice of dramatic text and the choice of performance language. When news spread about the Globe to Globe festival, artists, scholars and activists from various backgrounds joined forces to form a new theatre troupe. When I asked how the group was established Joseph Abuk recalled people's

> ...particular sensitivities. When you have a particular talent, you will also know that man [points at Derik Alfred] also exists over there. So when this moment came [...] they will just come. They are just like dancers. [...] It was not us who selected ourselves. People said, Derik is there, Abuk is there. Why don't you consult Taban as an advisor? And then we came together and said we can do this together! (Interview 5 May 2012)

The cast and the creative team came from all walks of professional life (teachers, chefs, social and health care workers, TV producers, writers, etc.) and they hailed from all regional states of South Sudan, among others, Eastern, Central and Western Equatoria, Western Bahr el Ghazal, Upper Nile State and Abyei, the latter a region contested between North and South Sudan. Ethnic backgrounds were rarely mentioned. And while the 'outside world' – the British Council and the London Globe – constituted the first official audiences for both the company and the play,[22] the opening of the production by Francis Paulino was again redirected 'inward'. To quote Solga again: 'This notion of performance as offering – as a gift given *first* to the absent and unfinished nation, and only *then* shared amongst the spectators in the global capital – framed the work ahead, and opened, for me, the stale corners of this messy play to fresh and compassionate readings' (2012).

Before I look at selected aspects of *Cymbeline* in performance, I would like conclude this brief overview by identifying the four most important 'human resource pools' for the establishment of the SSTC. While a number of company members worked or studied at the College of Art, Music and Drama, University of Juba,[23] most performers had connections with at least one of the following theatrical hubs: Skylark Dramatist Association founded by Joseph Abuk and others in 1979; Kwoto Cultural Centre established by Derik Uya Alfred, Al Sani Lual Aro and Stephen Affear Ochala in 1994 for displaced Southerners in Khartoum;[24] and drama activities in Christian, particularly Roman Catholic, churches. All of them are under-researched at this present stage, but these centres clearly constitute important landmarks in the history of theatre in South Sudan. While the church can be assumed to have had the most continuous and sustained impact on modern theatre practices in South Sudan,[25] details on Skylark, the oldest specifically theatrical group, have yet to be researched.[26] Kwoto's name and original cultural mission, however, are in line with the unification sentiments stated above and can be seen as the conceptual basis of the SSTC. As Derik Uya Alfred explained:

> We started in 1994 as Kwoto Popular Theatre Group. […] We had been very active in high school drama and in drama groups. Al Sani and I went on to study drama in Khartoum, in the College of Music and Drama. […] There was a lot of debate and discussion between us at the College. So when we graduated, we decided the best thing to do was to go home and do the drama there. But then the war broke out in 1983. There was no South to go to. People were coming from the South to the North as refugees. We started seeing people, the young generation born in Khartoum, living in the camps, the displaced areas. We thought it might be dangerous for these people to live in a totally different culture in the North. They would be [*recording unclear:* culturally?] wiped out. The best thing to do is to revive the idea of the old project going to the South, but the work could be done here. So that's why we initiated the Kwoto Popular Theatre Group in 1994. The word Kwoto is actually Toposa. They are a tribe in Eastern Equatoria. These guys believe that when their ancestors came to the present land […] on the borders with Uganda, they brought with them a certain stone of peace and love and reconciliation called Kwoto. […]. That stone, they believe, is the unification element when there is dispute, when there is misunderstanding, it is reconciled under that stone. (Interview 5 May 2012)

Following the model of 'Heartbeat of Africa', a successful traditional dance troupe established by Ugandan writer and cultural nationalist Okot p'Bitek in the 1960s as part of an independence-era African renaissance (Interview 5 May 2012; cf. Pier 2011: 413-14), Kwoto based their work on the long-established performance forms of various ethnic groups and combined them with short dramas, mostly in a mix of South Sudanese languages. This led to co-teaching and interaction not only between company members, but also their audience. If a play had five languages from South Sudan – 'a little bit of Juba Arabic, a little bit of Dinka, Nuer, Bari, Toposa' (Interview 5 May 2012) – audience members would translate the passages others did not understand, thus levelling ethnolinguistic differences and proactively creating a sense of community (cf. Miller 2002: 118). Similar dynamics developed in rehearsal for *Cymbeline*. Company members would teach each other their dances and, in turn, would learn dances of other areas. Alfred recalled that once a spectator tried to identify which of the Kwoto dancers did not belong to a particular group, judging from 'his movements, gestures, the way he deals with the song'. But then he found that 'all of them are, for instance, Zande. When they dance a Moru dance, they are all Moru. If they dance Dinka, you find that all these people are Dinka. He was just confused!

This man said you are the *ladari* of South Sudan which will make the food of South Sudan' (Interview 5 May 2012) – the *ladari* being the tripod, the supporting tool, onto which the cooking pot is placed over the fire.

Towards a South Sudanese *Cymbeline*: aspects of production process and performance

For the production of *Cymbeline*, Abuk and Alfred drew heavily on Kwoto's dance repertoire and their expertise in ethnic dress codes to transport the play into the context of South Sudan. The 'Roman'-looking costumes were borrowed from the Shilluk; the banished Belarius was dressed in a Zande cloth; Cymbeline's impressive headdress – a brazen helmet decorated with ostrich feathers – was Latuko; and the decorative beads were borrowed from various communities, among others Mandari, Shilluk, and Acholi. 'The only thing we thought of', Alfred explained, 'was that *Cymbeline* has to be done in our own way. [...] Characters should look like South Sudanese in terms of their costumes, in terms of their movements, in terms of their gestures and so on, so that it is actually our own story, our experience' (7 May 2012). As not all of the sixty-odd cultures could be presented on stage, a small selection were chosen as representative: 'a Shilluk dance from Upper Nile, a Dinka dance from Bahr el Ghazal, an Acholi dance from Equatoria',[27] amongst others. Unable to distinguish whether performers had already known or were new to the dances, movements or particular gestures, the new company had indeed become another *ladari* to my untrained eye. This was also confirmed by my brief post-performance encounters with South Sudanese spectators. Though statistically not representative (especially since most people seemed somewhat overwhelmed by the experience), everyone agreed with an elderly lady from Birmingham who declared that 'everything had been done very well' (Field notes 2 May 2012). By performing and participating in each other's cultures, the SSTC had begun to embody the idea of a new South Sudan.

Juba Arabic, the language chosen for the translation of the play, served as another *ladari* for the production; or at least it was presented as such. Considered a creole or 'stabilized pidgin' by experts in the field (Tosco 1995: 423), it initially developed in the late 19th century in the urban centres of Equatoria. Now, company members told me, it was gradually turning into the *lingua franca* of South Sudan.[28] Like the South Sudanese nation, Juba Arabic is a language still in the making and thus known for 'a high degree of variation' (Turco 1995: 424). While not necessarily 'a language without a dictionary' (Torbati 2012, Wynne-Jones 2012) as repeatedly maintained, the existing lexicon (Smith & Ama 2005) does not cater to all its varieties and offered little help to the translator, Joseph Abuk. For the translation of *Cymbeline*, this posed a major challenge. Abuk recalled that he sometimes wandered around waiting for inspiration to come; at other times he called for a collective reading with the cast to discuss possible alternatives and connotations. Once they sought help with a consultant to the Globe. Yet despite these difficulties, Juba Arabic was considered the only choice. 'In Juba Arabic,' Abuk explained:

> you find words from the Bari, some from the Dinka, some from Zande, and so on. It belongs to all. These languages are usually only spoken in their own areas, not in others. Even the Nuer who are a very large group – their language is not universally spoken, but Juba Arabic is. Some people still speak classical Arabic, but once they come to Juba, which is the capital of the South, you need to come down to Juba Arabic in order to be understood. Therefore it was the most normal choice for us to translate the play into Juba Arabic. We regard it as a unifier in the sense that it doesn't belong to anybody. It is ours. (5 May 2012)

While Juba Arabic once again catered to the internal dynamics of South Sudan – even if the 'local' audience had so far consisted of expatriates only – there was also the wider theatre-loving community in London to consider. After all, this was a South Sudanese *Cymbeline* initially conceived for an international festival, and thus exposed to the complex dynamics of a 'local' production within the framework of a global Shakespeare industry.[29] This led to another, non-verbal translation process in performance. Apart from the occasional casual English line, meaning was largely translated through the body of the performers, at times in direct physical contact with the groundlings around the stage. 'The language of the theatre is the language of the body,' Alfred pointed out.

> It was important to emphasise certain things – I am going to sleep, I am going to kill you, all these kinds of things. Using body language so that non-Arabic speakers could understand what is going on. I remember Abuk in rehearsal saying can we find a body language for that? [...] If you use your body effectively, you communicate a lot of messages to the audience. When Cloten is angry, he wants to fight, you can see it from his movements, his forceful energy. And you can see the two lovers, Posthumus and Innogen, want to be together, but every time the Queen comes in and they will separate, or in the last scene when they are embracing the King comes in. So you can see that the language of the body, the language of love coming in which is then interrupted. (7 May 2012)

Together with the copious use of ideophones – the 'uuaahs' and 'wheaas' meant to accentuate certain moments – this led to a perpetual sense of comedy. It had no link to a 'potentially laughter-inducing' Shakespearean prose (Gay 2008: 122), but was entirely related to performance. What we witnessed was overacting in the truest sense of the word. There was spectacular eye-rolling, overlarge gesturing and heart-wrenching wailing. It was bold and brash, and did not allow for subtleties. While the delicate rendering of Innogen has been crucial to many a famous British actress' career – Vanessa Redgrave as the gentle 'golden girl' or Judy Dench as 'sensitive but spirited' (Freedman and Sharpe 2011: 179-80), for example – Sarah John Bul played the role with unmatched verbal and physical gusto and a certain knowing sassiness.[30] This could be seen in her outspoken fights with the belligerent Cloten, played as a true warrior by Dominic Gorgory Lohore, in the interrupted love scenes with the smitten Posthumus or, unforgettably, during her examination of the decapitated corpse which she believes to be her husband's. Personified by a man-sized, blood-splattered rubber foam mannequin whose matching head (resembling the actual features of the actor playing Cloten!) had caused shrieks among the audience, there was a literalness to the production which appeared amateurish at times (cf. Truemann 2012), but which also caused unease for the ambiguities it produced. Matt Trueman of *The Guardian* wrote of his increasing awareness of the tragedy unfolding on stage even as he chuckled at its droll portrayal: 'Waking next to the decapitated corpse she believes to be her exiled lover Posthumus, Imogen [*sic*] nearly trips over the crudely stuffed dummy, before collapsing into overblown shrieks of grief. The more we laugh, the more she implores us to take it seriously' (Trueman 2012).

Trueman is very much to the point when he sets the tragic aspect of *Cymbeline* against the production's comical tenor. While this is not the place to go into elaborate models of laughter and comedy – with their various 'superiority', 'incongruity' and 'relief' theories (cf. Stott 2010: 17-39, 127-45), and a plethora of terminology 'at once mind-bogglingly extensive and still insufficient' (Reichl and Stein 2005: 4) – I would like to make a few general remarks at this point. My experience in the region has taught me that comedy in whatever form is vastly popular with audiences, but that it is less appreciated critically. In contemporary Ethiopia, for example, it has been linked with 'self-censorship' and an 'increasingly narrowing margin of artistic licence' (Köppen 2010: 26); often it is simply dismissed as trivial and lacking intellectual weight.[31] While I cannot offer a neat explanation for the general context of South Sudan or *Cymbeline* in particular, I believe there is a need to theorise comedy in African cultural production and that it had best start with audiences and practitioners themselves. 'The idea of theatre in Africa is very simple', as Francis Paulino, drawing on his long-standing experience with Kwoto, summarised:

> When you do a comic play it is to make people laugh. We are not compelled to stick strictly to the lines. [...] People in a camp or in a time of war – we think they need time to laugh. That's why back in North Sudan it was just comedy shows. But you know what comedy is like. You can put some tragedy into that to remind people of their situation, remind them back of South Sudan. We put it in a context of comedy. It makes comedy a tragedy also. (5 May 2012)

This double-coded function – echoing Trueman's experience of ambiguity – Paulino also saw in *Cymbeline*. Comedy, he explained, was a serious matter because you could not only entertain, but also teach and advise through humour. Due to its comic potential, Paulino started to identify with his role as Cornelius, the Doctor who prepares a strong sleeping potion rather than the requested poison for the Queen.[32] In Paulino's rendering Cornelius became a *kujur*, a traditional healer well versed in magical crafts. *Kujurs* 'are very funny people', the actor explained. 'They teach people through funny things. People are laughing, but they also learn some lessons. [...] I really liked the role. I even went to the rural areas where I could meet a real *kujur*, get to know the way he moves, the way he dresses, the way he behaves' (5 May 2012).

The *kujur*-Doctor was only one among many facets of the play that resonated with South Sudanese experiences. Abuk noted a number of social, religious and political aspects which led them to choose *Cymbeline* over other plays, such as *Hamlet* or *Coriolanus*, which had been discussed:

> The Europeans have a right to say whatever they want about their own stories, but we as human beings on the other side of the world, we also want to quote other stories from your library which we believe make sense in our own situation or resemble certain aspects of our own way of doing things. (5 May 2012)

Not all contextual allusions were necessarily readable by the motley crowd at the Globe. The idea of gods and ancestral spirits watching and advising the living through dreams and apparitions, for example, Abuk identified as prominent among many cultures in South Sudan. 'It is a very real situation', he explained. Jupiter and the ghosts of Posthumus's family translated extremely well into a South Sudanese context, with Jupiter being called upon more often on stage than in the various editions of Shakespeare's *Cymbeline*. Another local allusion was the administration of toxic substances, engineered by Esther Bagirasas' bullying Queen, which has a recorded history in Equatoria and can be linked to the dynamics of different socio-political interactions as part of knowledge production and a moral economy (Leonardi 2007). The most pertinent references, however, related to the experience of war, and were both personal and political in nature. Abuk, for example, compared the signing of the Comprehensive Peace Agreement of 2005 with the truce between Britain and Rome; other company members raised the continuing conflicts over border demarcations and oil as similar sources of contention between the two parties involved. There were also difficulties of a more personal nature in Cymbeline's court which resonated with the cast. There was, for example, the marriage of the King's daughter to a man of lower royal rank, and a pushy Queen who wanted to see Posthumus replaced by her aggressive son, Cloten. There was also the case of Cymbeline's missing sons, Guiderius and Arviragus, who had been abducted in childhood by Belarius. All three eventually fight for Cymbeline and are returned to the family fold. The ritualised death and rebirth of families – their breaking up and reunification – strongly reverberated with the company and was again corporally translated into the context of South Sudan. 'You might have realised that in the end', Abuk told the Warwick students that

> when Belarius reveals to the King that these boys are actually his children, he spits on their heads. These are original blessings we have in Africa, in our places

in the South. If somebody wants to bless, especially the elders or the parents, they used to spit on the children. It is very strong. You can do it two ways, you can curse with it and you can bless with it. So for you to find you own children and to say, I am blessing you, you spit at them. And then when the entering of the children through the legs [Abuk refers to Guiderius and Arviragus crawling between Cymbeline's legs in the final scene] it is also a kind of blessing. It means you are being born again. So in the different stages of your life, as a rite of passage, you have a lot of blessings, coming from your elders, coming from your parents and so on. These were the things we used a lot to emphasise that these are the South Sudanese cultures. (7 May 2012)

Finally there were not only figurative breakings and mendings, but also the issues of physical impairment, dismemberment and disintegration which had been the experience of many people during the civil wars. In the play, such bodily injuries were again followed by corporal reconstitution, such as the waking of the much-lamented Innogen or the re-appearance of a physically unharmed Posthumus at Cymbeline's court. While in Shakespearean times the reconstitution of the royal body was linked to the reconstitution of Britain's body politic (Hunt 2002), Abuk generally read these themes under the overarching umbrella of South Sudanese social and national reconciliation. Interestingly, he again did not link these issues primarily to the North, but to South Sudanese communities:

Following the final peace agreement in South Sudan, a process of pacifying the different members of South Sudanese communities started. People had fought each other so much during the war. People had stolen from each other. People had robbed or kidnapped people's daughters to make them their wives. But now they said, this is peace time, let us reconcile. If we become a new nation, we will need to settle our problems. So generally speaking, I think that *Cymbeline* is the nearest thing to the situation in South Sudan. (5 May 2012)

After the Globe to Globe: closing remarks

While forgiveness and reconciliation were certainly the most recognised themes in this Shakespearean utopia, they were only two among many issues to strike a chord in the performative creation of a South Sudanese national imaginary. For the expatriate audience, modes of representation were of equal importance. This had more to do with their life in the UK than with that of their compatriots in the new Republic of South Sudan. Tired of seeing their country being portrayed as a war-ravaged, poverty-stricken place, some spectators noted that for the first time they felt 'free' (Collins 2012) and were proud of themselves (Torbati 2012), their identity and culture. For Alfred 'one of the most satisfying aspects of coming to London' had indeed been 'performing for the South Sudanese expatriate community' (Torbati 2012). It had been worth the effort and toil, and despite a haphazard rehearsal period they had pulled it off (Bloomekatz 2012). But what would the future hold for the company back home? Despite being employed as the national cultural representatives of South Sudan, continuation of their work was far from certain. There also appeared to be underlying tensions with the authorities which belied the perpetual projection of reconciliation and peace. During the Warwick panel, one of the contributors joked:

> When you take a name like this [South Sudanese Theatre Company] they will ask you 'How legal is that name? Have you been registered?' These are the questions that will be brought to you. But I think because this project was so important, the government shut one ear and just listened to the side saying *Cymbeline, Cymbeline.* This question of registration has been a bit suspended. I think when we now go back the government will have time to ask 'Were you registered in the first place?' But we shall find this out then. I think with the success we have met here, they will just be smiling. If we had done badly, we might go there and they would say, 'Before you could shame us like that – did you register?' I think we will go back with testimonies [of our success] and will say, thank you for sending us. Because, of course, they would like to say that they were the people who sent us here. The government, you know. They might not be involved in a project, but in the end they make great speeches. (7 May 2012)

In his production review of *Cymbeline*, Trueman notes that it is 'power in general that's under suspicion here' (2012). Perhaps we as audience and critics should take heed. In mid-May 2012 the Director General of the Ministry of Culture, Youth and Sports, Charles Buth Diu, announced that after a successful return to Juba, the SSTC would perform their play in Nyakuron Cultural Centre at the end of the month for 'various dignitaries from various ministries and organizations' (Maring 2012). As yet, I am waiting for positive confirmation of this show, or any future plans to present the play to the general South Sudanese public.

When the company toured India at the end of 2012, newspaper reports suggested a slight shift in the company's narrative of the meaning of *Cymbeline*. In an interview with *The Hindu*, Abuk put more emphasis on the play's similarities to 'our war with the Arabs' (Datta 2012) than with processes of national reconciliation and peace. Obviously, it is impossible to draw conclusions from a short newspaper clip where the reporter's own reading might have influenced her selection of quotes. I do worry, however, about a potential appropriation of performance for a one-sided 'political vision' in South Sudan, rather than the multifaceted, contradictory 'national imaginaries' described by Askew. But perhaps this too is part of performing the nation, signifying the constant renegotiation and shifting of meaning.

'When we return the South', Abuk had told *Al Arabiya News*, 'we will be like other people in other places'. While the story of the company and their *Cymbeline* is perhaps too extraordinary for that, they have certainly demonstrated their being South Sudanese and citizens of the world. It is to be hoped that the South Sudan Theatre Company can continue their work in an environment of creative independence – and perhaps a semblance of 'normality', whatever that may mean.

NOTES

1 Cf. similar remarks by Sullivan 2012, Nice 2012, Wynne-Jones 2012. When in January 2013 the Globe's Executive Director, Neil Constable, picked up the London Theatre of the Year prize, he again felt the need to mention those nations with an 'extraordinary' background: 'I'd like to dedicate this award and share it with those countries that had huge problems coming to us for the Globe to Globe festival – from Afghanistan, from South Sudan' (Merrifield 2013).

2 For further information see: LeRiche & Arnold 2012; Johnson 2012; Natsios 2012: 194-221.

3 For examples see Lomong 2012, Gubek 2004, Deng 1986; 1989.

4 For examples see Buxton 1973; Evans-Pritchard 1976. Buxton's research was largely conducted prior to the first civil war, as was Evans-Pritchard's. His extensive studies on Southern Sudan can be found as early as the late 1920s in journals such as *Sudan Notes & Records*.

5 Taban is particularly known for his essays 'Can We Correct Literary Barrenness in East Africa' (1965), and the co-written 'On the Abolition of the English Department' (1968) with Ngugi and Henry Owuor-Anyumba. My MA dissertation had been on Kenyan women's writing, using the metaphor of 'literary barrenness' as the guiding question for my enquiry.

6 On the evening of 3 May I spent about an hour and half in the Globe's foyer prior to the performance as I was meeting a former artistic colleague of some of the company members, John Mairi, now based in London. While I was waiting the Globe filled to maximum capacity. There was also an opening event for VIPs on an upper floor. (Cf. Calderbank 2012.) According to the audience statistics of the New Globe, the two performances sold 71% of available seats. I wish to thank Penelope Woods, University of Western Australia, and Globe Communications for providing me with the data.

7 This, I believe, had to do with the different editions used for the production. While the scene synopses seemed to follow the 1955 Arden edition edited by J.M. Nosworthy (as seen, for example, in the spelling 'Imogen' used by Nosworthy), the company also used the new RSC Shakespeare from 2011 ('Innogen' in the programme flyer), a more accessible edition edited by Jonathan Bate, Eric Rasmussen and Will Sharpe. Though staying relatively faithful to the written texts, some scenes were shortened or merged in the production. Both editions can be seen used in the trailer for the show (http://yearofshakespeare.com).

8 South Sudanese sportsmen competed either for other nations, such as Lomong, or under the Olympic flag (DAPD/SID 2012).

9 The film can be watched online at thespace.org. It appears that this version was put together from both the matinee and the evening performance.

10 I would like to thank Yvette Hutchison, University of Warwick, for making the recording available to me.

11 Thanks also go to Cherry Leonardi, Durham University, for insightful comments on an earlier draft.

12 Ryle 2011: 31-42; [Kot] 2002: 19; www.goss.org, accessed 20 March 2013.

13 While 'participant observation' always requires a level of involvement with the group 'under research' (Jorgensen 1989: 12-25, Spradley 1980: 53-62), most of the audience members did not come to the Globe to do research of some sort, but to be entertained. For my understanding of 'participant-witness' I have loosely borrowed from Daria Halprin's understanding of witnessing in expressive arts therapy: 'simply by the act of paying attention, the witness creates a *holding environment* in which the mover [performer] feels seen and cared for. [...] Unlike having an audience, where the concern is on delivery, impact, and the performance as a presented piece of work, the relationship between enactor and witness requires unconditional acceptance and trust in entering the unknown together' (Halprin

2009: 116). In London, ticket-holders were both 'audience' and 'witnesses'. They came to see *Cymbeline* 'as a presented piece of work', but they also created a protective 'holding environment' in which the imagining of South Sudanese nationhood could take place and which many, I believe, primarily came to see. Unlike the participant-observer, the participant-witnesses responded emotionally to the performers and their complex history, rather than analytically or 'theatre critically'. A number of production reviews indeed spoke of 'their emotional responses' (Collins 2012) to the play.

14 As opposed to the much cited 'print-capitalism' in the emergence of a national consciousness in, for example, European nations (Anderson 1994: 44– 46, cf. Askew 2002: 9). In South Sudan, performance and radio are the most widely utilised media.

15 Bloomekatz 2012. For a list of founding patrons see http://www.southsudantheatre.com/founding-patrons.

16 Johnson 2003: 1-2, 12; cf. Interviews 5 & 7 May 2013. Abuk variously referred to the Closed District Ordinance, a British policy from 1914-1946 for then Southern Sudan, which effectively separated Southern and Northern administration. It also barred people from moving from one region to the other.

17 Mubarak 2000 & 2004; Sikainga 2011; Verney 2006; James 2011.

18 http://www.southsudantheatre.com/about-us, accessed 26 March 2013.

19 According to Cherry Leonardi, missionaries in the South also resorted to theatre in their work, such as the staging of nativity plays in schools. (Personal email 4 May 2013) The history of theatre in South Sudan certainly requires further investigation.

20 I am unable to give a clear outline of the selection and/or application process at this point. While, judging from my interviews, the idea of participating at the London Globe was not initially conceived in South Sudan but by the festival management in conjunction with the British Council, the above article suggests that the SSTC nonetheless had to apply to take part. Written inquiries to the New Globe and the SSTC have yet to be answered.

21 Assman 2010: 111, 117; Erll 2011: 27-33; cf. Walder 2012: 4, 9-12.

22 According to my interviews, *Cymbeline* had not been performed in South Sudan before coming to the London Globe. Only selected scenes had been presented to an invited audience of British Council members.

23 These were Esther Bagirasas, Margret Kowarto, and Buturs Peter who played Iachimo ('Jackimo' in the programme).

24 Please note that Ochala is spelled 'Stephen Afear Ushalla' and 'Stephen Affear Ushala' respectively in Miller 2002: 117-118. I am following the spelling provided by Derik Uya Alfred on 5 May 2013. Catherine Miller was the first to mention Kwoto's cultural work as part of her research on 'Juba Arabic as a way of expressing a Southern Sudanese identity in Khartoum'. I wish to thank Cherry Leonardi for drawing my attention to this article. For more detailed accounts of Kwoto's work see Dixon 2006; Thompson et al. 2009: 113-121.

25 In conversation, Esther Bagirasas mentioned the long-standing work of the Arch-Diocese of Juba Drama Society as an example, which also provided space for political plays. Bagiraras, an actress and accomplished writer of radio drama, noted that her first professional job in the mid-1980s was with the Drama Office of the Council of Churches. (Interview 4 May 2012).

26 So far I have not been able to find any sources on the running of Skylark. While the only South Sudanese company to be mentioned in a theatre historical overview of the old Sudan (Mustafa 2000: 226), time during the interviews was too short to go into historical detail. Another, London-based member of Skylark, John Mairi, was sadly unavailable for an interview. It can be assumed, however, that they followed patterns similar to other modern theatre companies in the region at the time (cf. Matzke 2003) and that their shows encompassed a variety of performance forms, including music and playlets, possibly also in English. Verney mentions a popular band, The Skylarks, as part of Juba's nightlife in the 1970s and 80s (Verney 2006: 402), though I have yet to establish whether they were part of Abuk's drama group. Given the way these theatre associations usually operated in nearby parts of Africa, it is highly likely.

27 Here, Joseph Abuk (panel 7 May 2012) referred to the three former provinces of Southern

Sudan which have now been divided into ten states: Central Equatoria, Eastern Equatoria, and Western Equatoria (formerly Equatoria); Northern Bahr el Ghazal, Western Bahr el Ghazal, Lakes, and Warrap (formerly Bahr el Ghazal); Upper Nile, Jonglei, and Unity (formerly Upper Nile).

28 According to Tosco and Manfredi, Juba Arabic is considered 'a "national" language according to the Sudanese People's Liberation Movement's language policy (although English is the only official language of South Sudan)' (2013: 507). I wish to thank Jonathan Owens for making this chapter available to me prior to publication.

29 On the dynamics of 'local Shakespeares in a global context' see Massai 2005: 3-11. The scope of this essay does not allow me to delve further into the matter, but the politics of *Cymbeline's* appropriation are certainly worth exploring at a later point. John Mairi suggested that the translation was a form of 'the empire striking back [...] which is probably subverting what it [the play] originally was' (7 May 2013).

30 Both programme and SSTC website give Margret Kowarto as Innogen, as do various reviews. In performance, however, this role was taken over by Sarah John Bul. Kowarto was one of the dancers and played various attendants at the court.

31 Cf. with a recent call for a 'South African Screen Comedy Conference' posted on H-AfriLitCine in April 2013 which points out that comedy is still considered 'lightweight' and an 'object of derision'. However, the convenors also indicate that it is 'a neglected area of research' (http://h-net.msu.edu).

32 Paulino also took on the role of Posthumus when three weeks before the show the actor originally cast for the part was sent on a training course by his employer. Paulino related his initial difficulties with the role because Innogen's husband was such a different character from the Doctor. He said he succeeded in playing both because he didn't want the production to fail. (Interview 4 May 2012).

BIBLIOGRAPHY

Anderson, Benedict (1994 [1983]), *Imagined Communities*, rev. ed. (London: Verso).

Askew, Kelly M. (2002), *Performing the Nation: Swahili Music and Cultural Politics in Tanzania* (Chicago: The University of Chicago Press).

Assmann, Jan (2010), 'Communicative and Cultural Memory', in *A Companion to Cultural Memory Studies*, in Astrid Erll and Ansgar Nünning, eds, in collaboration with Sara B. Young (Berlin: de Gruyter), 109-118.

Bloomekatz, Ari (16 May 2012), 'South Sudan Troupe Sees New Country's Struggle in Shakespeare', *Los Angeles Times*, available at www.latimes.com, accessed 24 May 2011.

Buxton, Jean (1973), *Religion and Healing in Mandari* (Oxford: Clarendon Press).

Calderbank, Tony (14 May 2012), 'South Sudan: All the Globe's a Stage', *British Council: Voices*, available at http://blog.britishcouncil.org, accessed 24 May 2011.

Carter, Lonnie (2010), 'The Lost Boys of Sudan', available at www.lonniecarter.com, accessed 6 March 2013.

Collins, Robert O. (2008), *A History of Modern Sudan* (Cambridge: CUP).

Collins, Toby (9 May 2012), 'South Sudan Theatre Company Perform Cymbeline in London', *Sudan Tribune*, available at www.sudantribune.com, accessed 25 May 2012.

DAPD/SID (20 August 2012), 'Eine Stimme für Südsudan', *Süddeutsche Zeitung* 184, 36.

Datta, Sravasti (14 November 2012), 'The Bard in New Lands', *The Hindu*, available online at http://www.thehindu.com, accessed 1 April 2013.

Deng, Francis Mading (1986), *The Man Called Deng Majok: A Biography of Power, Polygyny, and Change* (New Haven: Yale University Press).

—— (1989), *Cry of the Owl* (New York: Lilian Barber).

—— (2010), *Sudan at the Brink: Self-Determination and National Unity* (New York: Fordham University Press/The Institute for International Humanitarian Affairs).

Dixon, Luke (2006), 'Youth Theatre in the Displaced People's Camps of Khartoum: *Kwoto*', in *African Theatre: Youth*, guest ed. Michael Etherton, general eds Martin Banham, James Gibbs, and Femi Osofisan (Oxford: James Currey), 78–85.

Dromgoole, Dominic, and Tom Bird (2012), 'O for a Muse of Fire', available on http://globetoglobe.shakespearesglobe.com/, accessed 8 March 2013.

Erll, Astrid (2011), *Memory in Culture*, trans. Sara B. Young (Houndmills, Basingstoke: Palgrave Macmillan).

Evans-Pritchard, E.E. (1976 [1937]), *Witchcraft, Oracles, and Magic among the Azande*, abr. edn. (Oxford: Clarendon Press).

Frahm, Ole (2012), 'Defining the Nation: National Identity in South Sudanese Media Discourse', *Africa Spectrum* 47.1, 21–49.

Freedman, Penelope, and Will Sharpe (2011), '*Cymbeline* in Performance: The RSC and Beyond', in William Shakespeare, *Cymbeline*, in Jonathan Bate, Eric Rasmussen and Will Sharpe, eds, *The RSC Shakespeare* (Basingstoke: Macmillan), 155–187.

Gay, Penny (2008), *The Cambridge Introduction to Shakespeare's Comedies* (Cambridge: CUP).

Gellner, Ernest (1983), *Nations and Nationalism* (Oxford: Basil Blackwell).

Government of the Republic of South Sudan, 'Official Website of the Government of the Republic of South Sudan', available on www.goss.org, accessed 12 March 2013.

Gubek, Ladu Jada (2004), *Arrows and the Bow* (Trenton: Red Sea Press).

H-AfriLitCine, 'CFP: South African Screen Comedy Conference (deadline: 28 June 2013)', available online on http://h-net.msu.edu, accessed 11 April 2013.

Halprin, Daria (2009 [2003]), *The Expressive Body in Life, Art and Therapy: Working with Movement, Metaphor, and Meaning* (London: Jessica Kingsley).

Hobsbawm, Eric (2012 [1983]), 'Introduction: Inventing Traditions', in Eric Hobsbawm and Terence Ranger, eds, *The Invention of Tradition*, (Cambridge: CUP), 1–14.

Hobsbawm, Eric, and Terence Ranger, eds. (2012 [1983]), *The Invention of Tradition* (Cambridge: CUP).

Hunt, Maurice (2002), 'Dismemberment, Corporal Reconstitution, and the Body Politic in "Cymbeline"', *Studies in Philology* 99,4: 404–431.

James, Wendy (2011), 'Religious Practice and Belief', in John Ryle, Justin Willis, Suliman Baldo and Jok Madut Jok, eds, *The Sudan Handbook* (Woodbrigde: James Currey), 43–53.

Johnson, Douglas H. (2003) *The Root Causes of Sudan's Civil Wars* (Oxford: James Currey).

——— (2012), 'Briefing: The Heglig Oil Dispute between Sudan and South Sudan', *Journal of Eastern African Studies* 6,3: 561–569.

Jones, Kendra (4 May 2012), 'Review: Cymbeline by The South Sudan Theatre Company @ Shakespeare's Globe (Globe to Globe Festival)', available at http://impeltheatre.blogspot. de, accessessed 24 May 2012.

Köppen, Grit, (2010), 'Caught between Commerce and Censorship', in Rolf C. Hemke, ed., *Theater südlich der Sahara/Theatre in Sub-Saharan Africa* (Berlin: Theater der Zeit), 26–28.

[Kot, Peter Nyot] (2002) *The House of Nationalities: A Space for Preserving the Unity and the Diversity of the South Sudan*, report of a seminar on governance in the South Sudan, 1–3 November 2000, Aberdare Country Club, Nyeri, Kenya, available online at http://sudanarchive.net, accessed 13 March 2013.

Landry, D.E. (1982), 'Dreams as History: The Strange Unity of *Cymbeline*', *Shakespeare Quarterly*, 33,1: 68–79.

Leiter, Samuel L., ed., (1986) *Shakespeare Around the Globe: A Guide to Notable Postwar Revivals* (New York: Greenwood Press).

Leonardi, Cherry (2007), 'The Poison in the Ink Bottle: Poison Cases and the Moral Economy of Knowledge in 1930s Equatoria, Sudan', *Journal of Eastern African Studies* 1,1: 34–56.

——— (2011), 'Paying "Buckets of Blood" for the Land: Moral Debates over Economy, War and State in Southern Sudan', *Journal of Modern African Studies* 49,2: 215–240.

LeRiche, Matthew, and Matthew Arnold (2012), *South Sudan: From Revolution to Independence* (London: Hurst).

Lomong, Lopez, with Mark Tabb (2012), *Running for My Life* (Nashville: Thomas Nelson).

Maley, Willy (2008) '*Cymbeline*, The Font of History, and the Matter of Britain: From Times New Roman to Italic Type' in Diana E. Henderson, ed., *Alternative Shakespeares 3* (London:

Routledge), 119-137.

Maring, Monoja Anthony (19 May 2012), 'South Sudanese Actors' Return from London, to Perform in Nyakuron', *The Citizen*, available at www.thecitizen.info, accessed 24 May 2012.

Martell, Peter (12 January 2011), 'A Song for South Sudan: Writing a New National Anthem', *BBC News Africa*, available online at www.bbc.co.uk, accessed 25 February 2012.

Massai, Sonia (2005), 'Defining Local Shakespeares', in Sonia Massai, ed., *World-Wide Shakespeares: Local Appropriations in Film and Performance* (London: Routledge), 3-11.

Matzke, Christine (2003), '*En-gendering Theatre in Eritrea: The Roles and Representations of Women in the Performing Arts*' (University of Leeds, September 2003), available online at http:// etheses.whiterose.ac.uk/796/.

Mayen, Nadia (7 May 2012), 'South Sudan Troupe Give Historic Shakespeare Performance', *Al Alrabiya News*, available at www.alarabiya.net, accessed 24 May 2012.

Merrifield, Nicola (28 January 2013), 'The Stage 100 Award Winners 2013', *The Stage*, available at http://www.thestage.co.uk/, accessed 8 March 2013.

Miller, Catherine (2002), 'Juba Arabic as a Way of Expressing a Southern Sudanese Identity in Khartoum', in Abderrahim Youssi et al., eds, *Aspects of the Dialects of Arabic Today: Proceedings of the 4th Conference of the International Arabic Dialectology Association (AIDA), Marrakesh, April 1-4, 2000*. *In honour of Professor David Cohen* (Rabat: Amapatril), 114-122.

Mustafa, Khalid Al-Mubarak (2000 [1999]), 'Sudan', in Don Rubin, ed., *The World Encyclopedia of Contemporary Theatre*, vol. 4: The Arab World, (London: Routledge), 223-233.

—— (2004), 'Sudan', in Martin Banham, ed., *A History of Theatre in Africa* (Cambridge: CUP), 77-84.

Natsios, Andrew S. (2012), *Sudan, South Sudan, and Darfur: What Everyone Needs to Know* (Oxford: OUP).

Nice, David, 'Cymbeline of South Sudan', available at http://davidnice.blogspot.de, accessed on 24 May 2011.

Ngugi, James, Henry Owuor-Anyumba, and Taban lo Liyong (1972), 'On the Abolition of the English Department (24th October 1968)', in Ngugi wa Thiong'o, *Homecoming: Essays on African and Caribbean Literature, Culture and Politics* (Westport: Lawrence Hill), 145-150.

Pier, David (2011), 'The Branded Arena: Ugandan "Traditional" Dance in the Marketing Era', *Africa* 81.3, 413-433.

Reichl, Susanne, and Mark Stein (2005), 'Introduction', in Susanne Reichl and Mark Stein, eds, *Cheeky Fictions: Laughter and the Postcolonial* (Amsterdam: Rodopi), 1-23.

Ryle, John (2011), 'Peoples and Cultures of Two Sudans', in John Ryle, Justin Willis, Suliman Baldo and Jok Madut Jok, eds, *The Sudan Handbook* (Woodbrigde: James Currey), 31-42.

Sikainga, Ahmad (2011), 'A Short History of Sudanese Popular Music', in John Ryle, Justin Willis, Suliman Baldo and Jok Madut Jok, eds, *The Sudan Handbook* (Woodbridge: James Currey), 145-152.

Smith, Ian, and Morris Timothy Ama (2005), *Juba Arabic-English Dictionary/Kamuus ta Arabi Juba wa Ingliizi* (Kampala: Fountain).

Stott, Andrew (2010 [2005]), *Comedy* (London: Routledge).

Sharpe, Will, and Kevin Wright (2011), 'Director's Cut: Interviews with Dominic Cooke and Emma Rice', in William Shakespeare (2011), *Cymbeline*, eds. Jonathan Bate, Eric Rasmussen and Will Sharpe, The RSC Shakespeare (Basingstoke: Macmillan), 187-199.

Shakespeare, William (2011), *Cymbeline*, eds. Jonathan Bate, Eric Rasmussen and Will Sharpe, The RSC Shakespeare (Basingstoke: Macmillan).

—— (2007), *Cymbeline*, ed. J.M. Nosworthy, The Arden Shakespeare (London: Cengage Learning).

—— (2005), *Cymbeline*, ed. Martin Butler, The New Cambridge Shakespeare (Cambridge: CUP).

Smyth, ASH (4 May 2012), 'Globe to Globe: Cymbeline, Shakespeare's Globe: South Sudanese see the funny side of Shakespeare's romantic tragedy', *The Arts Desk*, available on www.theartsdesk.com, accessed 1 March 2013.

Solga, Kim (3 May 2012), 'The South Sudan *Cymbeline*, Shakespeare's Globe Theatre, 2 + 3

82 *Christine Matzke*

May 2012', available at http://blog.shakespearesglobe.com, accessed 24 May 2012.

Sorgensen, Danny L. (1989), *Participant Observation: A Methodology for Human Studies* (Newbury Part, CA: Sage).

South Sudan Theatre Company (2012), 'South Sudan Theatre Company', available at http://www.southsudantheatre.com, accessed April 2012 – April 2013.

Spradley, James P. (1980), *Participant Observation* (New York: Holt, Rinehart and Winston).

Sullivan, Erin (8 May 2012), 'Years of Shakespeare: Cymbeline', *Blogging Shakespeare*, available at http://bloggingshakespeare.com, accessed 24 May 2012.

Taban lo Liyong (1972), 'Can We Correct Literary Barrenness in East Africa? [1965]', in Taban, *The Last Word: Cultural Synthesism* (Nairobi: East African Publishing House), 23-42.

The Globe Theatre (2012), 'Cymbeline: The South Sudan Theatre Company', Globe to Globe: Shakespeare in 37 Languages, World Shakespeare Festival 2012, programme flyer.

Thompson, James, Jenny Hughes and Michael Balfour (2009), *Performance in Place of War* (London: Seagull Books).

Torbati, Yeganeh (8 May 2012), 'South Sudanese in Shakespeare Play, a Call for Peace', available at www.reuters.com, accessed 9 October 2012.

Trueman, Matt (4 May 2012), 'Cymbeline – Review, Shakespeare's Globe, London', *The Guardian*, available at www.guardian.co.uk, accessed 24 May 2012.

Tosco, Mauro (1995), 'A Pidgin Verbal System: The Case of Juba Arabic', *Anthropological Linguistics* 37, 4: 423-459.

Tosco, Mauro, and Stefano Manfredi (2013), 'Pidgins and Creoles', in Jonathan Owens, ed., *The Oxford Handbook of Arabic Linguistics* (Oxford: OUP), 495-519.

Verney, Peter, with Helen Jerome and Moawia Yassin (2006), 'Sudan: Still Yearning to Dance', in *The Rough Guide to World Music: Africa and The Middle East*, comps. and eds. Simon Broughton, Mark Ellingham, and Jon Lusk, with Duncan Clark (London: Rough Guides), 397-407.

Walder, Dennis (2012 [2011]), *Postcolonial Nostalgias: Writing, Representation, and Memory* (New York: Routledge).

Wynne-Jones, Ros (2 May 2012), 'Cymbeline: From War-Ravaged South Sudan to the Globe Theatre', *The Independent*, available at www.independent.co.uk, accessed 24 May 2012.

INTERVIEWS

Abuk, Joseph (translator, co-director) and Derik Uya Alfred (co-director), London, 5 May 2012. Interview and transcript: Christine Matzke.

—— (translator, co-director), Derik Uya Alfred (co-director) and John Mairi (London, former member of Skylark) University of Warwick, 7 May 2012. Interview: Yvette Hutchison, transcript: Christine Matzke.

Bagirasas, Esther Liberato (actress; The Queen, Jupiter, a soldier in the English army), London, 4 May 2012. Interview and transcript: Christine Matzke.

Paulino, Francis (actor; Posthumus, doctor, a soldier in the English army), London, 4 May 2012 Interview and transcript: Christine Matzke.

Matzke, Christine (2012), 'Field notes 2 May 2012, Globe Theatre, London'.

Leonardi, Cherry (4 May 2013), 'Final version of Cymbeline', personal email correspondence with the author.

Woods, Penelope (26 April 2013), 'Globe to Globe Stats', personal email correspondence with the author.

African Shakespeares
– a Discussion

MICHAEL WALLING with JUWON OGUNGBE,
ARNE POHLMEIER, KATE STAFFORD,
DEV VIRAHSAWMY

Michael Walling: Welcome to this discussion, everybody. This is a bit of an experiment in creating an article with multiple voices, as a way of bringing together theatre-makers from around Africa and the UK in conversation. To introduce you to each other, round the Google table we have:

Juwon Ogungbe (JO) is a musician and theatre-maker, whose musical version of *The Merchant of Venice* performed at the 2012 (Harare International Festival of Arts) HIFA.

Arne Pohlmeier (AP) is the director of Two Gents Productions. He has worked with two Zimbabwean actors – Denton Chikura and Tonderai Munyevu – to create versions of *Two Gentlemen of Verona* and *Hamlet*. *Two Gentlemen of Verona* was performed in Shona at the Globe to Globe festival (London 2012).

Kate Stafford (KS) was founding director of Nanzikambe in Malawi and is currently Artistic Director of Bilimankhwe Arts in the UK. Kate has directed a number of Shakespeare productions in Malawi, including *Macbeth* (2004), *Hamlet* (2003) and *A Midsummer Night's Dream* (2005), and has worked as producer with both companies on *Romeo and Juliet* for the 2012 World Shakespeare Festival.

Dev Virahsawmy (DV) is a Mauritian playwright who has been prolific in translating Shakespeare's plays into Morisien (or Mauritian Creole), as well as writing his own contemporary adaptations of the plays, including *Zeneral Makbef* (1981), *Toufann* (1991) and *Prezidan Otelo* (2003).

I am (**MW**) the Artistic Director of Border Crossings and Visiting Professor at Rose Bruford College. I directed *Macbeth* in Mauritius with a local cast (1997), and followed that project with a production of *Twelfth Night*, by the UK company which was created to tour Mauritius, the Seychelles and Zimbabwe for the British Council (1997-8). I also directed Dev's version of *The Tempest, Toufann,* at the Africa Centre in London (1999).

Let's begin the discussion by talking a bit about language and the power of language. I'd like to start with Arne, as I saw your Shona production the other night at the Globe. It sounded fantastic, and there were Shona-speakers in the audience responding to both the humour and the poetry – but I must say it seemed quite odd to me that a production which had started in English was translated into Shona specifically for a high-profile showing in London!

AP: I think we were all surprised by the aim of the festival to showcase productions of Shakespeare's plays in foreign languages. This seems to make sense in the case of languages such as Greek or Chinese, (that is, within countries and cultures where English is not a spoken language), but for productions from Zimbabwe or New Zealand, where English is a major national language, it does seem a little odd. We also had many discussions in the rehearsal room as to whether some use of English might be permissible, especially when the actors address the audience directly. In the end, however, a rigorous transposition of the play into Shona was an incredibly powerful act of liberation. Where and when else do you get the opportunity to showcase a language such as Shona in all its poetic and dramatic richness in front of a Global audience?

MW: I know you had plans to take the production to Zimbabwe, but that these didn't work out because of funding. It seems to be a bit of a pattern across the productions presented in the Globe to Globe festival, and I wonder if you can shed any light on that.

AP: The avenues of funding that we pursued to get the show to Harare did not lead anywhere... it's just a reality that what we want to achieve as artists does not always fit in with the aims of one or other funding institution. Of course we believe strongly that a performance of Shakespeare in Shona needs to be seen in Zimbabwe – (Has it ever happened before? Will it happen again?) – especially in such an instance, where many Zimbabweans will have heard about the show on the World Service and will rightly wonder why it's not being performed in Zimbabwe.

MW: We did make use of Shona in our production of *Twelfth Night* when it toured to Zimbabwe (under the aegis of the British Council, I should say), and that production was so popular there that people walked 200 miles to see it at Amakhosi in Bulawayo,[1] and there were disturbances in Mbare when some people couldn't get seats. So I can vouch for the demand. I don't know that there has ever been a fully Shona production of Shakespeare before yours, and it seems a great shame for it not to reach a majority Shona-speaking audience.

The Globe to Globe festival involved some major bodies like the British Council (at the development stage) and the Commonwealth Foundation. In each case, I'd have thought the desire would have been to see tangible benefits for the African cultures involved and for audiences in Africa itself, rather than mainstream audiences in wealthy places.

AP: I am not sure that the British Council's remit is to benefit economically less well-off countries. I think its remit is to bring the best of British culture to the world. Perhaps bringing our Shona show to a Shona audience does not fall within their remit. If it is a matter of benefitting the less well off, we would have been delighted to develop a programme of work that would have reflected this, such as performing our show in high density suburbs of Harare and in other parts of Zimbabwe, and workshops with schools and local artists, etc. My impression is, however, that funders want to be approached by artists with ready-made projects rather than working with artists to develop projects in collaboration. As a consequence, if you do not have a good (business/fundraising) sense as an artist you won't get the funding – even if your artistic idea is sound.

MW: I remember when I was first asked to direct Shakespeare in African countries for the British Council (which was in the mid-90s), there was still an element of 'bringing great culture to less developed people' in the agenda – and we had to work quite hard and quite deliberately within the project to overcome that. The use of local languages was an important part of this... The Mauritian *Macbeth*[2] had nine witches, three speaking English, three speaking French and three speaking Morisien[3], plus lots of passages in Morisien when its use reflected social realities. The Porter, of course, spoke the language of the audience and used very specific topical references – but there were also more subtle things, like the child Macduff talking Morisien with his mother, and then her switching to English when the murderers arrived, even though they answered her in Morisien. So the language cocktail started to raise questions about the cultural hierarchies present in the island, and the role that language and the survival of colonial cultural structures play in it. There was some umbrage in the British Council – who have the propagation of the language in their charter – but they also acknowledged that it worked, and that it allowed the performers and the audience a sense of ownership over the text, which seems to me crucial.

KS: What an interesting discussion – especially regarding the priorities of the British Council. My first African Shakespeare, *The African Hamlet,* was supported by British Council Malawi, who then commissioned me to produce *Macbeth* the following year. It was interesting that the British Council's Malawi Director at the time was particularly excited by what he saw as the 'mutuality' inherent in the work. He felt that in the past the British Council had been focussed on 'bringing British culture to the world', but that this was changing (this was back in 2003). He said that as I was a British director working with a Malawian cast to discover a way of performing Shakespeare to a largely Malawian audience, we fitted perfectly with the BC's new focus on bringing the cultures together. I'm interested to hear that Arne had trouble getting the British Council interested in bringing a Shona version of *Two Gentlemen* to Zimbabwe. I think that there is a huge difference between the British Council in the UK (who do still only seem to be interested in bringing the 'best' of British culture to ex-colonies) and the British Council in the countries themselves, who are much more interested in how the cultures can work together for mutual benefit.

My journey into African Shakespeare was a developmental one: in *The African Hamlet*, I used only the original Shakespeare but with Malawian traditional dancers and musicians providing the dumb show for the Players and entertainment for the wedding of Claudius and Gertrude (which I inserted as an introduction to the characters and the situation they were in). By the time I started work on *African Macbeth* I had developed a more confident approach. There were songs in Chichewa, sung by the witches (who were dressed as Malawian mfiti,[4] complete with goatskins and baboon tails) and some phrases of Chichewa sneaked in here and there. This, together with a programme in which I had a local artist do a comic-strip of the story with drawings which matched the actors, had the effect of making it much more accessible to an audience which was almost entirely made up of people for whom English was their second (and often third) language. The witches were played by a well-known afro-reggae band, so I cut all the 'double double, toil and trouble' and had some Chichewa songs instead. For *An African Dream* we used even more music and a lot of physical clowning, playing up the broad comedy which is very popular with Malawian audiences.[5] As before, we stuck with the Shakespearean text but added in music and original songs in Chichewa, which I commissioned from a local modern jazz musician.

MW: One of the most striking aspects of the Bilimankhwe/Nanzikambe *Romeo and Juliet* is the way the languages alternate, with the original text being used for the love scenes, and the bulk of the rest being in Chichewa. I know Amy Bonsall[6] directed this particular show, working very closely with Aaron Ngalonde Nhlane on the translation, but perhaps as producer you could shed a bit of light on the ideas behind this approach.

KS: Partly this was pragmatic, as we had a short rehearsal period and the actors were working in their second (and sometimes third or fourth) language, so it seemed sensible to have some of it in Chichewa. But then as the work started to progress, the rhythm and beauty of the Chichewa started to work its magic. The company did use some English phrases mixed in with the Chichewa: this reflects their natural way of speaking, as when they speak in their own language they often use English words and phrases. In this way they could sprinkle key phrases in English through the play so that a British audience would find it easy to follow the story.

MW: I hugely enjoyed the production, which I thought was really clear and direct, as well as bringing a very powerful (and non-literal) physicality to the piece. But I did wonder whether the use of the original English text for more 'poetic' passages didn't perpetuate a sort of colonial hierarchy of languages. After all, Romeo and Juliet become more themselves through their experience of love – at least, that's how I read the performances – and it seems odd to do that by abandoning your own language...

KS: Yes, I can see that this could be problematic. But in my opinion, what we were doing is Shakespeare, so it seemed appropriate that the central characters should express themselves in the original language of the play. The Shakespearean language therefore becomes the language of love. For me, that worked really well. But then my first language is English, so that's not surprising! However, the Malawian actors also felt that this worked well, and were not at all worried about whether English or Chichewa was a 'superior' language. Chichewa is a wonderfully poetic language in its own right, and the Malawians were confident enough in their own language not to feel at all threatened by Romeo and Juliet being the only characters to speak the original Shakespeare. Having said that, it might be interesting to reverse it, to have everyone speaking English except Romeo and Juliet. Aaron Ngalonde Nhlane is continuing to work on a translation of the entire text, so perhaps we could try it both ways.

MW: Dev, you're particularly well-known as a translator of Shakespeare, and I know from past conversations that much of this is to do with a kind of validation of the Mauritian language. It's in the same way that Julius Nyerere famously translated *Julius Caesar* into Kiswahili so as to prove that the African language was capable of 'great thought'.[7] I have to say that it astonishes me to find you still fighting that corner in the 21st century! Can Shakespeare actually prove the validity of Morisien, do you think?

DV: The Mauritian intelligentsia of the sixties and seventies were dead against any form of promotion of MC which for them was a dialect, a pidgin, a patois, some form of broken French, but not a language. They would argue that the profound thoughts found in Shakespeare could never be said in MC. I had to prove them wrong. So I started to translate Shakespeare... [*Enn Ta Senn Dan Vid* (*Much Ado About Nothing*, 1995), *Zil Sezar* (*Julius Caesar*, 1987), *Trazedi Makbes* (*Macbeth*, 1997), *Prens Hamlet* (*Hamlet*, 1994), *Lerwa Lir* (*King Lear*, 2006). Later came *Enn Afro Dan Veniz* (*Othello*, 2012), *Lerwa Bwar* (*Twelfth Night*, 2012), *Ramdeo Ek Ziliet* (*Romeo and Juliet*, 2012)].[8] If initially the main preoccupation was to support my claim that MC was fit to become the National Language of the Republic, my translation work started to develop new orientations. How could I use the prestige of Shakespeare to favour nation building? Could the theatre do to Mauritius what it did to the English or Irish Renaissance?

With the passage of time, language planning recedes into the background and the development of positive responses to the different challenges of social and cultural development starts to occupy the foreground. A good example is *Ramdeo ek Ziliet* [a rewriting of *Romeo and Juliet*, 2012]. It's about love between a Hindu boy and Christian girl, viewed from a feminist perspective, with reminiscences of *A Winter's Tale*.

Moreover, Shakespeare's works come in handy when taboo subjects are treated. Dr Hamlet helps a cancer patient to die; President Othello is gay; Cleopatra is a sex worker in love with a young man, Antony. Names from the plays of Shakespeare are used instead of local names to avoid fruitless and sterile polemics.

MW: It's interesting how your contemporary plays make this use of Shakespearean characters, sometimes in situations analogous to those in the original plays, and sometimes in completely new ones. What's the value in using these characters for a new play in Morisien?

DV: The old bard's plays can also be used to deal with and present powerful enduring values. *Trazedi Makbes* [1997] shows that evil will give you an egg to take an ox[9] ('donn enn dizef, pran enn bef'); *Lerwa Lir* echoes teachings of the New Testament, the Bhagavad Gita and the Koran – namely that life is a contradiction. The old king starts to think clearly when his wits are gone; he starts to win when everything is lost. As in Paul's letter to the Corinthians, he has to die to be born again [Corinthians 15:35-49]. Gloucester starts to see when his eyes are gouged out; Hamlet grows spiritually until he becomes a Christ-like figure ready to die to purge the world – there is a divinity in the fall of a sparrow – and Othello stabs himself to kill the evil in him – hell is not other people, it is in oneself].

I have often leant on Shakespeare to build a dramatic literature as part of the national culture of New Mauritius. Language planning, nation building and the teaching of basic values are done through tears, laughter, songs and dances, for like all lovers of Shakespeare I listen to the music of the spheres and watch Lord Shiva as He creates the world in a dance.

But most important of all, I have discovered God who is Mama-Papa (Mother-Father), an embodiment of love and mercy. That is the point I wanted to make in my translation-adaptation-Mauritianisation of *Romeo and Juliet*. A tragedy of fate (star-crossed lovers) becomes a tragi-comedy in which the benevolent Providence (Bondie) uses art (a statue as in *A Winter's Tale*) to bring reconciliation and reunion. Am I still following in the Bard's footsteps unconsciously?

AP: I think the process of taking ownership is what is crucial in staging Shakespeare, and working across cultures serves to highlight that. I think that a lot of 'established' productions of Shakespeare that I see in London do not make that process of taking ownership visible. Ownership is perhaps taken too much for granted. Sure, Shakespeare was white and British, so it seems only natural for him to appear in a white and British guise on stage today – this fails, however, to highlight how different Shakespeare's time was from ours and how edgy and contradictory his works are. Taking a more wilful approach to his works helps to highlight these edges and contradictions in a more honest manner, especially when you are letting the plays collide with other, seemingly disparate elements. For instance, there are other cultural practices (we always use the mbira, a musical instrument specific to Zimbabwe and Shona culture, in our productions) or other elements linked to our view of the world (this I suppose incorporates what Dev is speaking of).

MW: Maybe we could talk a bit about how particular African theatre styles have fed into these productions. Kate's been talking about some aspects of this in Malawi, and I also found the influence of township theatre on *Two Gents* to be very pronounced. It's not too hard to trace a line which starts with *Sizwe Bansi is Dead* and *The Island,* runs through *Woza Albert!* and arrives at your versions of Shakespeare for two actors with multiple doubling and creative use of minimal props...

AP: Barney Simon has actually had such a profound influence on my work, though it has only been tangential up until now ... My time as an intern at the Market Theatre in 2006 was actually saturated with his presence and influence, though he had passed away years before. But the plays I've read and what people have said about him has left a profound influence. If you see *Woza Albert!* staged, you see the care that has gone into creating beautiful, specific and precise characters, all drawn from the world around you. Mbongeni Ngema and Percy Mtwa, who co-created *Woza Albert!* with Barney Simon, speak about how they would go into the townships and study the people around them. They would then go and bring these observations into the rehearsal room to create the characters and situations. Even if our work is not devised but based on a classic text, you still have to employ a similar process of rooting the work in specifics drawn from your world of experience.

MW: The Border Crossings production of *Twelfth Night* for the British Council, which I mentioned before, was very interesting in that respect. It was originally commissioned for Mauritius and the Seychelles, so we made use of a very ethnically diverse cast to reflect the make-up of the islands, and we drew on a wide range of cultural traditions, including the Asian, which is very important in the Indian Ocean and which also allowed us an interesting route in to the gender games in the play. Indian folk theatre has a transvestite tradition similar in some ways to Shakespeare's own. We had a Mauritian composer working on it – Eric Appapoulay – and he worked with African instruments to construct a really beautiful score, which again localised the play. Then we were asked to go to the mainland with it, and perform in Zimbabwe. I felt we couldn't just transplant the whole thing. We had to be open to how our work might resonate in a very different space. And that's why I changed the casting – quite drastically in some instances. Reginald Tsiboe came into the cast as Antonio and the Sea Captain, so that there was a noticeably African response to Viola's 'What country, friends, is this?' It was wonderfully resonant to hear Reggie's accent meld with the verse when he said that he was 'bred and born / Not three hours' travel from this very place'.

Or take the very opening. In Mauritius, Orsino was white and Feste, who spoke Curio's lines, was South Asian. The relationship between them was quite easy, and the Mauritian audience read this as reflecting the very direct relationship between the better off groups in the island. It was a sort of race and class amalgam, which is the reality there. But in Zimbabwe, I didn't feel we could do the same thing. So I asked Wil Johnson, who is a very powerful black British actor, to play Orsino, and Peter Kenny, who is white, played Feste. The mere fact that they were master and servant suddenly became really important – there were gasps from the Zimbabwean audience when Wil's Orsino gave Peter's Feste an order.

Now, this got even more interesting later in the play, when Orsino is falling in love with Viola in her disguise as Cesario. Viola was played by a male actor, Gareth Corke, and so the gay subtext was very clear. I think it was quite discomforting for the audience to see Wil's Orsino, who they initially read as a powerful African hero, falling in love with this male figure. It was the time of Robert Mugabe's crusade against homosexuality as 'un-African', and I think it touched some important nerves.

Arne, you did some very interesting things with gender in *Two Gents* – tell us about that!

AP: Well, our *Two Gentlemen of Verona* has the two [male, Zimbabwean] actors slipping into all of the play's fifteen characters. This includes, of course, the women. Even more so than with the men, a lot of research and discussion went into the construction of these female characters. Single elements of costume are used to signify each character and in case of the women these were particularly feminine: a headscarf for the maid Lucetta, a long glove for Silvia, a hip-hugging sarong for Julia, and so on. This allowed the actors to slip in and out of character with great ease. It also meant that Denton and Tonderai did not have to 'over-act' femininity... For instance, by emphasising the put-on-ness (or 'prosthetic nature' to quote Sonia Massai) of gender and identity, the costumes actually liberated the actors and allowed them to take a more truthful approach, especially to the women.

Also, though our show was performed by only the two male actors, we didn't want this to undermine the plight of the female characters. In *Two Gentlemen of Verona*, both Sylvia and Julia, the two leading ladies, fall silent in the final act of the play. Sylvia actually has no lines after being attacked by Proteus, and Julia equally stops speaking after Valentine seemingly reconciles her with Proteus in Act Five. We felt we had to find a way of staging the women's silence in this final scene, and so our play ends not with the characters happily united in marriage, but with a tableaux of Julia and Silvia silently united in solidarity with each other. Describing it like this make it sound quite kitsch ... perhaps you need to see it to believe ... What did you make of it Michael?

MW: I didn't find it kitsch at all – I thought it was very moving. Given the play's title, and the fact that your performers were two men, the expectation was that the play's conclusion would focus on the Two Gents themselves, and it was actually quite shocking to see the emphasis move to the silent characters, the women. Because there were only two bodies on the stage, and they were male bodies, the decision to focus the ending on the characters who were apparently marginalised, the ones who weren't talking, the women, highlighted their journeys and their stories really powerfully.

It's interesting how far African Shakespeare tends to prioritise the silent figures. This came up recently [July 2012] when I had a public conversation with Peter Sellars at the Africa Centre about his production *Desdemona*. The whole conception of that piece is that Shakespeare's women tend to be passive and silent. In the new Toni Morrison text, Desdemona and her African nurse, Barbary, acquire a voice of their own in the afterlife, and begin the dialogue of forgiveness. It's almost as if the Shakespeare text leaves empty spaces for the contemporary, post-colonial, post-feminist age to fill in.

Thinking a bit more about gender and sexuality – Juwon, you've just done *Merchant of Venice* in Harare – I'm wondering how you dealt with the gay subtext of that play in that context.

JO: The performers constantly referred to the Antonio/Bassanio relationship as a 'bromance' during rehearsals. I didn't want to highlight the relationship dynamic. Negative attention isn't always useful...

At the end of the play, we had Portia with Bassanio, Gratiano with Nerissa ... and Antonio on his own, so we decided to have him sprinkle some confetti on the couples.

MW: The isolation of various characters at the end of the comedies often seems to me particularly powerful in spaces where there are social, political or cultural conflicts. Our *Twelfth Night* almost felt like a litany of isolations in the final song, the Fool is sounding pretty sad himself, and there's Malvolio plotting revenge, Antonio having lost Sebastian, Andrew nursing his broken head, Toby and Maria in that uneasy new alliance... The discomfort, the sense that things weren't complete and neat and finished, seemed to resonate very powerfully in spaces where the culture, the national identity, was perceived to be a work in progress. It seems to me that's a key reason why Shakespeare works so well in contemporary Africa. The political and cultural context he was writing in was also one of becoming – his London was in such a state of flux.

Merchant of Venice is also very sensitive in terms of racial politics, not only in relation to Shylock and his Jewish identity, but also more directly in relation to Africa in the figure of the Prince of Morocco. How did your musical version respond to this, and to the overt racism expressed by Portia against the Prince? How was your cast made up ethnically and culturally?

JO: The performers were all Black Africans (Shona-speaking Zimbabweans, except for me). I did set the Princes of Morocco and Arragon scenes [to music], but had to cut them, because performances at HIFA are supposed to run for no longer than one hour. Obviously, the guys that had been cast as Morocco and Arragon were disappointed... The upshot of this however, was that we didn't really address the issue of Portia's overtly expressed racist attitude.

MW: But it's also there in relation to Shylock, right?

JO: Yes, Michael, but in that regard it became much more of an issue of faith. When I look at a lot of people of Ashkenazi Jewish heritage in Britain and Europe, I don't really see the racial difference between them and Gentiles of Caucasian roots. I also believe that the Falashas[10] of Ethiopia don't look that different from other people from that country. There are a lot of problems in Africa related to ethnicity and religion, and it made more sense to go for the feeling of religious intolerance in our production. You might have heard of Boko Haram – the Islamic terrorist organisation currently wreaking havoc in Northern Nigeria. I think there is a similar stand-off between Christians and adherents of the Shona traditional belief system, for example, (though it isn't violent as far as I know). Shylock says a great deal about hating Christians... quite a provocative stance to take in a part of Africa where a lot of television programming features Nigerian Pentecostal 'Prosperity' preachers. I think some of the Pentecostal audience members were overjoyed to witness Shylock being forced to convert to Christianity.

MW: Kate, I remember you talking about some similar experiences with *Macbeth* in Malawi, and on tour in Zimbabwe, when the play seemed to reflect the political context.

KS: Yes indeed – we were sailing rather close to the wind with our production of *African Macbeth*. Performing it in Harare[11] under the dictatorship of Mugabe and in Malawi in an election year meant that in both places it had a strong resonance with the local situation. It was set in an unspecified African country and was in modern dress. Duncan and then Macbeth both had the chief's hat and flywhisk common to African dictators in both Zimbabwe and Malawi and the military opponents to Macbeth were dressed in camouflage uniforms and were clearly a rebel army. The Porter wrote his own speech – I was lucky to have an experienced actor/director/writer in the role – which lampooned the greed and excess of African leaders [and] went down a storm in both Malawi and Zimbabwe.[12] When we performed in Harare, the moment when Macduff finally kills Macbeth was particularly memorable. We did it as a knife fight, after Macbeth's gun jams. Macbeth is lying dead having been fatally stabbed, and Macduff lies exhausted and struggling to regain his breath after the fight. There is a silence in the audience and I clearly heard a man say 'and so should all dictators die'. There were armed guards at the venue, watching the show. Fortunately they didn't speak English.

MW: Juwon, I'd be interested to talk a bit more about the music in your production, and particularly how it related to your audience in Harare.

JO: My idea for *Merchant of Venice* was to set it in a Rastafarian/Ethiopian Orthodox Church sound world, so I drew inspiration from reggae, nyabinghi[13], dancehall, and several African music genres. The piece is totally music-driven and all-singing theatre. The performers had to sing, act and play instruments (marimba, drums, piano, recorders and light percussion). Some of the work is influenced by western art music and the performers had to learn a lot about devices such as recitative... The audiences seemed to be comfortable with all the twists and turns in the music.

MW: Arne, tell us a bit about the music in your production, which I thought was very exciting...

AP: Well, Denton plays the mbira, and the mbira is very typical of Zimbabwean/Shona music and so it focuses in all of our productions. We use music in *Two Gents* to evoke location/cultural context, to give an insight into characters' emotional states, to clarify the story or to give the audience a moment to breathe and relax... After all, we work them very hard in this show, where they have to believe that two actors on a bare stage actually are a dizzying array of fifteen characters, including a dog, in three major locations; Verona, Milan, and the forest. We draw on traditional songs – well, those that Denton can play on his mbira – as much as modern pop music, both typically Zimbabwean and generic Western. The music serves as a reminder that the production is both a modern and a Zimbabwean rendition of Shakespeare's classic story.

MW: Dev, music is very important in some of your responses to Shakespeare, isn't it? I'm thinking especially of *Sir Toby* (1998) now....

DV: A genuine Mauritian theatre can naturally use songs. It is part of our culture. Mauritians of all ethnic backgrounds love musicals. Bollywood films are full of songs and dances. During World War Two when films could not be imported from India, Mauritian artists created dance dramas called 'Natak'. French musicals [*4 Jours à Paris*] and Hollywood musicals have a great appeal. I use songs to express certain views but also to generate the mood I need for my story to get through. Moreover the contribution of the rock-opera *Zozef Ek So Palto Larkansiel* [*Joseph and His Amazing Technicolour Dreamcoat*, 1984] to language planning and nation building can never be overlooked.

JO: I think music does play a central role in rituals and ceremonies and theatre in most of Black Africa. Islam sometimes has a way of interfering with this, but I sense that the heritages that are more musically inclined tend to transcend such interventions... Bambaras and Mandinkas of Mali spring to mind... I say this, because I don't think each and every heritage in Africa is equally musical. Some ethnic groups have more of an inclination to express themselves musically than others. My heritage is Yoruba, and the Yorubas have a long history of producing music theatre... I'd even go as far as saying 'singing theatre'. I've worked on a Nigerian based poetic drama in New York, [Off Broadway] and the producer couldn't understand the convention of having characters speaking in courtly English and then singing songs in an African language in the same scene. This is a device that is taken for granted by theatre makers and audiences that are *au fait* with the genre. My setting of *Merchant of Venice* would sit comfortably with the works of pioneering Nigerian actor/manager/makers such as Hubert Ogunde or Duro Ladipo,[14] except for the differences in my musical vocabulary, when compared with theirs, of course. What was exciting in that context was the opportunity to combine my knowledge of Black British nyabinghi-based music theatre with an art music sensibility. The performers were willing to go on that journey with me.

MW: Did anybody else see the RSC's recent foray into Africa with *Julius Caesar*?[15] In some ways it highlighted a lot of the questions we've been discussing, although this was very emphatically not 'Shakespeare in Africa' but 'Shakespeare set in Africa'. Perhaps this made overt what was a hidden agenda in the Globe to Globe season − the fact that a lot of this work is actually being made for western audiences, and not for Africa at all. It makes me wonder what the western audience is getting out of this. If something like that *Julius Caesar* were done in Sierra Leone, we'd all be talking about its relevance; but done in England, it almost seems like a way of disengaging the audience and exoticising the play.... Turning the politics into entertainment.

JO: I haven't seen the RSC's *Julius Caesar*, but I agree with the idea that the setting could disengage the audience and exoticise the play. Greg Doran has done a lot of Shakespeare work with South Africans and I guess that a sort of 'African theatre' ambience is part of his vocabulary that he likes to draw from occasionally.

KS: I saw *Julius Caesar* and while I really liked it, it was definitely not African theatre. The entire company was black British as far as I could see, and while it was done very well, I agree with Michael that it was Shakespeare set in Africa, not African Shakespeare. Having said that, setting a Shakespeare play in sub-Saharan Africa is perfectly appropriate ... so long as it is not mistaken for the real deal. Incidentally, my Malawian cast went to see it and one of them commented on how interesting it was that from their accents they all seemed to come from different parts of Africa (not, I feel, Greg Doran's intention!).

MW: I just worry about productions for Western audiences that construct a fantasy of modern Africa as 'how the West used to be in more barbaric times'. The discourse around the production involved people saying things like 'The Soothsayer actually makes sense because in Africa they still have witch doctors.' It smacks of primitivism to me... And Shakespeare wasn't talking about 'the primitive'– this is a play about the immediate, current moment. People always say he made a mistake in putting chiming clocks into the play, but I think he knew exactly what he was doing. Everyone in the play keeps asking, 'What's the time?', and the chiming clock proves to the audience that the time is now!

DV: What I would like to say on *Julius Caesar* may not be totally irrelevant to the discussion you want to trigger, Michael, but it may have some relevance. I think that for Shakespeare, since Rome was no longer a city state but an empire, it needed very strong leadership to develop and control it, a kind of king with divine rights, according to Tudor ideology. The play is not the tragedy of Julius Caesar, for he becomes stronger after his death and his name is mentioned more than seventy times after the coup and his assassination. It is rather the tragedy of Brutus, a good man but a blundering politician. According to Shakespeare, I think, he was not the political animal with political intelligence that Rome needed. I would like to see more of this in modern productions, for the political message is clear and relevant for our times. A good and honest person does not always make a good political leader with strong political clout and acumen.

MW: I totally agree about the contemporary relevance, Dev. I know you translated, rather than adapted, this play as *Zil Sezar*: did you find yourself drawing out any specific parallels with contemporary Mauritian politics, or with African politics more generally?

DV: The African leaders who championed the cause of independence and led the battle to obtain it had a major preoccupation: how to keep together the different tribes within 'artificial' boundaries drawn by colonial powers. The 'empire' (multi-ethnic country) had to be consolidated and civil war avoided and many young post-independence leaders, including me,[16] driven by 'noble ideals' thought they had to 'get rid' of the old Caesars to pave the way for a more progressive set-up. Have we always been right? Take the present situation in Libya, for example. Will the new regime be able to keep the territorial integrity of a tribe-ridden country? I'm aware that I'm oversimplifying an extremely complex situation. But the question remains... My translation of *Julius Caesar* as *Zil Sezar* was influenced by such thoughts.

MW: And so was my production of *Macbeth*, which I remember you saw in Mauritius. People often present that play as a comment on 'African dictatorship' – Kate's production being one example – and to a degree I suppose that's what your adaptation *Zeneral Macbef* does too, through setting the post-colonial state in a global context, caught between superpowers scrambling for its natural resources. What I found particularly resonant in the Shakespeare text when I approached it for an African production, was that the colonialism comes at the end, with the English army invading Scotland, supposedly to install the rightful ruler after the overthrow of the tyrant. Sound familiar? You can't help feeling that Malcolm, schooled at the English court to become a duplicitous Machiavellian schemer, is not going to be the same sort of king his father was, and that the process of regime change will in fact lead to English domination. In much the same way, modern relationships between Africa and the current global powers may offer 'development' and 'aid', but this is actually the front for an exploitative neo-colonial agenda. As Macduff says, 'Such welcome and unwelcome things at once / 'Tis hard to reconcile.'

DV: Works of Shakespeare are replete with Tudor and Stuart propaganda. This is clear in *Macbeth* in which the English court is pious and the Scottish court devilish. King James the First must have been very pleased with this play. When initially I started to translate *Macbeth*, I was put off by the Manichean outlook and finally chose the satirical vein, and the end result was *Zeneral Makbef*, an original play which lampoons the two superpowers and political doormats of the seventies. Some people have suggested that the play has now lost its lustre, [and] is irrelevant because of the demise of the USSR. Is that really so? Don't we still have quite a few Zeneral Makbefs in today's world (in Iraq, Afghanistan, Libya, Syria and so on)? Is not the world through the media literally harassed by US imperialist propaganda? Are we free to build our country in a way which reflects our history, reality and culture? Are we free to protect our economy from US dumping? Are we free to move towards a green economy? ... Maybe I should think of writing *Zeneral Makbef 2*.

NOTES

1 Amakhosi is a leading independent theatre company in Zimbabwe which is based in the second city of Bulawayo.

2 This production was staged in Rose-Hill, Mauritius, in 1997, with a local cast.

3 The term Morisien is the Mauritian word for the local language, which in English tends to be called Mauritian Creole. Later in the conversation, Dev Virahsawmy abbreviates this to MC, although he strongly believes that it needs to be regarded as a language in its own right, and not a Creole or patois.

4 *Mfiti* is someone who uses evil spiritual forces to hurt/kill others. (Thanks to Elinettie Chabwera for this definition.)

5 Malawi has both English and Chichewa language drama traditions, but theatre in Chichewa is always comic.

6 Amy Bonsall is Associate Director of Bilimankhwe, and has a background in African Shakespeare: she assisted Janet Suzman on her production of *Hamlet* at the Baxter Theatre Centre in South Africa.

7 Julius Nyerere, the first president of Tanzania, promoted the use of Kiswahili as a *lingua franca* and a focus for the nationalist struggle against colonialism. He translated both *The Merchant of Venice* and *Julius Caesar* into Kiswahili to prove the sophistication of the language.

8 Dates for these later plays are as recorded in the scripts published on Virahsawmy's website, www.dev-virahsawmy.org.

9 This means to cheat someone by giving a trifle to take something important. Dev Virahsawmy saw this as echoing Banquo's words: 'And oftentimes, to win us to our harm;/The instruments of darkness tell us truths/Win us with honest trifles, to betray's/In deepest consequence.'

10 The Falashas are Ethiopian Jews who were cut off from all other Jewish people for many centuries. According to Ethiopian mythological history, the Queen of Sheba converted Ethiopia to Judaism, but the ruling Amhara people were then converted to Christianity in the 4th century AD. The Falashas were discriminated against in modern Ethiopia and most were taken to Israel in the 1980s, where they are now often discriminated against because of their race and because some people do not see them as properly Jewish.

11 The production toured to HIFA with British Council support.

12 This sounds very similar to the approach taken to this speech in the 1997 production in Mauritius. [MW]

13 Nyabinghi is the name of the music-making used during Rastafarian praise and worship ceremonies.

14 Hubert Ogunde and Duro Ladipo were actor-managers of famous Yoruba Nigerian theatre groups in the period spanning the 1950s to the late 1970s.

15 This production took place in 2012.

16 Dev Virahsawmy was one of the founders of the MMM (Mouvement Militant Mauricien), a radical socialist party which was formed in 1969, the year after the island became independent of Britain. He was imprisoned in the early '70s for his political stance. The MMM has since become a more conventional party, and has entered government, but not with Dev's participation.

'Sa bezsominn Shakespeare la' – The Brave New World of Dev Virahsawmy

ASHISH BEESOONDIAL

Inspired by the fact that two of his predecessors at the University of Edinburgh – Julius Nyerere, who was later to become the President of Tanzania, and Thomas Decker from Sierra Leone – had translated Shakespeare's *Julius Caesar* in Swahili and Kriyo respectively, Dev Virahsawmy took the decision to delve into translating Shakespeare during his university days in the mid-1960s. For Virahsawmy, this was concrete evidence that Shakespeare was perennial and accessible to all. Urged by his university lecturer to explore Mauritian Creole (Kreol) as a language, Virahsawmy's endeavour became even more pressing. However, his first translation was not that of *Julius Caesar*, but of *Much Ado about Nothing*.[1] It was done with one objective in mind: he felt that comedy, being culturally loaded and more difficult to translate, would prove the opponents of Kreol wrong. Stirred by the post-independence nationalist spirit and an appreciation for a national language that was not yet officially recognised, the dramatist sought to prove that his mother tongue, like any other foreign language, could articulate philosophical thoughts. Shakespeare was to become his instrument to popularise Kreol and to contest the bias of the elite against the language, for at that time, Mauritian writers preferred the colonial modes of expression – English and French.

Transacting with Shakespeare was to serve another purpose too. As a socially engaged writer and politician in the 1980s, Virahsawmy felt that the Bard's ubiquity and cultural authority would permit him to recreate and adapt his plays to the Mauritian context. By negotiating the canon, Virahsawmy gives Shakespearean plays new life through a language and staging that is closer to home. Not only are characters appropriated but Virahsawmy also reshapes events derived from the Bard's plays and experiments with genre-mixing. Virahsawmy's repertoire of tradaptations is wide-ranging. This essay seeks to bring out how the playwright engages in the deconstruction of Shakespearean plays and the subsequent reconstruction of his own to express his ideology and establish Kreol as a literary tool.

Perhaps the play that best illustrates Virahsawmy's transposition of

Shakespearean characters into a different time zone and condition is *Dernie Vol* (The Last Flight, 2003), an adaptation of *Antony and Cleopatra*. A guilt-ridden, blind Antwann meets an aged Kleopatra (a sex worker in her past) at an airport. He affectionately calls her 'Klekle' – a figurative image representing life. After imploring Kleopatra's forgiveness for leaving her for a richer woman in the past, Antwann departs and she is left alone. *Prezidan Otelo* (President Othello, 2003) is equally intriguing: the play reveals Othello as a homosexual President, Iago as the Prime Minister and Desdemona, Othello's closest friend, as the Vice-Prime Minister. While the plot retains the themes of suspicion and betrayal, the symbol of Othello-Desdemona's bond – the handkerchief – is replaced by a book of poems by Khalil Gibran. *Tabisman Lir* (Lir's Estate, 2003), Virahsawmy's adaptation of *King Lear*, projects Kordelia as a victim of the HIV virus who is banished from her rich father's estate.

Can Shakespeare be used in this way? While the legitimacy of this question can be debated in a postcolonial context, Virahsawmy's answer remains in the affirmative, emanating from his belief that Shakespeare belongs to humanity. One can almost sense the fun that Virahsawmy has in taking extreme liberties with the Bard: Shakespeare is made to function both in the 'now' and in a local context, understood to be Mauritius. *Dokter Hamlet* (Doctor Hamlet, 1996) finds the eponymous character having to contend with important social issues such as marriage, abortion and euthanasia against a backdrop of political manipulation. The 'play-within-the-play' technique is employed as Virahsawmy tinkers with a new genealogy of Shakespearean characters: Hamlet is the brother of Mrs Ermionn Kapilet (Hermione Capulet) and Ziliet (Juliet) is his niece. Moreover, his other version of *Romeo and Juliet*, *Ramdeo ek so Ziliet* (Ramdeo and her Juliet, 2012), comprises characters who are, in fact, Mauritian descendants of Shakespeare's play. The play's ending is reminiscent of *The Winter's Tale* with the statues of Ramdeo, Ziliet and their baby coming to life again. By mingling tragedy with tragic-comedy Virashsawmy is creating a hybridised vision of his own.

Of all his adaptations, *Toufann* (The Tempest, 1991) is the most famous, having been (re)-translated into English and staged in London under the direction of Michael Walling in 1999. Virahsawmy pits eclectic characters from Shakespeare's plays against each other: Alonso is replaced by Lir (Lear), Polonius is his adviser, Miranda is replaced by Kordelia, Sebastian by Edmon (Edmund) and Yago (Iago) becomes Antonio. By revisiting the characters, Virahsawmy has Yago questioning his status as the perennial villain; he hits back at his own creator – Shakespeare: 'Depi ki sa bezsominn Shakespeare finn servi mwa pou li bez Othello ek Desdemona tou dimoun kwar momem responsab tou problem dan lemon' (32). [Since Shakespeare, this son of a bitch, has used me to harm Othello and Desdemona everyone thinks that I am the one responsible for all the troubles in the world] before adding, 'Mo espere ki bann kritik literer konpran ki mo pa move net' (39). [I hope literary critics understand I am not all that bad.] Such metatextual elements encapsulate the nature of Virahsawmy's tradaptations and are a reminder that Virahsawmy's characters are extensions of the original version that can evolve as personae in their own right, as he often takes characters from Shakespearean plays, but only as a starting point, as these beings may then develop in ways which radically depart from the original.

'Shakespeare's plays overlap with post-colonial concerns...they regularly provided a vocabulary for theorizing the colonial encounter and psyches', (10) observe Loomba & Orkin (1998). Many writers have adopted a deconstructive approach, questioning the Bard's status and rewriting Shakespeare, while others have utilised a more reconstructive strategy by using Shakespeare to articulate their own realities. Virahsawmy's rewriting of Shakespeare has taken both approaches. The intertextuality in *Toufann* can be specifically interpreted as a challenge to the meta-narrative of Shakespeare – an endeavour which is reinforced in his rejection of the 'master tongue' and in is his re-presentation of Kalibann. Different from Octavio Mannoni, Virahsawmy's delineation is closer to Retamar's in his projection of Caliban as a symbol of hybridity. Far from being 'a thing most brutish' (*The Tempest*, 1: ii) and a demonised character, here Kalibann is an intelligent, handsome twenty-five-year old Métis whose lineage can be traced back to his mother being a slave and his father a pirate. The re-presentation and valorisation of Kalibann reaches its pinnacle when Prospero agrees that Kalibann may marry his daughter and become king. This is Virahsawmy's answer to the racially Manichean vision of *The Tempest*, as his hero is clearly mixed race.

Toufann is also very clearly situated in a contemporary context. As Prospero himself discloses to Kordelia, their revenge plot is in three phases, much like a modern play in three acts. Prospero's control-room replaces his magic books; the prison housing Prince Ferdinand has surveillance cameras; Aryel is not a spirit but Prospero's invention, and to top it all, there is mutual attraction between Aryel and Ferdinand as the latter admits his homosexuality. Prospero's mastery of illusion propels him to omnipotence. An interview with the playwright reveals that he wrote the play as a 'disguised message' to local Hindu leaders that abuse of power can be detrimental.[2]

Virahsawmy's Shakespeare tradaptations – whether adaptations or re-creations – fall under two broad categories: political and social. While these two categories can be seen to overlap, the playwright's tumultuous political involvement makes it vital that his political plays be examined separately. Having joined the Mouvement Militant Mauricien (MMM) as one of its young leaders in 1968, Virahsawmy embraced the fight for equality of rights and the post-independence struggle to create a national identity by recognising Kreol as the national language. The MMM, which had originated as a students' movement, triggered new political thinking in Mauritius as socialist ideology swept through its ranks. In 1971, the promulgation of the Public Order Bill paved the way for the then government to impose a state of emergency to counter the political activities of the MMM. This was seen as a serious lapse in democratic practice, especially when the state of emergency lasted till 1976. Along with other leaders of the MMM, Virahsawmy was jailed for nearly a year in 1972 because of his involvement in a series of national strikes. Fellow activists from the party were also attacked. The ruling Labour Party remained in power through an alliance with other political parties despite the fact that the MMM had won the majority of seats in 1976. The popularity of the government continued to plummet because of unpopular economic policies and what was felt by many to be a culture of favouritism. This culminated in the landslide victory of the MMM in 1982, only for general elections to be held again in 1983, that put the MMM back in opposition. However, Virahsawmy had already left the MMM in 1973 in order to form his own political party, the MMMSP: though his participation in active politics subsequently dissipated within a few years. Disillusioned by what he perceived as a corrupt political arena, he steered away from party politics. It is against this activist background that Virahsawmy's interrogation of the body politic has to be understood.

It may be hard to demarcate a space between Virahsawmy the politician and Virahsawmy the playwright. The playwright is very much shaped by his political beliefs and his writing becomes a political act to expose corruption and the misuse of power. Based on the idea that Shakespeare's dramas were political, Virahsawmy's political plays question leadership and, in this way, become an indictment of corrupt and abusive power and its pervasiveness in society. His works speak out against despots who have taken on the role of political leaders, typifying the central idea in *Macbeth* that the titles of the leaders hang 'loose' upon themselves. *Zeneral Makbef* (General Makbef, 1980), a political satire, depicts a new ruling philosophy put in place by Makbef, built on a rhetoric of humanism, freedom and democracy – all of which is antithetical and incongruous because Makbef and his military leaders are mere power seekers who are inept politicians. Poor farmers are taxed for personal enrichment as the leader basks in vanity and self-glorification in his personal 'Pale-di-Pep' (Palace of the People) and his 'Stad-di-Pep' (Stadium of the People). The irony in the names is palpable. Virahsawmy also pushes the boundaries further in his depiction of the world of politics as being rotten to the core. Madam Makbef (Lady Macbeth) is swayed by Mazor Kaskontour to gradually oust Makbef from his throne so they can jointly rule. While grounding his play in the theme of 'vaulting ambition' (*Macbeth*, 1: vii), Virahsawmy's adaptation of *Macbeth* veers a long way from the internal torment of guilt that ambition provokes in Shakespeare's protagonist.

The subject of corrupted politics is also treated in *Sir Toby* (1998), a re-creation very loosely based on *Twelfth Night*. Lord Orsino, a visionary and reliable leader, is undermined by the destructive forces of despots. Sir Toby, on the other hand, shuns politics, in order to retain an independent identity. The play opens in a bar with free flowing booze – a sign that overindulgence has trickled down to the people. 'Onon Zwisans San Fren' (113), that is, in the name of limitless enjoyment, both politicians and the common people find solace in merry-making and are totally oblivious to good governance. Once again Virahsawmy condemns a corrupt and degenerate body politic.

In *Sir Toby*, Virahsawmy stresses the different levels of power associated with politicians. Apart from mercenaries, the dramatist introduces other dark and even more powerful elements in order to reveal the depth of corrupted ideology. Kleomatari (derived from Cleopatra) and her army of women overpower Zeneral Marto and are linked with the Godfather of the Mafia, the 'Paren-en-Sef' also known as the 'Supreme Mind'. The forces of evil join hands to perpetuate their leadership, even when this means abducting Sir Toby and threatening to inject him with AIDS in order to thwart the rise of Beatrice-Shakti, his girlfriend and the heroine of the play. The playwright ascribes a mythical and religious status to this figure, drawn from the Hindu goddess Durga, who is the destroyer of evil forces. In *Sir Toby*, Virahsawmy heightens the violent trend inherent in politics by exposing corrupt leaders who have been willing to intimidate pregnant women with the the threat of contamination with AIDS if they do not support the ruling party. The play ends with a battle between Thanatos and Eros, following a rebellion by the people to save Sir Toby. As in Shakespeare, the play ends with the restoration of a moral order and a cleansed society.

Virahsawmy's response to political excesses is also a reminder of Africa's leading dramatist, Wole Soyinka, and his castigation of power seekers. In 'The Writer in a Modern African State' (1968), Soyinka concludes that, 'the artist has always functioned in African society as the record of the mores and experiences of his society and as the voice of vision in his own time. It is time for him to respond to this essence himself.' It is a fervent statement; a call to fellow African writers to stand up for their people. Like Soyinka, Virahsawmy uses the language of satire as a powerful medium through which he expresses his revulsion and rebukes the vice and folly of contemporary national political leaders. Zeneral Makbef's fixation on the throne and power is reduced to an infantile obsession through his hypocritical leitmotiv of personal sacrifice for the country; as is the absurd decorum manifested by the army in their grand salute. Virahsawmy's naming technique also contributes to reducing a politician to a laughing stock. Makbef is a combination of two Kreol words: *Mak* and *Bef* [stooge and ox] and the name amusingly bears the Mauritian maxim "donn dizef, pran bef" (29), which literally means, "give an egg, take an ox", indicating an unequal exchange involving a valuable item and a worthless one.

Farcical situations in *Toufann* ridicule the corruption typified by Edmon who hears 'the voice' (of his own conscience or Prospero's) talking to him, and goes berserk. Neither is Lir spared. He becomes a target of the farce too and his confession can be read as an important manifesto for the playwright: 'Mo abdike. Power corrupts...absolute power corrupts absolutely. Donn pouvwar lepep. Organiz eleksion.' [I give up... Power corrupts...absolute power corrupts absolutely. Give back power to the people. Organise elections...].

The leaders are further caricatured as sexual perverts to reflect Virahsawmy's interpretation of 'rank sweat of an enseamed bed/ stew'd in corruption…' (*Hamlet* 3: iv). Eroticism is blown out of proportion as sexual deviance develops into a fetish in *Sir Toby*. The 'raag erotic-santimantal' (84) [sentimental erotic melody] is associated with Zeneral Marto who clearly admits his preference for 'ti-garson' (102) [boys], while Kleomatari's army of women performs an 'erotiko-militer' (113) [erotic-military] dance. The effeminacy of Lakord Pandi undermines the power he supposedly holds in *Sir Toby*. More significant are Zeneral Makbef's constant attempts at fondling Sooklall, the representative of the people – a metaphor denoting the politician's abuse of the people.

Virahsawmy repeatedly underscores how politicians manipulate the common man. As pointed out by Edmon in *Tablisman Lir*, 'Pa ekout dimoun plengne. Zot memwar kourt. Nek donn zot enpe maja… Tou rant dan lord' (74). [Don't listen to the complaints of people. They easily forget. Provide them with some fun and everything will be fine] – an adage used by numerous leaders in Virahsawmy's plays. The advisor to the President, Klodjous (Claudius) in *Dokter Hamlet* contends that given the anti-government feeling, the ruling cabal will need to project themselves as a conservationist government by bribing journalists and by emphasising traditional values and cultural beliefs in order to gain the sympathy of voters.

In retaliation to corrupt political excesses, Virahsawmy's plays are a direct appeal to the people for genuine action – hence, the dramatic function of Sooklall. In line with Brecht's concept of alienation, Sooklall is judiciously used and made to comment on events, even to the extent of mocking the ruling party. As a dramatic device, this is significant because he represents the 'people' who go against their leaders. Sooklall leaves Zeneral Makbef and his phony 'progressive-socialist-humanist government' (44) in order to join the army of 'Front Trankilis'. The last words of the play are addressed to the audience and form a passionate defence of a just cause: 'Zot bann bon spektater. Me mo espere ki zot pa pou kontinie res spektater. Zot bizen vinn akter. Me avan, swazir bien ki rol zot pou zwe. Toultan lezot ki desid pou zot, bann gran-gran panser pans pou zot; bann gran-gran akter zwe pou zot…'[You are good spectators. But I hope you will not remain spectators. You must become actors. But before, choose what role you would like to play. Every time, others decide on your behalf, thinkers think for you; actors act for you…] (53). A dynamic relationship between actor and audience is struck as Sooklall exhorts the reader/audience to take action and become – to borrow a term from Augusto Boal – spect-actors. Sooklall's dual identity is convincing: not only is he a representative of the people but he is also Virahsawmy's mouthpiece. *Zeneral Makbef* is permeated with a powerful message, triggering reflection on a most pressing issue: the role of the mass in politics. Virahsawmy knows that the challenge is not an easy one as others have tried to confront corruption and fallen victim to the ruling class. Varrouna, the new messiah in *Ziliet ek so Romeo* is killed, as is Shakti

Devi. References to Christ and the Goddess Durga in Varrouna and Shakti Devi respectively show them as archetypal sacrificial figures. The playwright hopes that his audience and readers realise that sacrifice should not be wasted. Virahsawmy therefore presents free thinking and independent characters such as Dokter Hamlet, Sir Toby and Desdemona as heroes for his readers to identify with. He wants us to free ourselves from social prejudices and narrow mind-sets which are symbolised by the metaphor of the crossroads in *Hamlet II* (1996), an allegorical play where the only reference to Hamlet as liberator is made at the end.

'Uneasy lies the head that wears the crown' is a theme that recurs most persistently in Shakespeare's tragedies and historical plays as he explores the inner conflict of his protagonists. Virahsawmy, however, while focusing constantly on the theme of power politics, does not seek to dwell on the psyche of his characters. It is around their acts and discourse that he constructs his political plays. The question then arises: how complex are the characters? Far from possessing the depth of Shakespearean characters, Virahsawmy's protagonists are mostly depictions of exacerbated violence and corruption. Yago emerging from his coffin, vampire-like in *Prezidan Otelo*, and Zeneral Makbef's self-promotion from chief to emperor make them both more stock characters or character types than convincing and rounded protagonists..

While this may reveal a lack of depth on the part of the playwright – a regular criticism levelled against him, it is, in fact, in his creation of character types that Virahsawmy needs to be understood. Rather than searching for any psychological correspondence with Shakespearean heroes, Virahsawmy's characters must be interpreted as symbols, because they incarnate his social vision.

Much of the drama in Virahsawmy's plays emerges through the ominous presence of powerful global or international forces. In *Prezidan Otelo*, for instance, the country is threatened by a powerful neighbour, the Gridi Empire, that seeks to flood local markets and exploit local resources. The Othello-Iago conflict is reflected at another level: the schism between protecting the local economy, which is Otelo's goal as the president, and the promises of opulence which the Gridi Empire guarantees and which Yago supports. Otelo's vision, which relies on the values of solidarity, honesty and sincerity (45), is juxtaposed with the world of commerce that Yago favours. Virahsawmy's stance against uncontrolled globalisation which he perceives as a form of neo-colonisation is clear. He belittles the forces of globalisation in *Prezidan Otelo* as he portrays them as mafia agents in the style of Al Capone. 'Peyna sak pei. Ena vilaz global sou lidership Paren'(40). [There cannot be different countries. There is a global village under the leadership of the Godfather.] These are hegemonic forces that can erase local identities: 'Pou konstrir lape iniversel bizen detrir santiman primitif kouma "mo pei", "mo kiltir", "mo dinite". Yago, Paren panse ki se twa ki bizen pran labar isi.' (41). [To achieve universal peace, we must destroy notions like 'my country', 'my culture', 'my dignity'. Yago, the Godfather feels you need to take control in this country.] The projection of foreign supremacy as the international mafia is also seen in his other plays such as *Zeneral Makbef* and *Sir Toby* while *Tabisman Lir* and *Ziliet ek so Romeo* also underline this dangerous obsession with capitalism. Romeo is obsessed with his get-rich-quick scheme and converts Ziliet's small bar – 'Kot Ziliet' – into a huge 'Kot Romeo' commercial brand of hotels, bars and restaurants. In *Tabisman Lir*, the Rigann-Gomon quartet develops into a corporate entity through their association with the biggest multinational on the planet. Part of Virahsawmy's parody is also to magnify the threat posed by political machinations. The use of hyperbole allows him to drive home his vision of a society cleansed of nepotism and corruption.

In Virahsawmy's tradaptations, the playwright expresses many contemporary concerns. Feminism and human rights are both issues of particular concern to Virahsawmy. Otelo as president posits a new philosophy: the abolition of any kind of discrimination, including opposition to gay marriage. Other equally bold statements emerge from other plays through Virahsawmy's afflicted characters. Other than HIV and prostitution, which are significant social problems in Mauritian society, Virahsawmy also highlights two other important and contentious issues – abortion and euthanasia – as these have met with moral resistance from various quarters locally. Through the emotional stress that they undergo, Ziliet and Dokter Hamlet are used as the means by which the playwright can provoke reflection on taboo issues in Mauritius.

Ziliet ek so Romeo – a rewriting of the creation myth and clearly a feminist take on the story of the Garden of Eden – is written in response to the often-quoted argument that Eve caused the downfall of Man. While the prologue places the action in the Balfour Garden, a public park in Mauritius, the play deals with Ziliet and Romeo on earth, caught up in their mundane lives with Ziliet striving to retain her identity and running her business in contrast to the lethargic, inebriated dreamer, Romeo. Virahsawmy once more takes a swipe at people's inaction and chastises armchair feminists who are more concerned with biased Darwinist comments rather than concrete social engagement. Comments downgrading the Creole community such as 'enn letap anretar dan levolision' (38) [a belated phase in the process of evolution] smack of social bias which the playwright condemns. Virahsawmy does not fail to acknowledge the difficulty of being a woman in a patriarchal set-up, especially in the world of politics. It is telling that in *Sir Toby*, despite Lord Orsino's wishes, Beatrice-Shakti forsakes her belief that she can change the course of things and usher in a new philosophy, simply on the grounds that the people are not ready for a female Prime Minister in the country.

Born in a country with a sensitive ethnic and religious fabric,[3] another chief concern of Virahsawmy is community tolerance. *Ramdeo ek so Ziliet* takes place in Varouna Siti, a peaceful place undermined by clashes between two distinct communities: Creoles and Hindus, that is, the communities of

Ziliet and Ramdeo respectively. The 'Kabri'[4] metaphor is quite catchy as the play exposes the conflict between the *Kabri lafrik* (African descendants) and the *Kabri lenn* (Indian descendants) while the argument over the naming of the baby of Ziliet and Ramdeo is as funny as it is symbolic, because the name reflects the ethnicity of the child. By declaring her name as 'Saroj Zorzet Kapilet-Moutalou',[5] Ziliet and Virahsawmy may have opted for an easy way out, but it is an important statement: the future lies not in myopic ethnic essentialism but in both biological and cultural miscegenation, a sentiment that is also echoed in *Toufann*. The solution to this disharmony is characterised by Sheik Soufi (Sheikh Sufi, belonging to the Muslim-Sufi religion), who is Virahsawmy's adaptation of Friar Lawrence. By making Ramdeo and Ziliet disappear for a year, Sheik Soufi forces their respective communities and families to take cognizance of their regretful acts and realise their mistake. The absence of the protagonists has the desired impact, putting an end to the communal feud. In many ways, Soufi is Virahsawmy's ambassador for peace and harmony:

O Bondie Lamour-Pardon	(God of Love and Mercy
dir tou bann zenerasion	tell the people of the world
toulezour met dan later	to sow a seed in the soil
enn lagren ousa enn plant	every day or plant a tree
pou dir nou Mama-Papa	as a way of saying to Mother-Father
ki nou bien sagren erer	we are very sorry about the lapse that
ki finn fer zoli zarden	has turned a beautiful garden
vinn dezer ek simitier (19)	into a desert and a graveyard)

Overall, Virahsawmy's adaptations are politically and socially charged. They build awareness, castigate and raise consciousness and provoke through entertainment. Through the language of Kreol, the playwright saw the appropriate medium through which he could convey his ideas and reach out to people. Above all, Virahsawmy believes that Kreol Morisien (Mauritian Kreol) is the only unifying language for all Mauritians,[6] which explains why he is among the pioneers of it in Mauritius and is often regarded as the father of the language. It is the common spoken language of all Mauritians, going beyond any ethnic or linguistic divisions.

While his involvement in the formalisation of the language has been well documented,[7] Virahsawmy needs to be recognised for his genuine attempt to give the Kreol language vibrancy – both on and off stage. Not only does Kreol acquire certain oxymorons with a literary status, such as 'dous-amer' (sweet-sorrow) or 'dife-fre' (cold-fire) in *Ramdeo ek so Ziliet*, but also Virahsawmy's translation of key Shakespearean dialogues are in verse and have endorsed the iambic pentameter verse form. Moreover, by using idioms of common parlance such as 'ladling pena lezo' (*Tabisman Lir*, 74) [i.e. 'the tongue has no bone', implying that one can say anything] and by creating new idioms such as 'Tonn al fer pak avan karem' (*Ramdeo ek so Ziliet*, 20)

[You have celebrated Easter even before fasting] or by inventing words that defy morphological rules, like 'sanepepasekontinie' (4) [thiscannotgoon], Virahsawmy has added to the local register. His writing is further enriched as he borrows words such as 'garrbarr' [trouble], 'bourbak' [idiot] and 'nimakarram' [ingrate] from Bhojpuri and Hindi – which is where the term 'Toufann' [Tempest] originates, thus giving it a more folkloric touch than the more obvious 'Siklonn' [Cyclone]. Virahsawmy aptly catches the Kreol spirit in his use of repartee, as the language relies heavily on metaphor. Interesting code-mixing may arise in the writing process. His typical use of 'sega' (local music and dance) and 'sirandann'[8] (or riddles, that are brilliantly used as a reworking of the witches' predictions in *Zeneral Makbef*) endow his works with unique elements of comedy and theatrical syncretism. Virahsawmy's Shakespearean adaptations further reflect the folkloric tradition in the choice of the names of his character-types. Zeneral Marto (literally translated as General Hammer), Kapitenn Koulou (Captain Nail) and Misie Lakord Pandi (Mr Hangman's Noose) in *Sir Toby* all reflect the propensity for nicknames within the comic elements of Kreol.

In many ways, Shakespeare remains a literary guru for Virahsawmy but the Bard also provides a literary refuge for Virahsawmy by paving the way for his own denunciation of abuse of power and of corruption. For all the national discourse on multi-culturalism, Mauritius still harbours a strong undercurrent of ethnic and religious tension. Names denote a specific ethnicity. While openly castigating the political rulers, Virahsawmy stands clear of any possible religious controversy through ethnic associations or representations. The names of Shakespearean characters allow the playwright to retain a neutrality through which he can safely assert his views over taboo subjects.

With the diversity in character-types, themes and buoyancy of Kreol, it may come as a surprise that only three of his tradaptations have been staged, namely, *Zeneral Makbef* (Mauritius Drama League, 1982 and 1993), *Toufann* (Mauritius Drama League, 1988) and *Sir Toby* (a musical, Mauritius Drama League, 2009). *Zeneral Makbef* achieved resounding success locally. This was due to the fact that 1982 was a year of profound political change in Mauritius, with Virahsawmy's party, the MMM, coming to power. The people found echoes of the political situation in Virahsawmy's satire as the play reflected their sentiments. *Zeneral Makbef*, in fact, followed Virahsawmy's other political and highly successful play, *Li*, written in 1972 when he was in jail. At a time when the two Mauritian theatres – Plaza and the theatre of Port-Louis – were showcasing plays in French and sometimes in English, *Li* and *Zeneral Makbef* brought about a radical change in the theatrical landscape. The language of the people – Kreol – was finally being used for full-length plays on stage, as a tool for constructing national identity.

However, *Toufann* did not have similar success in 1995. Quisnarajoo Ramanah, the director of Virahsawmy's adaptations, opted for a large cast, some of whom were 20-year-old prison inmates, in the hope that theatre could rehabilitate them. The audience responded predominantly to the joking punch-lines and the songs, which was not much of a surprise. Perhaps the production did not do full justice to the play being, above all, a fantasy of the modern era. The fact that it was less successful than *Zeneral Makbef* is also understandable. The 1990s were the years in which Mauritius experienced a boom in its economy; political theatre could not thrive in a society hankering more for pleasure then controversial political engagement. *Sir Toby* opened to a mixed response in 2009 even though it had all the ingredients that would usually appeal to the Mauritian audience. Their undisputed preference for the comic and the farcical is well known. However, the production did not work as a musical satire, perhaps because of its realistic staging. A strict adherence to all the elements in the text and a linear and realistic presentation of the drama led to a production lacking the vibrancy more commonly and particularly conveyed by character-types.

Virahsawmy's plays cover a gamut of genres, from poetry, verse, songs, comedy, to the grotesque, the serious, and even the sinister. All these must be depicted with special effects, whether in lighting, sound, multi-media screens or through puppetry. With these numerous threads woven into these adaptations, they run the risk of being too busy, even indigestible. The plays need theatrical devices, such as masks, for example, to depict the stylisation and externalisation of malevolence, together with different staging from the conventional, realistic mode. Moreover, for a contemporary audience that is disconnected from political theatre, Virahsawmy's plays may seem to be overburdened at the ideological level.

Virahsawmy remains at the forefront of Mauritian theatre in Kreol. Other playwrights, such as Asgarally, and theatre practitioners such as Favory have followed suit. However, Virahsawmy's repertoire is well rooted in the local context, especially at a time when the role of theatre has been to hold up the social mirror to the people. Besides *Li*, Virahsawmy's other plays such as *Basdeo Inosan* (Basdeo is Innocent, 1977), *Lincolnsing Finalay* (*lit.* Lincolnsing has gone/ He has gone to Lincoln's Inn, 1979), *Bef dan Disab* (The Ox is in the Sand 1979), *Dropadi* (based on the mythological character from the Mahabharata, Draupadi, 1982), *Zozef ek so Palto Larkansiel* (an adaptation of Joseph and the Amazing Technicolour Dreamcoat) and *Dokter Nipat* (*lit.* The Barefoot Doctor, 1983, inspired by Ben Jonson's *The Alchemist*), have followed the same pattern as his Shakespearean tradaptations and have all been very well received by the Mauritian audience. To date, Virahsawmy remains the most active playwright in Mauritius, having written over twenty plays, many of which have been performed.

Political and social issues aside, it is the linguistic aspect of his work that has interested Virahsawmy. Using Kreol in verse form, and for Kreol comic effect, Virahsawmy has given Kreol different dimensions, employing it as a tool for dramatic expression. The writer has also gone to the extent of translating the Bible, the Bhagavad Gita and even Sufi poetry. He is currently involved in bilingual education, and especially functional literacy with prison inmates. Despite the atrophy of the culture of theatre in Mauritius, Virahsawmy's works have been outstanding, and remain a reference in terms of creativity and expression in Kreol.

Over and above these achievements are Virahsawmy's audacious and imaginative attempts at adapting Shakespeare to express his own reality. His plays are not 'art for art's sake' but carry the weight of a writer with a social commitment who tries to get his message across in an innovatively entertaining manner. Numerous post-colonial writers have challenged the cultural authority of Shakespeare while others have drawn inspiration from his plays. The array of themes and characters in Shakespeare account for the Bard's universality; like many other writers from the Third World, Virahsawmy has found elements in these works that enable him to articulate his personal, social and political vision. It is one of unification, especially through the means of the Kreol language. As a result, he would like to see a 'brave new world' (The Tempest, 5: i) for his people:

> I have often leant on Shakespeare to build a dramatic literature as part of the national culture of New Mauritius. Language planning, nation building and the teaching of basic values are done through tears, laughter, songs and dances…

NOTES

1 The play was published much later, in 1995.

2 Interview conducted with the playwright for the purposes of this article on 16th April 2013.

3 Comprising different ethnic groups of European, African, Indian and Chinese descent, Mauritius is widely regarded as a melting pot of cultures. However, despite its pluri-culturalism, Mauritius has known two major inter-ethnic conflicts in 1968 and 1999, and communal tensions have been regular, particularly during election time. Nationalistic sentiments, which peaked during the period of independence, are now fast being replaced by ethnic identification.

4 This is a pejorative term in Mauritius (lit. goat), to designate Indians and people of Indian descent.

5 Saroj Moutalou is the mother of Ramdeo and Zorzet Kapilet that of Ziliet.

6 With reference to the previous note on ethnic identification, Mauritius has a diverse language policy. 'Ancestral' languages are taught as optional languages right from primary school. These include Hindi, Tamil, Telugu, Marathi, Urdu, Arabic, Mandarin. English and French were the official languages, and it is only since 2012 that Kreol has been introduced, again as an optional subject. There are now attempts to introduce Bhojpuri at Standard 1. It is the common language spoken by the majority of Indian immigrants, but is fast disappearing. While all of this validates a multi-cultural discourse, it conceals a strong undercurrent of ethnic and linguistic divides. For example, Hindus study Hindi, Muslims opt for Urdu or Arabic, etc. Under the broad category of 'Hindu community' are others that are Tamil-, Telugu-, or Marathi-speaking (depending on which region of India their ancestors hail from). Kreol was introduced at school because it would represent the language of the 'General Population'. Virahsawmy's view of Kreol, however, is different. He sees it as the only language that can unite the people of Mauritius in a shared culture.

7 Virahsawmy was initially part of The Akademi Kreol Morisien (Academy for Mauritian Kreol, 'AKM') which worked towards standardising written Kreol. The first draft was published in 2011. It was important to synthesise the orthography for Kreol (hitherto

only a spoken language), out of all the attempts by various people and groups in the past. Virahsawmy has been at the forefront of this effort since the 1970s.

8 Both 'sega' and 'sirandann' are part of a long history of oral culture in Mauritius, right from the period of slavery. While sega, which was considered the music of the slaves, has gained in stature and popularity, becoming the national music of the island, 'sirandann' is losing its place in the rapidly evolving Kreol language.

REFERENCES

Chow, Brian & Chris Banfield (1996) *An Introduction to Post-colonial Theatre*, Cambridge: Cambridge University Press.

Loomba, Ania & Orkin Martin (1998) *Postcolonial Shakespeares*, London: Routledge.

Ramharai, Vicram (1990) *La Littérature mauricienne d'expression créole. Essai d'analyse socio-culturelle*, Port Louis Mauritius: Editions Les Macareignes.

Soyinka, Wole (1968) 'The Writer in a Modern African State' in Per Wästberg, ed., *The Writer in Modern Africa*, Uppsala: Scandinavian Institute of African Studies, 14-20.

—— (1993) *Art, Dialogue and Outrage*, London: Methuen.

Toorawa, Shawkat (2012) *Flame Tree Lane*, London: Pink Pigeon Press.

Virahsawmy, Dev (2012) 'Border Crossing Shakespeare', in *Mauritius Times*, 1 June 2012, http://www.mauritiustimes.com/index.php?option=com_content&view=article&id=1663:dev-virahsawmy&catid=1:latest-news&Itemid=50

—— *Works*, available in the original language at http://www.boukiebanane.orange.mu/

Crioulo Shakespeareano &
the Creolising of
King Lear

EUNICE S. FERREIRA

The late Cesária Évora, celebrated 'barefoot diva' of the Cape Verde Islands, shone a global spotlight on the small island republic located approximately 600 km off the West African coast. The intercultural fusings of the music and her vocal style represent aspects of the Crioulo culture of this former Portuguese colony, a country that has been under-researched in African studies and certainly in theatre studies. Of all the performance traditions, it is music that is most celebrated throughout the Cape Verdean diaspora as a marker of national and cultural identity. The Grammy Award-winning Évora, notably lauded in her *New York Times* obituary, was often referred to as a cultural ambassador, introducing Cape Verde and its Crioulo culture to an international stage.

The Cape Verde Islands provide a rich opportunity, which only in the last few years scholars have taken up, to examine theatre at the crossroads of Africa, Europe, and the Americas, with a particular focus on how Cape Verdeans negotiate national and international identities in and through performance.[1] Theatre in the islands reflects interplay along a Crioulo spectrum with Europe on one end and Africa on the other. The post-independence theatre movement in Cape Verde and the theatrical tensions manifested on and off stage continually raise questions of what it means to be Crioulo – racially, culturally, nationally, and internationally.

The complexity of Cape Verdean identity and its unique Crioulo culture is rooted in the history, politics, and geographical separateness of the island republic. In order to avoid confusion, I use the word 'Crioulo' specifically to refer to the Cape Verdean language or culture and 'creole' to indicate a more inclusive word that embraces the Caribbean and other creole cultures.[2] The ten-island, strategically located, archipelago was supposedly uninhabited when the Portuguese laid claim to it in the mid-15th century to advance the transatlantic slave trade. On 5 July 1975, the first Cape Verdean National Assembly declared its independence from Portuguese rule, but the hybridisation of European and African traditions (which emerged from the various populations of Portuguese settlers, bonded and free West Africans

111

Fig 1 Romeu e Julieta, *at the 1999 Festival Morrer d'Amor, Teatro Municipal Rivoli, Porto, Portugal, with Ludmilla Tatiana Evangelista Évora and Flávio Hamilton. (Cape Verde premiere was in 1998 at Mindelo Cultural Centre.)*
(Photo courtesy of Mindelact Association)

and other Europeans) remains evident throughout the islands and is a central characteristic of its Crioulo culture.

In the immediate post-independence years, the re-Africanisation theories of Amílcar Cabral (assassinated PAIGC leader in Cape Verde's liberation struggle) influenced the shaping of national identity and are evident in the pioneering work of the theatre troupe *Korda Kaoberdi* (Wake up, Cape Verde). Under the direction of Francisco Fragoso (a.k.a. Kwamé Kondé) the troupe attempted to reclaim performance traditions which had been suppressed during the period of colonialism. In the 1980s there developed a stronger emphasis on regional variations via the popular comedies of *Juventude em Marcha* (Youth on the March), to date, the islands' longest-running theatre troupe. It was only in the late 1990s that Shakespeare was seen on the Cape Verdean stage.

The first recorded Shakespeare production was the 1998 *Romeu e Julieta*, a Crioulo language adaptation produced in Mindelo, São Vicente. Directed by the Portuguese João Branco and presented by the GTCCPM (*Grupo de Teatro do Centro Cultural Português do Mindelo*/Theatre Group of the Mindelo Portuguese Cultural Centre), the production was a benchmark for Branco's approach to the creolisation or '*crioulização*' of western canonical plays. Adapted by Branco, with Crioulo language translation by Mário Matos, the action was relocated to 1990s Mindelo where two gangs from rival neighbourhoods of Monte Sossego and Ribeira Bote replaced the ancient family feud of Shakespeare's tragedy. The Montagues and Capulets became respectively the Monteiros and the Cardosos, while pistols replaced swords. Since the GTCCPM travelled to Portugal the following year to participate in Porto's Festival Morrer D'Amor, this *crioulização* can also be read as a commodification of Shakespeare, one that allows for international prestige and feeds both academia and the general public's seemingly insatiable fascination with Shakespearean adaptations.

As for the appetites of the Cape Verdean public, Shakespeare's plays have been strictly a Mindelo affair with few, but influential, offerings. One of the reasons for Shakespeare's late introduction is that his plays were not taught under the Portuguese colonial education system. With no Shakespeare reading public, students' first encounter with the Bard is in Branco's introductory theatre programme. It should be noted that Branco's students, for all of whom Crioulo is the first language, are reading Portuguese translations. Thus, it is what Shakespeare signifies that is arguably more important than any particular play title, as audiences are unlikely to be familiar with the originals.

Shakespeare production history in Cape Verde includes GTCCPM's *Romeu e Julieta* (1998), *Rei Lear – Nhô Rei já bá cabéça* (*King Lear – The King's Gone Mad,* 2003) and two adaptations in 2005 by Teatro Solaris (an experimental theatre company consisting of Branco's alumni) of *Julietas* (*Romeo and Juliet*) and *Sonho de uma Noite de Verão* (*A Midsummer Night's Dream*). Forthcoming productions directed by Branco include *Muito Barulho Por Nada (Much Ado About Nothing)* and GTCCPM's anticipated *A Tempestade* to be premiered at the 2013 Mindelact International Theatre Festival. Branco also promises various performance/art installations on Shakespeare throughout the festival, leading him to write in a recent personal message that 'Shakespeare is alive in Mindelo!'

The islands with the most theatrical activity are Santiago, Santo Antão and São Vicente, but 'Crioulo Shakespeareano' reigns only in Mindelo, São Vicente. It is difficult to imagine Shakespeare productions on any other island, since only in Mindelo has formal theatre training been made available, due to the influence of Branco, co-founder and artistic director of the Mindelact International Theatre Festival, founding director of GTCCPM, and director/teacher since 1993 of The Introductory Theatre Programme of the Portuguese Cultural Centre of Mindelo. For their annual final projects, students devise performance pieces inspired by a Shakespearean play. In this way, Branco reinforces Shakespeare as a creative fount for Cape Verdean theatre as almost every graduating class has led to the formation of a new theatre company, including the GTCCPM, which just celebrated its twentieth anniversary. It is arguably the most active theatre company in Cape Verdean history with almost fifty productions and forty international appearances. In recognition of their contributions and the success of the Mindelact Festival, the city of Mindelo was officially pronounced the 'National Capital of Theatre,' by the musician-playwright Minister of Culture, Mário Lúcio.

In this article, I introduce four categories of *crioulização* examined through a textual and performance analysis of *Rei Lear* – *Nhô Rei já bá cabéça* (*King Lear* – *The King's Gone Mad*) presented at the 2003 Mindelact International Theatre Festival. Translated into the Crioulo language, *Rei Lear* offers an example of how Shakespeare engages performers, audiences and the wider public reached by the media in a cultural discourse on language at a local, national and global/lusophone level.

The drama of language on and off the Cape Verdean stage

Cape Verde's colonial past and its unique geographical location – part of, yet not attached to Africa – is central to the negotiation of Cape Verdean identity and how the country positions itself on the global stage. This is particularly significant in terms of Cape Verde's relationship with the United States, Africa, and Portugal/Europe. In strengthening ties to the United States and other diasporic communities, the Cape Verdean government actively promotes an idea of nationhood that reaches beyond the geographical boundaries of the archipelago to form a 'Global Caboverdiano Nation'. In 2005 the United States bestowed a Millenium Challenge Corporation award of $110 million dollars to address poverty, water and agricultural management, infrastructure, and private sector investments. After successful fulfilment of the award, a second compact of $66.2 million was granted, making Cape Verde not only the first country to complete a MCC compact, but also the first to receive a second award.[3] Recognised as a 'model' African country, Cape Verde also strategically positions itself in relationship to Europe, reducing its role in ECOWAS (Economic Community of West African States) while attaining 'special status' with the European Union. These examples represent ways in which Cape Verdean national policy is driven by identity politics and an ability to seamlessly shift along the African/European poles of the Crioulo spectrum, a fluidity with echoing counterparts in theatre.

Almost forty years after independence, the official language remains Portuguese, while the first language of Cape Verdeans is Crioulo, which draws upon Portuguese and West African languages.[4] Given Cape Verde's recent colonial history, language choice is a significant factor in artistic conceptualisation and audience reception as Cape Verdeans grapple with issues of national and cultural identity. The interests of bourgeoning tourism, government agencies, education, and increasing globalisation efforts continue to privilege the place of Portuguese over Crioulo as the vital means to connect the islands to Lusophone (Portuguese-speaking) and international communities. While Portuguese may be an 'international tongue,' impassioned battles for the co-official status of and standardisation of Crioulo are waged at all socio-economic levels both in the islands and throughout the diaspora. The officially approved and highly contested orthographic system for writing Crioulo is ALUPEC, an acronym for *Alfabeto Unificado para a Escrita da Língua Cabo-verdiana* (Unified Alphabet for the Written Cape Verdean Language). ALUPEC is based on the Crioulo of Santiago where more than half of the archipelago's population of 500,000 live. During the production of *Rei Lear*, former Minister of Culture Manuel Veiga led a controversial campaign to officialise the Crioulo language based on ALUPEC, a system whose merits continue to be debated on the basis of linguistic theory and cultural discrimination, since the orthography arguably privileges the Crioulo variant of Santiago over that of the other islands.

Language play can most certainly be viewed as a political act (Gilbert and Tompkins) and many acting troupes have used Crioulo as a means to subvert the political, historical, and cultural dominance of the Portuguese language in original plays. In productions of Shakespeare, however, the Portuguese director João Branco, who clearly supports the officialisation of Crioulo, has attempted to utilise the Bard to 'elevate' the status of the *lingua materna* in a similar – and yet very different – spirit to productions from former British and French African colonies. For example, Thomas Decker's 1964 translation of *Julius Cesar* (*Juliohs Siza*) into the Krio language of Sierra Leone premiered in the early years after independence, as 'an act of linguistic and political independence.' As Caulker notes, Decker sought to make Krio 'a legitimate literary language'.[5] Similarly, Shawkat M. Toorawa describes Dev Virahsawmy's intentions in *Toufann*, a Mauritian Kreol adaptation of *The Tempest*, as 'to redeploy, exploit (in the good sense) and wield Shakespeare in order to elevate Kreol – the language in which all his plays are written – to the status of a world language'.[6] Branco also acknowledges a Creole-connection with Virahsawmy in an April 2013 Facebook posting to '*Shakespeare em Crioulo*', highlighting Virahsawmy's contributions to promoting creole languages.[7]

The inter-island language variant distinction earlier noted is significant when examining Shakespeare's presence in Cape Verde. Located on the island of São Vicente at the end of the island chain, Mindelo's history as a port city has shaped its identity as the intellectual and cultural centre of Cape Verde, boasting a number of writers, artists, musicians and an array of annual cultural events including a boisterous carnival, Mindelact International Theatre Festival, and *Baia das Gatas*, a Woodstock-inspired music festival. Perhaps the most significant characteristic of Mindelo lies in its claim to be an international nexus that fosters an arms-wide-open embrace to the forces of globalisation.

Crioulização – Creolising Shakespeare

Branco became a galvanising force in Cape Verdean theatre not long after moving there in 1991. The son of two artists, Portuguese musician José Mário Branco and theatre director Isabel Alves Costa, Branco grew up in the wings of the theatre where the plays of the western canon were his teachers of the 'universal' stage, undoubtedly moulding his directing aesthetic. Although GTCCPM has drawn from Cape Verdean writers, traditions and historical accounts, it is Branco's theory of *crioulização* that has distinguished the work of his group, garnering both praise and criticism. Under his artistic direction, GTCCPM has presented creolised adaptations of Shakespeare, Lorca, Molière and Beckett.

He claims that *crioulização* introduces a new theatrical term and dramaturgical approach for Cape Verdean theatre. The objective is to take the 'universal classics of theatre' and 'make them our own', with translation into Crioulo as the primary adaptive strategy. For Branco, this means that the tiny archipelago of Cape Verde can participate in the 'patrimony of humanity'. When he reads Portuguese translations of Shakespeare (or watches a favourite film like *Shakespeare in Love*), he usually latches on to something that makes him say, 'We too have this in Cape Verde.' Thus, extolling Shakespeare as a 'treasure of humanity', Branco creolises the bard, claiming that, 'Shakespeare is a little a bit Cape Verdean, too.'[8] He argues that canonical works allow Cape Verdean artists to access and participate in a historical repertoire that puts them on the global stage and often opens doors to international travel. Branco also recommends foreign plays as a source for theatre troupes in search of new material, challenging them that '[t]he world of universal dramaturgy is out there, ready for the taking.'[9] Again, Branco's sentiments align with Virahsawmy who defended *Trazedji Makbess* as a means 'to proclaim loudly that we are part of a large planetary culture known as humanity; our own way of saying that you cannot shut away Shakespeare, Moliere, Mozart, Tagore, Picasso.'[10]

The four main categories of *crioulização* are: linguistic, adaptive, cultural and performative creolisation. Based on observations of Branco's directorial work, various writings and other production research, I offer these four perspectives as a means to examine how and to what degree *crioulizacão* functions in his *King Lear*.

Adaptive creolisation refers to the overall process that guides the director's interpretive vision of the original text in selecting elements of theme, plot and character that strongly resonate with a Cape Verdean experience. Branco's 2002 adaptive strategy to Samuel Beckett's *Waiting for Godot*, for example, was to offer a metaphorical play. Centuries of drought and famine cycles on the islands, coupled with neglect from the former metropole, have etched tropes of drought and famine into the cultural imagination, particularly in music and literature. Renamed *Espera da Chuva* (*Waiting for Rain*), the production replaced longing for Godot's long-awaited arrival with a national rain angst.

One of the adaptive strategies in *Rei Lear* was to delete all references to war, several characters and subplots, including Gloucester and the antagonistic fraternalism between Edgar and the illegitimate Edmund. As McMahon notes, since war never took place on Cape Verdean soil, its absence from *Rei Lear* is a justifiable deletion.[11] It is also standard practice in Cape Verde to perform a play without intermission for both aesthetic and practical reasons. Thus *Rei Lear* was abbreviated to just ninety minutes. Wishing to focus on Lear's paternal bonds, Branco also radically altered the ending by making Lear die in the arms of Cordelia.

Once a general adaptive interpretation and directorial concept has been established, a **linguistic creolisation** begins in the process of translating the source text into the Crioulo language. Linguistic hybridity is a central characteristic of *crioulização* and is most apparent in code-shifting: when a character either intentionally or subconciously mixes and shifts from one style, language or linguistic variant to another. When a lower status character, for example, wishes to achieve higher status, a playwright may give him a butchered version of a Portuguese line to great comic effect, revealing the absurdity and discriminatory practices of postcolonial linguistic authority as embodied in the character (and, in some cases, in the actor). Similarly, a Cape Verdean character's affinity with Portuguese may reveal clues about her education and family background. In *Três Irmãs*, a *crioulização* of Chekhov's *Three Sisters*, the characters spoke significantly less Crioulo than in *Rei Lear*, but when it was spoken it illuminated colonial tensions and upset the social harmony of the household. Thus, the crucial question is not how much is translated into Crioulo, but *how* Crioulo is utilised in the translation, including linguistic variants. This fluidity of language is not restricted to the practices of the GTCCPM but can be found throughout Cape Verdean literature and music.

The use of code-switching as a manifestation of postcolonial heteroglossia is prevalent throughout postcolonial theatre practices and as Marvin Carlson notes, the characteristic has been especially identified with the creole theatres of the Caribbean.[12] Cape Verdean linguists Dulce Almada Duarte and former Minister of Culture, Manuel Veiga, describe Cape Verde not as heteroglossic but as a diglossic nation, where Portuguese is the official language and Crioulo the mother tongue, with social circumstances dictating which language to use.[13] Theatre reflects this quotidian reality in the strategic code-switching employed in writing and script translation. This creative process continues into the rehearsal period as actors begin to embody their roles. Also at work in language play are historical and cultural influences including emigration patterns and the hegemony of English in the global market. In *Rei Lear*, for example, the Fool, whose costume suggests a blend of hip hop and court jester, raps Shakespearean verse in both Portuguese and

Crioulo, often ending his phrases with 'yo'.

In keeping with the publicity promise of a 'Crioulo Shakespeareano,' almost all of *Rei Lear* is translated into the São Vicente variant. The disinction between adaptation and translation is evident in the GTCCPM programmes. For *Rei Lear*, the adaptation of the text is credited to both Branco and actor Fonseca Soares, while the translation is solely attributed to Soares, who based it on Alvaro Cunhal's Portuguese version. Soares also played the role of Lear. In fact, it was his performance two years earlier in the final Shakepeare project of Branco's course that inspired *Rei Lear*. A radio journalist by profession, Soares explained that they wanted to capture some of the poetry of the original text and so '[w]e invented a new Crioulo... [n]ot your everyday Crioulo. It's new. It's different but it's Crioulo. . .a Shakespearean Crioulo.'[14]

To achieve his aim, Soares researched words that had fallen out of use and attempted to creolise Portuguese words. The linguistic hybridism of *Rei Lear* is a fusion designed to transform Crioulo into something new. Here, code-shifting is at the service of the translator's poetic goals as opposed to being rooted in character revelation or motivation. As Branco further explains, this reinvention of Crioulo was meant 'to follow – and serve – the poetry of the original text...the Crioulo that one hears has different phrase structure than we hear in everyday life, a different resonance, a more accentuated poetry: a Shakespearean Crioulo.'[15]

Soares attempts to retain some iambic pentameter, and in many cases the Crioulo translation is far more poetic than Cunhal's Portuguese, offering a distinctly Crioulo idiomatic flavour. Some of the most eloquent passages take place in the opening scene when Lear questions the fidelity and love of his daughters. Soares acknowledges the first scene as representative of the best of his translation effort to infuse a certain level of the poetic. More important than a close recreation of iambic pentameter, the Crioulo translation privileges poetic capture of the lilting cadence of Mindelo Crioulo. Goneril's pledge of filial love is below compared with the Portuguese translation followed by the original:

> Um t'amá bocê más du ki palavra podê dzê.
> [A]mo vos mais do que as palavras podem exprimi-lo.
> I love you more than word can wield the matter. (I: 1, 56) [16]

This *crioulização* also suggests a more earthy and physical world than the original text and Cunhal's translation. One of the most evocative examples takes place at the close of the traditionally designated Act I, Sc. 5, as Lear cries out to heaven in a plea for his sanity. In both the original text and Portuguese translation, Lear attempts to invoke the compassion of a Christian heaven. Soares' Crioulo translation endows heaven not with the qualities of Shakespeare's 'sweet heaven' or Cunhal's '*céu misericordioso*' (merciful heaven) but rather employs a physical metaphor with heaven as 'the hat of the world'.

Fig 2   Lear's fool (Nuna Delgado) was costumed as court jester meets rapper in Rei Lear – Nhô Rei já bá cabéça, *by GTCCPM at Mindelact Festival, 2003.*
(Photo by Luis Couto, courtesy of Mindelact Association)

Fig 3   Lear dies in the arms of Cordelia in this 'crioulização'. Helena Rodrigues and Fonseca Soares in Rei Lear – Nhô Rei já bá cabéça, *by GTCCPM, Mindelact Festival, 2003.*   (Photo by Luis Couto, courtesy of Mindelact Association)

'Oh, un ka krê vrá dod, un ka kre ba cabeça, oh céu, chapéu de mund;
conservam nha juize; un ka krê vrá dôd!'

'Oh, que eu não endoideça, não endoideça, céu misericordioso;
conserva-me a razão; não queria endoidecer!'

'O let me not be mad, not mad, sweet heaven!
Keep me in temper; I would not be mad! (I., v., 48-9)[17]

The translation of madness itself is also grounded in a commonplace
reference that humanises the regal Lear through his use of language. In both
Shakespeare and Cunhal's texts, Lear uses 'mad' respectively as adjective
and verb to address his fear of insanity, whereas in Crioulo, Lear literally
exclaims, 'I don't want to turn mad, I don't want to lose my head.' The
literal translation of 'lose my head' is a common reference to insanity that
translates to the everyday Cape Verdean ear as 'go crazy' or 'lose my mind'.
Although the phrase '*ba cabeça*' is not taken literally, the reference to Lear's
physical head is a poetic partner to heaven as the 'hat of the world.'

Lear's monologue also foreshadows the promise of the Crioulo subtitle
Nhô Rei já bá cabéça (*The King's Gone Mad*) and represented Soares'
finest acting moment, unfortunately undercut by the Fool's improvised
interjections. Branco tends to infuse his works with seemingly inexplicable
comic interpolations (further discussed under performative creolisation).

A significant question might be to ask whether Soares and Branco's
modification of Crioulo by varying syntax and 'creolising' Portuguese
words in order to 'elevate' and demonstrate its ability to express the revered
language of Shakesepeare, has enhanced Portuguese influence further over
the peoples' language? In spite of their claim that the translation was a
crioulização of Portuguese words, Cape Verdean linguist Duarte suggested
that the GTCCPM contributed to a 'decreolisation' of the national language
by rendering Crioulo more Portuguese-sounding.[18]

In conjunction with linguistic adaptation, **cultural creolisation** occurs
when cultural markers are interpolated or substitute references in the source
text in an attempt to move the piece closer to the target audience. *Rei Lear*
features fewer specific substitutions or additions than there have been with
other creolisations, such as *A Casa da Nha Bernarda* (*The House of Bernarda
Alba*)and *Três Irmãs* (*Three Sisters*) set in 1940s Mindelo and teeming with
cultural signifiers. In spite of Branco's stated wish to evoke a more 'universal'
world in *Rei Lear* with an ambiguous locale and time period, the linguistic
choices and text alterations clearly indicated a strange but nonetheless
recognisably Cape Verdean world. The highest concentration of cultural
markers in *Rei Lear* centre around the Fool, the character Branco ironically
describes as the 'most Crioulo'.[19]

Indeed, the barefoot Fool reflects the teasing and playful quality Cape
Verdeans hold dear, particularly in language play. The Fool's repeated tag
line of 'yo' is not only an allusion to the international influences of hip
hop and rap culture but additionally serves as a Crioulo cultural marker.

The international music genres are indeed expressive threads of Cape Verdean youth culture and reference contact with the significant diasporic communities in the United States. Thus, this non-traditional signifier of Cape Verdean culture nonetheless identifies contemporary expressions of global youth culture. The rap recording that underscored the Fool's first entrance was a clear shift from the instrumental music that guided other transitions. His costume and demeanor suggested a cross between court jester and rapper, while his oversized hat invoked the outrageous costumes of Mindelo's carnival tradition.

In the setting of the Mindelact Theatre Festival, where the audience is slightly more diverse than at other times during the year, a *crioulização* of a canonical work can also defamiliarise the canon to patrons acquainted with the original texts. The Fool's first encounter with the conniving Goneril (Act I, Sc. 4) contains several specific textual insertions, performance choices and cultural markers that problematise Branco's intention to 'neutralise' the setting of the play. Goneril inexplicably attaches a false belly panel and, feigning pregnancy, she sings a Crioulo lullaby. Insulted by his daughter's disrespectful and patronising behaviour, Lear curses his daughter's womb. As he and the Fool begin to exit, the Fool addresses Goneril as '*bruxa*' (witch) and asks when the '*guarda-cabeça*' (a loud, merry-making ritual on the eve of a newborn's seventh day to ward off witches and other evil spirits) will take place. Rapping his way out of the scene, the Fool tops off his verse with an offensive gesture and the departing line '*mi jambai*', the colloquial equivalent of 'I'm out of here.'

These cultural references to superstitious practices and contemporary culture have little bearing on the play except to further demonise Goneril and generate laughter in response to the Fool. I suggest that the audience's laughter stemmed not only from actor Nuno Delgado's comic antics but also from the pleasure of hearing street Crioulo in an internationally venerated theatre classic. It was an actor-audience exchange that recognised that, at least in that specific moment, the play had been truly made 'ours.'

The most concentrated and significant use of cultural signifiers occurs in Act I, Sc. 4 as the Fool probes Lear with riddles of sanity and displaced power. In a *crioulização* that closely adheres to Cunhal's Portuguese translation, textual alterations warrant special attention. The changes here are crucial for the slight alterations clearly localise the setting and emphasise political overtones in the play.

In the Fool's riddle sequence, translator/actor Soares makes minor substitutions in order to reference the vegetation and animal life of Cape Verde. As opposed to Cunhal's literal translation, a silver banana replaces Shakespeare's apple and a sea turtle replaces an oyster. The Fool's following riddle goes beyond a mere cultural substitution, however, and clearly invites a critical and political reading of the play. In both source texts (Shakespeare's and Cunhal's translation), the Fool muses, 'The reason why the seven stars are no more than seven is a pretty reason', to which Lear responds, 'Because they are not eight.' Congratulating Lear for his insight, the fool answers 'Yes indeed. Thou wouldst make a great fool.'[20] In the Crioulo version, however, the fool's reference is not to heavenly constellations but to the Cape Verdean flag.

> BOBO: Titio, nôs bandeira tem dez estrêla ka é por acase.
> LEAR: Porque é k'el ka tem nove?
> BOBO: Justim: bô dá um bobo de kel bom!
> LEAR: Um tem ke t'má o ke é de meu! Oh ingratidon!

> FOOL: Uncle, our flag has ten stars by the way.
> LEAR: Why doesn't it have nine?
> FOOL: Exactly. You would make such a great fool!
> LEAR: I have to take what is mine! Oh, ingratitude!

The ten stars in the Fool's comment represent the archipelago's ten islands as symbolised on the Cape Verdean flag. Lear's nine star retort humorously comments on the fact that only nine of the ten are populated.

Working in tandem with textual cultural markers is **performative creolisation.** This most collaborative phase of the creolisation process occurs when actors begin to embody the text. Some lines are translated during rehearsal as the actors' instincts and character familiarity organically generate a Crioulo version of a Portuguese line. (This technique is also used by other troupes who begin with a Portuguese-written text.) The *Rei Lear* production also reveals how actor-generated *crioulização* may be improvised in performance, as in the case of actor Nuno Delgado who played the Fool and inserted Crioulo asides that are not in the final version of the translated script. Thus, the actors are an integral part of the *crioulização*, for it is through their voice and bodies that particular Crioulo performance codes are transmitted.

In *Rei Lear*, however, Branco implemented highly stylised movement patterns and mask work in his attempt to achieve a 'universal' setting and style for the play. Masks are not traditionally used in Cape Verdean theatre and the hand-held face-masks of the three sisters and Kent's attachable mask created a distancing effect. Full front, off-stage focus replaced the more accustomed practice of profiled, on-stage focus so that characters often did not face one another when conversing.

The movements of Goneril and Regan in particular were highly choreographed and replete with theatrical conventions unfamiliar to the local audience. The sisters incorporated a ritualised use of the mask for speaking, often addressing their respective masks instead of Lear and using their masks to kiss and embrace in place of physical contact. It is a hallmark of Branco's directing style to physicalise and make literal that which is alluded to in a text. For example, upon the announcement that Lear will split Cordelia's inheritance between Goneril and Regan, the offended king instructs the elder daughters to divide the crown. Branco took the order literally and initiated a pantomimed interlude underscored by a dissonant and warped-sounding instrumental recording. Goneril and Regan leaned over the top of their father's head while their masks 'kissed' and then together they lifted Lear's crown from the top of his head and placed it on the back of the throne. Slowly they crossed to their husbands who were still genuflecting to the king. The husbands pivoted on their knees to face diagonally upstage left while their masked wives straddled their raised thighs in a copulating celebration. The couples remained intertwined as the scene proceeded and the loyal Kent attempted to talk sense into the duped king who was seemingly oblivious to his daughters' blatant, vulgar behavior.

The Fool carried the most Crioulo signifiers in performance. He was free to move and speak as he pleased without restriction by Branco's stylised approach to the play. The Fool's entrance was underscored by hip hop music as he began to rap and perform a dance sequence resembling the combined moves of a novice capoeira (Afro-Brazilian martial arts) and a 1980s break dancer. A perplexing aspect of Branco's 'most Crioulo' character, however, is that most of his rapped verses were in Portuguese. It is possible that Soares and Branco did not want to translate multiple lines of similarly rhymed endings. Since Cape Verdean performers routinely rap in Crioulo, it was a most unusual choice in an otherwise all Crioulo translation. In spite of the choice to use Portuguese verse, Delgado was able to kinaesthetically transform the words into a corporeal Crioulo expression that simultaneously conveyed Cape Verdean and global youth culture.

There were two basic elements at work in the performative creolisation of this production. On the one hand, the stylised movements and masks of the court introduced a foreign theatrical convention to the local Mindelact audience. The vocal and physical patterns do not have counterparts in Cape Verdean performance idioms and so suggested a non-Cape Verdean world. The Fool, however, consistently performed a Crioulo identity, even when given a Portuguese text, showcasing Delgado's ability to take the inexplicable Portuguese verse and transform – or creolise – it through performance.

Creolising the Portuguese Prospero[21]

By transforming Shakespeare's Anglophone identity into something new, that is, claiming that the bard is a 'bit Cape Verdean, too,' Branco reveals yet another significant aspect of *crioulização* – he presents *himself* as an object of creolisation.[22] By doing so he refocuses the public gaze and therefore, the public reception of himself and of his artistic work. Branco situates both Shakespeare and himself as creolised. This inversion and performance of Branco's shift in identity from coloniser to colonised is repeatedly noted in the press and in own Branco's own writings. I believe in the sincerity of Branco's love and passion for Cape Verde and her people. Even during our interviews and conversations he is more likely to speak in Crioulo than in Portuguese. He genuinely enacts this self-perception in daily life, but what must be considered is that the *crioulização* of Branco is intensely performed and promoted in various forms of media.

In his book *Nação Teatro* as well as in other writings, Branco identifies himself as 'Cape Verdean by choice'. It is the media promotion of Branco's transformation, however, that is most significant in this personal *crioulização*, especially when it is endorsed by notable figures such as author Germano Almeida or writer/politician Onésimo Silveira. Almeida shifts any possible perception of Branco as neocoloniser by attributing agency to the people of Mindelo. Recalling his first impression of Branco, Almeida asserts that Branco was 'anxious to be colonised by Mindelo' and that now he is a 'completely Cape Verdean man'.[23] Silveira, a figure of great political stature, described Branco as being 'more Crioulo than Crioulos'. One of the most compelling portrayals of Branco's *crioulização* appeared in the newspaper *Expresso das Ilhas* in response to a much heated debate over 'authenticity' in Cape Verdean theatre. In an article entitled 'Mindelo ate João Branco', Eduino Santos defends Branco by reversing the paradigm of Branco, the Portuguese coloniser to Branco, the object of Cape Verde's consumption. Mindelo, as subject, has consumed the Portuguese Branco and 'transformed him into a Cape Verdean product ... we synthesise all the good we can bring in and transform it into products *made in Cape Verde*.'[24] This act of consumption and transformation of 'the other' (language, food, music) is celebrated as a facet of Cape Verdean culture and directly relates to Branco's justification for creolising western plays.

Rei Lear and the politics of *crioulização*

The Crioulo language, or 'Crioulo Shakespeareano' as Branco coined it, was heavily promoted preceding the play's premiere and its subsequent remounting. Media announcements emphasised the prestige of producing Shakespeare in Cape Verde and that most importantly, 'the greatest playwright of all time' would be heard in the Crioulo language. Banking on the cultural cachet and literary authority of Shakespeare, the media reinforced Mindelo's assertion as a capital of culture, particularly in celebration of its designation as the 2003 Lusophone Capital of Culture. A survey of headlines attest to the linguistic focus: '*Rei Lear ou o Crioulo Shakespeareano*', '*A magia do criouloshakespeareano*', '*João Branco encena Shakespeare em crioulo*', and the sub-heading '*Rei Lear ou Shakespeare na Língua di Terra*'.[25] International announcements for Portuguese-speaking countries called the production 'a bold adaptation into Crioulo based on Alvaro Cunhal's Portuguese translation', leading one to question if the descriptor of 'bold' referred to the troupe's audacity in performing *King Lear* in Crioulo rather than Cunhal's much praised Portuguese translation.[26]

With promises of poetic linguistic display, the showcasing of Crioulo in *Rei Lear* may be read as a challenge to the hegemony of Portuguese, particularly to its authoritative literary claim as the language of Luís Vaz de Camões, the 'Portuguese Shakespeare'. Although it may not have been Branco's intention, the *crioulização* of *King Lear* with its somewhat earthy subtitle *Nhô Rei já bá cabeça* (*The King's Gone Mad*), valorises the western canon while simultaneously questioning the literary prestige of Portuguese by supplanting it with 'Shakespearean Crioulo.' That Branco and the GTCCPM chose to present *Rei Lear* when the gaze of the lusophone world had been directed to Mindelo further underscores political readings of the play. After all, the troupe's name reveals its intimate relationship with the Portuguese Cultural Centre – Camões Institute.

On a national level, the production may also be read as a challenge to the prevailing position of Santiago Crioulo which serves as the basis for ALUPEC, the officially recognised orthographic system for the writing of Crioulo. As a salaried employee of the Mindelo Portuguese Cultural Centre, Branco would seem unlikely to position a Crioulo translation as a critique of the dominance of Portuguese in influential political and intellectual circles. However, media releases along with Branco's outspoken position on cultural matters, suggest that the 'bold adaptation' was critical of national politicians, linguists, and cultural critics who espouse ALUPEC and Santiago Crioulo.

In a Mindelact website notice on the remounting of *Rei Lear* on the 19th and 20th November 2005, Branco (who also serves as web editor) offered excerpts from the play to illustrate '*Shakespeare em Crioulo*'. Perhaps as a jab at the former Minister of Culture, Branco acknowledges that the cited Crioulo passages written in the style of the São Vicente variant may not follow the rules of official standardised (ALUPEC) but nonetheless, 'the beauty [of the text] is the same.' Additionally, he takes a passive–aggressive tone when he defends the company's style of writing Crioulo as not due to any 'unfamiliarity or inability' to apply ALUPEC. The implication here is that GTCCPM especially wanted to convey Shakespeare in 'Criol de Soncent' and use Shakespeare to legitimise it.[27] In keeping with previous publicity campaigns emphasising language, posters prominently announced '*Shakespeare Na Kriolu*' (Shakespeare in Crioulo). Ironically, the two-weekend Shakespeare cycle which opened with *Rei Lear*, was primarily funded by the Portuguese Cultural Centre and the Cape Verdean Ministry of Culture.

In an analysis of the historical, political and personal factors which surround Cunhal's translation of *King Lear*, Rui Carvalho Homem attributes the translation's success to 'the canonical status of the text, the high profile of the translator and the text's complicated history'.[28] Upon news of Cunhal's death in June 2005, massive crowds filled the streets of Lisbon in memory of the romanticised communist leader. Homem contends that what compelled the crowds to gather was the 'the memory of an era of resistance to dictatorship and political repression, a memory they believed was best embodied in the man styled, in a front-page obituary, 'the last icon'.[29]

O Rei Lear: Nhô Rei já bá cabeça premiered in 2003, less than two years before Cunhal's street-lined memorial. His name certainly would certainly have been recognised by Portuguese administrators and guests during Mindelact 2003, as well as by many Cape Verdeans and other readers of lusophone news. With a full-press emphasis on the national tongue of Crioulo, I argue that anyone who recognised Cunhal's name and his former leadership role in the Portuguese communist party would have been immediately prepared for a political reading the play. Although Homem notes that the political overtones in Cunhal's translation are subtle, they nonetheless reveal his ideology. Other Portuguese translations were available but Branco chose to creolise the version by the former communist leader, one who would have been sympathetic to the cause of Cape Verdean liberation.

The GTCCPM clearly invited a political reading of their production, foregrounding Cunhal's translation in the official programme of the 2003 Mindelact Festival. The uncredited portion that Branco reproduces is from an editorial introduction to the former communist secretary's translation. Since programme notes are routinely used to influence an audience's reading of play, it is significant that it glosses over Lear's domestic issues and focuses instead on the political ramifications of a megalomaniac, 'whose passions and personal vanity supplant the wisdom of life experience and the art of governing'. Additionally, a preview article in *A Semana* described Lear as a dethroned and powerless man who nevertheless wanted to continue to influence affairs of the state. In praise of the cast, Branco further promoted a political critique by praising the actors for 'successfully communicating the sharp manner in which Shakespeare attacks the theme of power and the way in which people generally behave when they lose power'.[30]

Could Lear then be perceived as a dethroned or current Cape Verde politician or cultural leader? Perhaps the depiction of Lear's madness, evident in Branco's staging of the first scene, is an attempt to debunk those in authority by revealing the instability of power. Yet another reading of Lear is as one of those Cape Verdean theatre artists/critics who long for the days when they reigned in Mindelo's theatre scene, before they were displaced by younger generations of theatre practitioners. Such interpretations would certainly explain Branco's somewhat callous treatment of Lear in his production.

It makes sense that in a festival year that attracted more than usual international media attention, Branco would want to showcase the strengths of the GTCCPM by having the actors perform in their first language. Opting to perform in Portuguese might instead have magnified the postcolonial condition since the actors have varying degrees of fluency with the Portuguese language. Branco could have selected a national playwright for the festival. Instead, his choice to adapt Shakespeare in Crioulo not only aligned GTCCPM with other European festival offerings but can also be read as a highly political act with multiple layers of possible interpretation.

For some it may have challenged the discriminatory view of Crioulo as a bastardised Portuguese, while others may have regarded the production as a challenge to the hegemony of both Portuguese and the regional Santiago basis for ALUPEC.

Crioulo imagination in flux

The creolisation of western plays has received a mixed reception. Mindelo theatre patrons, many of whom are former students in Branco's training programme, faithfully support GTCCPM productions which routinely sell out the newly remodelled 225-seat Mindelo Cultural Centre. During the Mindelact Festival, a more diverse audience includes international artists, government dignitaries, performers from various islands and a small group of loyal attendees who annually journey to São Vicente for the festival. It is important to note that while press notices and television lavish praise on the festival, there exists no tradition of theatre criticism on the islands. In private conversations, however, other theatre artists repeatedly express bewilderment and frustration over Branco's emphasis on producing creolisations of foreign plays and the resulting media attention received. It is especially disheartening for national playwrights who question Branco's positing of adaptations as part of the national dramaturgy. Cape Verdean director Francisco Fragoso (a.k.a. Kwame Kondé), who is dubbed the 'father of Cape Verdean theatre' for his post-independence efforts, has openly contested Branco's views and incited heated debates on what constitutes 'authentic' Cape Verdean theatre.

One of the most adventurous theatre companies is Teatro Solaris (2004), the only other troupe to have formally presented Shakespeare and whose radical departure from the *crioulização* practices of GTCCPM introduced an alternative approach. Director/playwright Herlandson Duarte (Branco's former star student) does not adopt his mentor's *crioulização* theories but freely employs the Portuguese language and the 'authority' of Shakespeare to critique local and national issues. In *Julietas*, a 'free adaptation' of *Romeo and Juliet*, the young Duarte used Shakespeare's tragedy to critique societal norms in Cape Verde, where homosexuality is taboo and lesbianism even more so in its macho culture. *Julietas*, presented March 2005 during the annual 'Month of Theatre,' attempted to shock audiences and challenge views on female sexuality by pairing two similarly dressed women as the star-crossed lovers, backed by a chorus of three loin-clothed men. Duarte further invoked the canon by pairing Shakespearean authority with biblical allusions to address sexual taboos in this predominantly Catholic country. A cloud of secrecy surrounded the rehearsal process for a production that promised to 'examine love between human beings'. Publicity carried an 'advisory warning' that it was not appropriate for anyone under sixteen, which of course boosted even greater interest and advance ticket sales. As an audience member, I could not help but also monitor the varied responses of other

Fig 4 Julietas *by Teatro Solaris, directed by Herlandson Duarte, with Patricia Leite and Joseline Rocha, in 'March, Month of Theatre', 2005 at the Mindelo Cultural Centre.* (Photo by João Barbosa, courtesy of Teatro Solaris)

Fig 5 Titania (Milanka Vera-Cruz) and her attendants dote on Neca Fundos (Nick Bottom) played by Nuno Costa. Mindelact Festival, 2005. (Photo by João Barbosa, courtesy of Teatro Solaris)

patrons to Solaris' experimental and visceral style. Duarte's appropriation of venerated source material provided an opportunity to introduce themes that had otherwise not been treated on the Cape Verdean stage. The play was only the second Solaris production, but it was a clear indication that the young troupe was intent on carving out its own place in Cape Verdean theatre, unrestricted by audience expectation, language choice, and the theoretical philosophy of their principal theatre mentor.

Branco does not recognize *Julietas* as a Shakespeare production, since he claims most of the text has nothing to do with the original. I opt to include it in my listing since it was Branco who ironically introduced the notion that adaptations of Shakespeare can contribute to national dramaturgy. In fact, it was Solaris' adaptation of *Sonho dum Noite Verão* (*A Midsummer Night's Dream*) that premiered at Mindelact 2005 in tandem with the remounting of *Rei Lear*. While GTCCPM employed Crioulo to engage the nation, Solaris strategically used Crioulo, Portuguese – and Shakespeare – in a critique of audience tastes and the Mindelact Festival, offering a type of neocolonial counter-discourse to power structures of local theatre on the stage of an international festival.[31]

Duarte planned to direct *A Midsummer Night's Dream* in Portuguese, but the lively argument I witnessed between him and Branco on the choice of language may have fuelled Duarte's neocolonial interpretation of the play as a critique of local theatre practices. Acquiescing to Branco's insistence, Solaris presented a predominantly Crioulo *Sonho dum Noite Verão*. The Duarte-Branco exchange, lending itself to a Prospero-Caliban analogy, also has its counterpart in Solaris' *Dream* adaptation. Duarte explained to me that he saw real-life parallels between the play's fictional actors and Teatro Solaris. In empathising with the amateur actors who must please Duke Theseus, Duarte further challenged hierarchal structures by casting the mechanicals as slaves, rather than free manual labourers. In the setting of Cape Verde, such an alteration inevitably echoes the islands' former slave culture and the legacy of colonialism, while also heightening criticism of Mindelo theatre dynamics.

In opposition to the *crioulização* of previous Shakespeare plays, Duarte chose to write and direct *Julietas* in Portuguese. Determined to present a 'serious piece of work' (in contrast to Branco's comic tendencies), Duarte believed Portuguese would create an aesthetic distancing effect that would allow the audience to reflect on the play.[32] Duarte's strategic language choice may unfortunately have also reinforced the colonial mind-set, that the Portuguese language is more suitable for intellectual engagement than Crioulo.[33]

One of the risks of producing western canonical works in a postcolonial context is the possibility of perpetuating the myth of colonial superiority. Unlike Aimé Césaire's acclaimed postcolonial adaptation of *The Tempest*, Branco's creolisations do not deconstruct texts in order to provide a critique of colonial power systems. Nor does he question the absence of African playwrights from the western-based theatre programme that he offers through the Portuguese Cultural Centre. This exclusion seems painfully ironic for a theoretical approach to creolising theatre in Cape Verde, but it is indicative of his own training and reflected in the 'Five-Act' structure of his book *Nação Teatro*, a history of Cape Verdean theatre. With chapter sections designated as 'scenes', his carefully researched book further testifies to his western dramaturgical tendencies and, of course, his love of Shakespeare.

As I write, GTCCPM is preparing for the *crioulização* of *The Tempest* to premiere at the 2013 Mindelact Festival. Given the history of postcolonial interpretations of *The Tempest*, I have long been curious about how Branco, as director of the festival, might approach this play. I was excited to visit his Facebook page '*Shakespeare em Crioulo*', designed to engage readers in an online discussion prior to the festival premiere.[34] As with other creole adaptations, Cape Verde's Crioulo culture presupposes a multi-lingual production with references to slavery, mulatto characters, island superstitions and, of course, colonial powers.

A central question in adapting Shakespeare is whether Branco and GTCCPM assume the subjugated position of the colonised in highly esteeming the 'works of the masters' to the detriment of the emerging national dramaturgy. Is it possible to perform the canon and avoid the hold of colonial mimicry that Edward Brathwaite laments?[35] These questions are further complicated by the fact that GTCCPM's creolisations are directed or at least supervised in some capacity by the Portuguese Branco. Teatro Solaris, however, has not produced any new adaptations since 2005, choosing to focus instead on writing original plays that might bolster a national body of work, thus opposing (like other theatre artists) Branco's championing of *crioulização* as national dramaturgy.

With increasing attention focused on globalisation, what is the efficacy of language, then, in locating a place for oneself on the global stage? This question is especially significant as the Cape Verdean government actively promotes the idea of a global Cape Verdean nation that reaches beyond the geographical boundaries of the archipelago to its diasporic communities in the USA and elsewhere. Sociolinguist Donaldo Macedo passionately argues that '[i]t is through their own language [Crioulo] that Capeverdeans will be able to reconstruct their history and their culture.'[36] Can creolisations of Shakespeare serve this function or does the historical weight of the canon make 'colonial mimicry' an inescapable component of the process?

The cultural roots of Cape Verde are undeniably both African and European, a central characteristic that emerges from more than five centuries of asymmetrical co-influence. Just as the Cape Verdean government positions itself somewhere between these two poles, so too theatre draws from a variety of sources. While troupes on the main island (characteristically more African) employ traditional cultural practices in order to archive the history and language of Santiago, Branco and GTCCPM recreate theatre practices by appropriating the most canonical western playwright to engage the nation. Even as Branco attempted to emphasise the 'universal' in *Rei Lear*, the embodied performances localised his interpretation. At its best, *crioulização* may contribute to the promise of Cape Verdean theatre to transform the postcolonial tensions that exist within a Crioulo society into creative acts of political engagement and freedom – what Bhaba might describe as 'the liberatory signs of a free people'.[37] Positioning Shakespeare at the service of Crioulo, Branco recreates his own self-creolisation by making Shakespeare a little Cape Verdean, too. I surmise that the undeniable hybrid nature of Cape Verdean culture and its far-reaching historical practice of absorbing and transforming 'the other', moves beyond the practice of a *crioulização* of Senhor Guilherme Shakespeare to a conceptualisation of theatre and Crioulo performance theory that is fundamentally hybrid and essentially Crioulo.

NOTES

1 This article builds upon my dissertation and excerpts are reprinted here. All translations into English are mine. See Eunice Ferreira, 'Theatre in Cape Verde: Resisting, Reclaiming, and Recreating National and Cultural Identity in Postcolonial Lusophone Africa.' Ph.D. Dissertation, Tufts University, 2009. See also Christina S. McMahon, 'Theatre in Circulation: Performing National Identity on the Global Stage in Cape Verde, West Africa.' Ph.D. Dissertation, Northwestern University, 2008.
2 Crioulo is also referred to as Kriolu, Kriol, Kriolu Kabuverdianu, lingua caboverdiana and the Cape Verdean language (CVL).
3 Official website for the Millennium Challenge Corporation (MCC), a United States government corporation whose 'mission is to reduce global poverty through the promotion of sustainable economic growth.'http://www.mcc.gov/mcc/countries/capeverde/index. shtml. See also http://www.state.gov/e/eb/rls/othr/ics/2013/204617.htm.
4 Richard Lobban (1995), *Cape Verde: Crioulo Colony to Independent Nation*, Boulder CO: Westview Press, 70.
5 Tcho Mbaimba Caulker (2009), 'Shakespeare's "Julius Caesar" in Sierra Leone: Thomas Decker's "*Juliohs Siza*", Roman Politics, and the Emergence of a Postcolonial African State', *Research in African Literatures*, 40, 2: (Summer), 209.
6 Shawkat M. Toorawa (2001), 'Translating The Tempest, Dev Virahsawmy's *Toufann*, cultural creolisation & the rise of Mauritian creole' in Martin Banham, James Gibbs, and Femi Osofisan, eds, *African Theatre: Playwrights & Politics*, Oxford: James Currey, 129.
7 See https://www.facebook.com/pages/Shakespeare-em-Crioulo/271731509629637?fref= ts.
8 Branco, *Nação Teatro*, 354-355.
9 Ibid., 364.
10 Toorawa, 130.
11 McMahon, 'Theatre in Circulation,' 237.
12 Marvin Carlson (2006), *Speaking in Tongues: Language at Play in the Theatre*,Ann Arbor MI: University of Michigan Press, 113.
13 See Dulce Almada Duarte (2003), *Bilinguismo ou Diglossia?: As Relações de Força entre o Crioulo e o Português na Sociedade Cabo-Verdiana*, 2nd ed.,Praia, Cape Verde: Speen Edições; Manuel Veiga (2004), *A Construção do Bilinguismo*, Praia, Cape Verde: IBNL.
14 Fonseca Soares, personal interview, March 9, 2005.
15 Branco, *Nação Teatro*, 362-3.
16 William Shakespeare, *King Lear*, I.i:56. All Crioulo lines cited henceforth in this article

are taken from Soares' translation. The Portuguese translation by Alvaro Cunhal is from the GTCCPM's working translation script. Texts are archived by the GTCCPM in the Mindelo Portuguese Cultural Center.

17 William Shakespeare, *King Lear*, I. v.: 48–9.

18 See '*Estruturação e Descrioulização*,' in Dulce Almada Duarte (2003), *Bilinguismo ou Diglossia?* 52–74.

19 Branco, personal interview, August 1, 2005.

20 *King Lear*, I,v: 39.

21 I borrow the term 'Portuguese Prospero' from Boaventura de Sousa Santos. Evoking a metaphor to convey Portugal's 'national inferiority complex,' he repositions the former colonial empire as somewhere 'Between Prospero and Caliban'. See Boaventura de Sousa Santos (2002), 'Between Prospero and Caliban: Colonialism, Postcolonialism, and Inter-Identity', *Luso-Brazilian Review* 39: 2, Special Issue: Portuguese Cultural Studies, (Winter, 9-43).

22 Branco, personal interview, 1 August 2005.

23 Branco, ed., *Dez Anos de Teatro*, 17–18.

24 Eduino Santos (2005), 'Mindelo "comeu" João Branco' *Expresso das Ilhas* 169, March 2, 25. See also Abílio Tolentino and Américo Antunes, 'João Branco: o rosto do teatro' in *NJC Fim-de-Semana*, Saturday, 19 July 1997, 8-9. In the two-page feature, the authors describe Branco as 'on the verge of becoming black'.

25 TSF [Teresa Sofia Fortes] (2003), '*Rei Lear ou o Crioulo Shakespeareano*', *A Semana*, 12 September 2003. Fortes' article is cited here as a specific example, but variations were repeated in all forms of media.

26 'Centro Cultural Português encerra comemorações com Rei Lear,' 10 December 2003, http://www.noticiaslusofonas.com/view.php?load=arcview&article=4409&catogory=news.

27 In keeping with the spirit of the production, the name of the São Vicente variant, *Criol de Soncent*, does not employ the ALUPEC orthographic system. The '*Ciclo Teatral Shakespeare*' also featured *Sonho dum Noite Verão* (*A Midsummer Night's Dream*) presented by the Solaris Theatre Company.

28 Homem, Rui Carvalho, (2008), 'Memory, Ideology, Translation: King Lear Behind Bars and Before History,' in Diana E. Henderson, ed., *Alternative Shakespeares*, vol. 3: 204-220; 206.

29 Ibid., 204-205. Here Homem quotes an excerpt of Cunhal's obituary which appeared on June14, 2005 in the Portuguese newpaper *Público*.

30 Mindelact 2003 official program, 11. Available at the Mindelact Documentation Center. See also TSF [Teresa Sofia Fortes], '*Rei Lear ou o Crioulo shakespeareano,' A Semana*, September 12, 2003.

31 See McMahon's insightful, comparative analysis of the two productions within the festival context in McMahon, 'Theatre in Circulation,' 253–65.

32 Herlandson Duarte, personal interview, March 2005.

33 I am thankful to Donaldo Macedo for reminding me of this linguistic prejudice. Macedo's play *Descarado* was the first Cape Verdean play published in Crioulo. It examines the emigrant culture of the island of Brava, challenging the prejudices and privileges of class, race, gender and ethnicity. One of the primary reasons that Macedo wrote the play was to demonstrate that Crioulo is a viable language for Cape Verdean literature, which to this day is written primarily in Portuguese.

34 See https://www.facebook.com/pages/Shakespeare–em–Crioulo/271731509629637?fref=ts. See the bibliography for more online resources.

35 Edward K. Brathwaite, 'Nation Language,' in *The Postcolonial Studies Reader*, ed. Bill Ashcroft, Gareth Griffiths, and Helen Tiffin (London: Routledge, 1995) 309-13.

36 Donaldo Macedo, 'Literacy in Post-Colonial Cape Verde,' *Portuguese Literary and Cultural Studies 8: Cape Verde Language, Literature and Music*, ed. Ana Malfalda Leite (North Dartmouth, MA: Center for Portuguese Studies and Culture, 2002):405. Ibid., 405. This essay challenges language instruction in Cape Verde's educational system.

37 Homi K. Bhabha, 'Cultural Diversity and Cultural Differences' in *The Post-Colonial Studies Reader*, eds. Bill Ashcroft, Gareth Griffiths, and Helen Tiffin, (London: Routledge, 1995), 209.

BIBLIOGRAPHY

Archives of the GTCCPM and Centre for Theatre Documentation and Investigation (Mindelact Association), Mindelo, São Vicente, Cape Verde. The collections contain festival programmess, production records, photographs, videos and audio recordings, publicity material, correspondences and press clippings. All notices referenced in this article are included here.

Ashcroft, Bill, Gareth Griffiths and Helen Tiffin, eds (1995) *The Postcolonial Studies Reader*, London: Routledge.

Branco, João, ed. (2003) *Dezanos de Teatro,* Praia: Centro Cultural Português.

—— (2004) *Nação Teatro: História do Teatro em Cabo Verde*, Mindelo: Instituto da Biblioteca Nacional e do Livro (IBNL).

Carlson, Marvin (2006) *Speaking in Tongues: Language at Play in the Theatre*, Ann Arbor: University of Michigan Press.

Caulker, Tcho Mbaimba (2009) 'Shakespeare's 'Julius Caesar' in 'Sierra Leone: Thomas Decker's "Juliohs Siza"', Roman Politics, and the Emergence of a Postcolonial African State', *Research in African Literatures*, 40, 2: Summer, 208–27.

Correira e Silva, António (2000) *Nos Tempos do Porto Grande do Mindelo*, Praia, Cape Verde: Centro Cultural Português.

Duarte, Dulce Almada. (1998) *Bilinguismoou Diglossia?: As Relações de Força entre o Crioulo e o Portuguêsna Sociedade Cabo-Verdiana*. Praia: Spleen Ediçoes.

Ferreira, Eunice S. (2009) 'Theatre in Cape Verde: Resisting, Reclaiming, and Recreating National and Cultural Identity in Postcolonial Lusophone Africa.' Ph.D. Diss., Tufts University.

Fernandes, Gabriel (2006) *Em Busca da Nação: Notas para uma Reinterpretação do Cabo Verde Crioulo*. Florianópolis, Brazil: Editora da UFSC; Praia, Cape Verde: Instituto da Biblioteca Nacional e do Livro.

Gilbert, Helen and Joanne Tompkins (1996) *Post-Colonial Drama: Theory, Practice and Politics*, New York: Oxford University Press.

GTCCPM online:http://jgbprivate.wix.com/gtccpm#and also https://www.facebook.com/GrupoDeTeatroDoCentroCulturalPortuguesDoMindelo?fref=ts.

Halter, Marilyn (1993) *Between Race and Ethnicity: Cape Verdean American Immigrants, 1860-1965,* Chicago: University of Illinois.

Homem, Rui Carvalho (2008) 'Memory, Ideology, Translation.' In *Alternative Shakespeares 3*, ed. Diana Henderson. London: Routledge, 204–220.

Kondé, Kwame (Francisco Fragoso) (1981) *Caderno 'Korda Kaoberdi': ano de 1979-1980*, Praia, Cape Verde: Imprensa Nacional.

Lobban, Richard (1995) *Cape Verde: Crioulo Colony to Independent Nation*. Boulder: Westview.

Lobban, Richard and Paul Khalil Saucier, eds (2007). *Historical Dictionary of the Republic of Cape Verde.* 4th ed. Lanham, MD: Scarecrow Press.

Lopes, José Vicente (2002) *Cabo Verde: Os Bastidores da Independência.* 2nd edition, Praia, Cape Verde: Spleen Ediçōes.

Wẹsóo, Hamlet!
or The Resurrection of Hamlet

FEMI OSOFISAN

CHARACTERS
Masks
Messenger
Hamlet
Claudius
Ophelia
Létò [*pronounced 'Lay-toe'*]
Ìyámọdẹ
Aṣípa
Òjẹ̀
Olorì
Ọba Ayíbí
Ọba Sayédẹ̀rọ̀
Túndùn
Àdùkẹ́
Citizens / Townspeople
Drummers

NOTE
The diacritics to the Yoruba names have been supplied here in order to indicate how the names should be pronounced. But they will be omitted in the body of the text except where absolutely necessary.

PLAY HISTORY
The first version of this play was written, and premiered, at Greencastle, Indiana, USA, during my stay at the DePauw University as the Lee G. Hall Distinguished Playwright-in-Residence in 2003. The workshop production was directed by Professor Ron Dye at the Moore Theatre of DePauw's Performing Arts Centre, with music provided by Francis Awe and his Nigerian Talking Drum Ensemble. The present script has only been slightly modified.

134

A Note to the Director

The play takes place in Yorubaland, Nigeria, in a period deliberately set in a non-specific year within the last half of the 20th century. Thus, some of the references will recall the early 50s, and some the later part of the century. This will not matter however to those not normally familiar with the history of the area.

Similarly the location of events is, generally, the Ilaje-Ijebu Waterside, but I have also, for my own dramaturgical purposes, introduced elements from other parts of Yorubaland, especially some aspects of Yoruba Oyo traditions. Again, this would not matter at all for those not normally familiar with Yoruba traditions. The intention is to make the situation general to the whole of Yorubaland – indeed, to Africa – rather than restricting it to a specific Yoruba area.

The stage should therefore depict a general playing area, with minimal sets, allowing for a swift and fluid movement between the various scenes either immediately in front of, or somewhere inside, the palace. Thus only two areas need to be specifically mapped out: the palace courtyard, and the *bàrà* (the shrine-like mausoleum where the bodies of dead kings are buried and worshipped. Note that each corpse normally has its own separate room there, and so only one needs to be shown, without the set designer needing to bother with elaborate details).

The Casting

The play has been conceived for a mixed cast of black and white actors. However, given our situation in Africa, it is quite possible there are no white actors readily available for performance. In such circumstances, the practice so far has been to make up the black actors, either by painting their faces or noses white, and/or giving them wigs, etc. This never quite works as far as I am concerned, except for comic characters. I will therefore prefer that even the white characters be played by black actors, and so have included in the text appropriate dialogue to explain this to the audience. However these areas of the text can be easily identified, and expunged or modified where the appropriate mixed cast is available.

Prologue
[*Lights come up on a swirling mass of dancing* **Masks**, *of different shapes and colours, all in an atmosphere of merriment. Enter the* **Messenger**, *with a tablet. The dancing stops.*]
Messenger
How beautiful it is to see you all, preparing
For your annual reunion with your human offspring.
From reports, they are also eagerly waiting for you on earth.
As you know, however, Ọrunmila sometimes
Finds it necessary to ask some of you to return to the world,
Not in this ancestral form, but as human beings, as
Your former selves. That is why I am here.
[*General excitement rises among the* **Masks**]
Right now, a situation is brewing
Somewhere in Yorubaland, which echoes another one
Of many centuries ago, a drama that you,
Shakespeare—are you there? Yes, the story that
You once put in a play that has become famous
Ọrunmila has decided that some of you
Who were prominent in that earlier drama
Should return now, to participate again,
In its recurrence in Yorubaland, all in the hope that
The tragedy that is about to break may be averted
So as I call you out now, you will go and prepare
To regain your former human forms
But—I warn you this time as Africans,
The same colour of skin as your hosts
[*He consults his tablet as he calls out*]:
Hamlet! Claudius! Ophelia! [*The* **Masks** *step out*]
Please come with me now for further briefing
[*They go, as the dance resumes. Lights*]

ONE

[*Early evening. The open space in front of the palace, with only a few stragglers around.* **Létò**, *in partial disguise, is making his way to the palace, trying as much as possible not to attract attention.* **Ìyámọdẹ**, *who has walked past, in the company of* **Baba Aṣípa** *and his drummer,* **Ọjẹ̀**, *turns to look at his retreating back. Puzzled, she calls out to him*]

Ìyámọdẹ Ọmọ baba! Ọmọ baba!
  Ṣé ìwoni? Or is it not you?
  Létò, ọmọ baba, Akanni ọ̀gọ̀—àbì ìwọ̀ kọ́?
  Baba Aṣipa, do you see who I see,

Or am I dreaming?

Baba Aṣípa [*Exclaims*] Indeed, **Ìyámọdẹ**, it must be him! [*At his gesture, his drummer, **Ọjẹ**, begins to play **Létò**'s oriki, while **Aṣípa** translates.*]
'Ọmọ aláso ẹtù—se ìwọ ni?
Ọmọ A-jí-faṣọ àrán bora!
A-sùn-fi sányán bojú!
Oníle òpọ́-wọ̀'lẹ̀ kẹ̀, wọ-aṣọ-nlá!'[1]
Don't pass like this without a word of greetings! Or don't you know us any more?

[*Létò is obliged to turn round at this solicitation*]

Létò Ìyámọdẹ! And you, Baba Aṣípa, I'm sorry, I—

Ìyámọdẹ Of course it had to be you! Oh I am old, and my eyes are failing but still how can I miss that princely gait, that shift of royal haunches that the lineage of Oba Sayedero alone has perfected into its single trademark?

Létò Forgive me, Ìyámọdẹ—

Ìyámọdẹ A little bigger no doubt, but it's still the same restless buck I once carried on my back!

Létò It is, Yeye! But as you know, several months have passed since my father died, and I've not been free to come home since then to mourn him. That's why I wanted to get to the palace quietly.

Ìyámọdẹ Quietly! Ah ah ah ah ah! Do you hear that, Baba Aṣípa?

Baba Aṣípa Prince, did we hear you right?

Ìyámọdẹ Quietly! Is it a thief who died then, that his son should sneak back unnoticed into the town?

Baba Aṣípa Quietly, Son of my Master! [*Shakes his head in disbelief*]

Ìyámọdẹ Is it a poor man without means, or a villain with a burden of crimes, waiting to be punished?

Baba Aṣípa Prince, your father was the best ruler we have had in this land, since the days of Ọba Abiodun, our venerable ancestor! And it was the whole town, you hear! The entire town went into a rage of celebration to mark his death!

Ìyámọdẹ And now—ẹ gbà mìí, káá mà kàn?[2] —his son, his only son, wants to slip into town 'quietly!'

Ọjẹ No, Létò, you are doing us a great injustice by sneaking in like this! What would your father say where he lies there in the bàrà among his ancestors? Is this how to remember him and reward him for all he did for us, that his son should be welcomed back into town without honour?

Létò It isn't like that, Baba Aṣípa, please.

Ìyámọdẹ [*Shouts suddenly*] Come, people! Come and see!

Létò No, please, Yeye, don't.

---

[1] 'Son of the owners of etu cloth—is it you?
Son of those who wake to be draped in velvet!
Son of those who sleep covered in silk!
Whose house posts are draped in beads and rich cloth!'
[2] Oh dear, what is this? (Ijebu dialect).

[*Too late, some townspeople have gathered*]

Ìyámodè See who we have here.

Voices Who? Who is it, Yeye?

Ìyámodè 'Who is it?' Could you so soon have forgotten then? That forehead! Those lissom limbs?

Voices Tell us, Yeye.

Ìyámodè You mean you don't know? Ah, *ó mà se o!*[3] I ask you: What animal takes a walk and the whole forest trembles?

Voices The elephant of course!

Ìyámodè He alone! What animal rumbles and rumbles like gathering rain, and sends the baby hunter scrambling up the nearest tree?

Voices The buffalo!

Ìyámodè Yes, no other one! And when we talk of the god who is as equally at home in the heat of battle, as in the midst of a drinking party?

Voices Ogun! Ogun of course!

Ìyámodè So, look again! The elephant is the elephant! The buffalo has no clone! And Ogun! ah, what other god rivals the god of the fiery forge! Look again, my friends, and tell me which other offspring could come from the loins of our late Oba Sayédèrò?

Voices Omoba Létò! Our Prince!

[*Reluctantly,* **Létò** *takes off his disguise. Recognising him now, the people pay obeisance jubilantly. Someone starts the song, 'Káábò o, káábò! Omo abílè sòrò, kílè yanu, káábò o!', and a dance of welcome begins*]

Asípa Dance for Omoba. Létò, son of our departed king! Ah, the king who brings destruction and destitution to the land will be remembered–

Voices Just as the one who brings laughter will never be forgotten!

Asípa Yes, thank you! Your father it was, Prince, who brought prosperity to every home, so how can we ever forget!

Létò Baba Asípa, my friends, please, later! Later! Please, I beg you, let me go now–

Ìyámodè Later? Oh when we call him to dance the cripple pleads–

Voices 'I am in a hurry!'

Ìyámodè We call him to dance and the ungainly says–

Voices 'Please give me another date!'

Ìyámodè But how can one be in a hurry, tell me, when one is the son of Sayedero, father of festivity himself?

Voice Come, let's see you dance too in his honour, omo Oba Létò! Dance the way you used to teach us right here on these sands when you led your age-group on your numerous outings!

Voice Prince, you cannot be in a hurry today! For, let me tell you, your father our father who left not too long ago: when he was here, he was never in a hurry, especially when it came to spending! Freely his hands scattered largesse whenever we gathered at his feet, as we do now to his son...

---

[3] What a pity!

[*They kneel round him, gaily supplicating, calling his praise names*]

Létò [*Yielding gradually to the merriment*] Oh do not misunderstand me, excellent people, you remember me, I'm not afraid of spending here, take! [*He takes out some bills and distributes*] You see? But I have just arrived after such a long absence I am tired, and besides I am still to get to the palace to see my widowed mother! Yes, I'm yet to visit my father's grave and pay my due respects! I'm still to perform my own rites of mourning...

Voice Your rites of mourning, Prince and master, they begin here! Where we are dancing! Shower us with money, *o jare!* as your family is known to do!

[*The dance hots up*]

Voice The death of a mighty hero like your father brought us grief.

Voice But it was also the occasion for a great celebration!

Voice Look, we've been dancing these many months of his going.

Voice And the feast is not over yet!

[*The drum leading, they sing:*
Ọ̀tọ̀ lamúgboro dùn,
Ọmọba!

Létò, Létò! Ọmọba![4]
Circling him, they urge him to join the dance]

Voice Or have you forgotten already those styles which made you champion of the dancing ring? Lost your nimble tricks?

Voice Have those years away in the white man's country stiffened your limbs so much that you can no longer swing gracefully to the tunes of the drum?

Ìyámọdẹ Ọmọba! It's for you so many feet are dancing, but do I see you standing there, rigid like the plinth of Ọranyan?

Asipa Ọmọba! The songs are calling your father's praise-names and do you simply watch like a newly-arrived stranger who cannot interpret the drums?

Ìyámọdẹ Or like a love son too ashamed to acknowledge his birth?

Létò Ah, as for that—never Iyámode, keeper of the dead at bàrà. The only woman whom we all call 'Baba, our father'! You know me—I am a trueborn and can beat my chest anywhere my father's name is called! But try to understand. If I choose to stand still when the drum of my father calls to summon us for dancing, it's because the right occasion is—

Ìyámọdẹ Is now! Show us, and show the spirit of your father what you still remember, Létò! And let your people feel again the generosity of those hands!

Aṣípa I say, shower us with bills as only a Prince of Sayédèrọ can! And you others, you'd better shake and bend to it as he rains them down! Dollars, you know! Foreign exchange! For we are not too bush to know what

---

[4] We have our own way of bringing joy to the town / O Prince!/

they spend over there! Nothing like our niggardly naira notes that only minions spend nowadays!

Létò All right, I surrender! I'll dance with you, but just for a short while...

[*Laughing now, infected by their jollity and the chanting of his oriki he joins the dance and begins to paste money on the foreheads of the dancers. But suddenly, the drums alert the crowd to a new arrival, with the customary homage, 'Èrù Ọba ni mo bà, Ọba to!'*[5]

Enter **Ọba Ayíbí**, *with a few attendants. He is in a casual dress, wearing only the cap for informal occasions.*

The people throw themselves on their faces, saluting and crying 'Kaabiyesi!']

Ọba Ayíbí We heard the singing and drumming, And in front of our palace too...

Ìyámọdẹ Yes, Kabiyesi, it's because of...

Létò [*Comes forward to salute, down on one knees*] Kaabiyesi!

Ọba Ayíbí What! It's you, our son? You're back!

Ìyámọdẹ We caught him right here just now, Kabiyesi, trying to sneak into the palace 'quietly'!

Ọba Ayíbí What! But why, Létò? Hey, someone, run and call our Olòrì. Tell her to come and see who we have here! Ah, Létò, sneaking into town like a thief? You do us great injustice. You know you should have sent us advance notice of your arrival, so we could receive you as royally as you are worth!

Létò Forgive me, Kabiyesi, I meant no disrespect. But not having been able to come all these months to mourn my father, I thought—

Ọba Ayíbí Your father! Congratulations, my son, you are now a full man on your feet! [*Sees his fallen face.*] Or don't tell me you're still shedding tears over such a glorious transition! Come, rejoice instead, Létò, as we have all been doing! His life ah, that kind of exemplary life! One can never finish celebrating it! Or, my people, what do you say?

[*The crowd responds enthusiastically with the song:*

Láyé Ólúgbón, mo ró'bórùn mẹta
Egbinrin baba aṣọ;
Láyé Arèsà, mo ra ṣààkì mẹrin
Ọba ló semí lóge:
Láyé Ọba Ṣayédèrọ̀, ìlú dùn,
Ó fayé tu ni lára.[6]

The Ọba too showers money on the dancers who surround him. Just then, the **Olòrì** *arrives, with those who went to fetch her.*

The crowd hails her too, and some gather round her. But just then, **Létò**'s *cry of shock brings the dance to an abrupt stop.*]

---

[5] 'It's the King I fear, all-powerful King!'

[6] In the time of King Olugbọn, I owned many wrappers / of royal Egbinrin cloth / In the time of Aresa, owned many shawls / The King made me rich / In the time of King Ṣayédèrọ̀, life was sweet / He made life of great comfort for us...

Létò Mother! Mother?

[*Hurrying towards him, her arms open*]

Olórì Yes, Létò! So you have come at last! Ah, *kaabo, omo mi!* Welcome! How long we've waited, to see you back here.

[*Goes into his oriki:*]

'Aremo Oríómádéga, Ariówósáye
A fìgbá wọnwó
Ọmọ èyí ò jọ tèèkan
Tèèkan ò jọ tèyí, Ọmọ' [7]

[*But he steps away from her embrace, forcing her to stop, confused*]

Létò Mother? So it's true—you are the Olórì, wife to the new king?

Olórì Létò...

Ọba Ayíbí Oh, of course, you haven't been informed, we forget! Welcome back then to a double celebration, my son! First, your father's death, which we fêted lavishly! And then afterwards the joy of our marriage! This woman, your mother, is a priceless jewel, a true adornment of the palace! When our brother, your father, was alive, remember, she served our people devotedly as the Olórì. And so, when your father left, there was a clamour from all our citizens, and especially the market women, that they did not want to lose her services. Well, since a good king must listen to his people at least that is what your father's example taught us we yielded to their demand. And graciously, your mother consented. So, nothing has changed, son. As you left the palace, so you are returning to it: Welcome to the palace, and welcome, as before, to your home! That is your mother, the Olórì of our palace! Come with us, let us go in now and—

Létò No!

Olórì What?

Létò No, Kabiyesi, I cannot come with you

Olórì Why? Something the matter, Létò?

Létò You're Olórì. You sleep in a different bed now. So how can you also be my mother!

[*Cries of shock all around. Létò turns and begins to walk away*]

Olórì Létò!

Ọba Ayíbí Let him go. Poor son, we'll talk to him later.

[*Lights*]

---

[7] First son and heir of King Orimadega, / Who has enough money for merriment / whose wealth is carried in calabashes / son of 'This is unlike the previous one,' / 'The previous one is unlike this one'! son of ...

TWO

[*Túndùn, with her friend, Àdùké*]

Túndùn [*Dancing*] He's back, Àduké! He's back! Létò's back!

Àdùké Yes, I heard—

Túndùn You heard! At last, he's back!

Àdùké I am happy for you!

Túndùn Comb, my hair! Quick, plait it for me! Make me up as only you know how to! I must be at my finest to receive him!

Àdùké Easy now, easy! *(Teasing)* È-è-é-é-o! Ìyàwó! Ęlęyin'jú ęgę!⁸

Túndùn Come on, we have no time! You know it's my house he'll be coming to straight after seeing his mother!

Àdùké I know, but—

Túndùn Then don't waste time, my friend! You know how many years I've been waiting! What I've suffered because of it! The humiliation from all those spurned suitors! Their abusive songs! Because they all thought he wouldn't ever return! That I would die a jilted spinster! Now it's going to be my turn to sing back at them! Come, Àdùké, o *ya!*⁹ My hair!

[*Begins to hum happily. Lights*]

THREE

[*Létò is pacing around, brooding and deep in thought. Enter (the Spirits of)* **Hamlet** *and* **Ophelia**. *They are holding their heads i.e. their ancestral masks in their hands, such that they seem to be headless.*]

Hamlet So now you know how it feels.

Létò [*Looking up*] What did you say?

Hamlet The pain. The disappointment. Like a cold knife in the heart.

Létò Who are you?

Hamlet Hamlet. And this is Ophelia, once my girlfriend.

Létò You mean ... as in Shakespeare?

Hamlet Yes

Létò I see! You can wear your heads properly? Like normal human beings?

Hamlet, Ophelia. Oh sorry [*They do so*] Węsóo,¹⁰ Létò!

Létò Ah *węsóo*, Hamlet. And you ... you say you're Ophelia?

Ophelia Yes. Węsóo!

Létò But you're the wrong colour, both of you! You're not black!

Ophelia You forget, we're reincarnations.

Hamlet The dead have no colour.

Ophelia Which means we can come in any colour we choose.

Hamlet Just like the egungun.

Ophelia Yes, I see. So what are you doing here?

Hamlet It's the season again, have you forgotten? When the dead return?

---

⁸ Bride of the jewel eyes!

⁹ Get going!

¹⁰ *Węsóo*: Hello/Good day/Hi, etc.

Létò Ah yes, of course. The annual Dance of Ancestral Masks.

Hamlet We've come to take part in the festival.

Létò But ... what do you mean? You are not real! You're figures in a fable.

Ophelia Isn't that what the whole festival is, a fable?

Létò It's a reunion with ancestors. You were not born here.

Hamlet Ọrunmila sent us.

Ophelia Over there, among the dead, there are no tribes or races.

Hamlet The ancestors come from everywhere.

Ophelia From the Word that was the beginning.

Hamlet From the beginning that was the Word.

Ophelia One day you too will die, Létò, and become our ancestor.

Létò Now you speak in riddles! You said Ọrunmila sent you?

Ophelia Yes. But don't ask us why, we've forgotten.

Hamlet Just as it was planned that we should.

Ophelia All we know is that we can help you, if you let us.

Létò I see. What was it you said again?

Hamlet I said, it wounds, doesn't it? To return like that, with the intention of mourning your father. But only to discover that your mother has already married again!

Létò I don't see how that is a business of yours.

Hamlet But it is. Remember, we've gone through it all, before you. [*Létò turns away*] At first, it's shock and disbelief that you feel. Then anger. And finally, a terrible sense of loss.

Ophelia Come on, talk to us. We're friends. [*Létò hesitates*] It always helps to let it out.

Létò Terrible, isn't it? My mother, she was the only true friend I thought I had.

Hamlet She's still your friend.

Létò No, not any more.

Ophelia Have you stopped to consider that she too, has her own right to happiness?

Létò Happiness!

Ophelia Plus the right to take it wherever she finds it?

Létò She doted on my father! Till I went off to college abroad, we three were always together, inseparably. She called him her special *orisa*—

Ophelia And she meant it too—

Létò So I thought—

Ophelia While he was alive. But life has to go on...

Létò [*Ignoring her*] Six months of mourning, that's all that was required! But she could not even wait to complete them! She'd found a new lover quickly, in my father's successor. And his brother too!

Ophelia I suffered too, when it happened to the man I loved. Hamlet here, yes. But I am a woman. And so, after these many years, I am now able to understand—

Hamlet My dear mother, I said in disbelief! But, Létò, women think little of us, the children! In the name of happiness, suddenly and without warning, they will cut us adrift!

Létò I didn't believe it when the news first got to me. No, I said, it couldn't be true. Not the mother I knew and remembered! I just hurried home. And then ... [*Stops, unable to continue*]

Hamlet Don't break yet, Létò. You're going to need all your courage soon.

Létò What do you mean?

Ophelia The worst is still to come. You are going to need a lot of compassion.

Létò Compassion?

Hamlet Or anger. Whichever way you choose to play it. But your life will not be the same again after this.

Létò You have news for me?

Hamlet Your father. He wants to talk to you.

Létò My father!

Hamlet He has a sad message, waiting to be spoken.

Létò I too would love to speak to him! But he's dead, and gone to the other side.

Ophelia He's waiting for you.

Létò Where? Oh he's coming too for the dance?

Ophelia No, not for the dance. Not yet.

Létò Then ?

Hamlet In the bàrà, the royal burial house, where he lies with the other kings of the past. That's where he'll meet you.

Létò But the bàrà! It's forbidden to go there.

Ophelia Not if Iyámọdẹ allows it. As the keeper of the shrine, she alone can take you there.

Létò Iyámọdẹ! You mean she—

Hamlet Yes. Here she comes to take you to the bàrà.

[*As **Hamlet** and **Ophelia** withdraw, **Ìyámọdẹ** arrives. Lights cut off*]

FOUR

[***Túndùn**, accompanied by **Àdùké**, comes over to **Baba Aṣípa***]

Túndùn Baba, where's he? I was told he was with you!

Aṣípa Who?

Túndùn You know, Baba, don't tease me! Who else have I been waiting for all these years?

Aṣípa Létò?

Túndùn Where's he now? Tell me! Please!

Aṣípa Eh, softly, young woman I saw him, but—

Túndùn How does he look? Fatter? Taller? Oh Baba!

Aṣípa Túndùn! I said, easy! You'll see him in good time—

Túndùn When? You told him where I am?

Aṣípa He has other things on his mind now, I'm afraid.

Túndùn [*Crestfallen*] You mean ... he's not asked for me?

Aṣípa He ... How shall I put it? You see, he came home, and found something he did not expect. So—

Túndùn I understand. He's forgotten about me.

Aṣípa That's not what I mean. Just that you may have to be a little more patient, my child.

Túndùn Patient! Hear that, Àdùkẹ́! After how many years! Patient! Baba, he made promises to me! He gave me his word! And because of that I've stayed faithful to him, watching myself grow into this sterile spinster! What songs do they not sing of me, all over the town, because of it! All these years! You know all about it, Baba! You were one of the few who encouraged me to wait! Now he's back and he's not come to see me, and you, Baba, you say patient! No, no more! This corpse he's turned me into, he'll have to bury it now, with his own hands! Yes, baba! So, wherever he is, I'm going to find him!

[*She storms out. Lights*]

FIVE

[**Ìyámọdẹ** and **Létò**, *at the bàrà*]

Létò You say you called but he did not respond?

Ìyámọdẹ It was very strange, my son! Aṣípaọdẹ, Jagun, and others of the hunters' guild were all here with me. After we sang the customary songs and poured libation, we called his name. Three times, as is the custom. We waited. Not a word! We tried again, this time seven times! But not even the briefest rustle in the air. Your father did not answer us. He would not give a message to those he left behind!

Létò And you say this has never happened before?

Ìyámọdẹ Once perhaps. Long, long ago. Older than any of us can remember.

Létò What was the cause at that time, do you know?

Ìyámọdẹ Well, some say the king at the time had died in unhappy circumstances. So he was angry with the world he left behind.

Létò Ah!

Ìyámọdẹ But it doesn't fit in this case. What would your father be angry for? He was a good king, he lived a happy life. And he spread the happiness to all of us. You know yourself how the palace was always a hive of laughter in his time. Ah, those were truly prosperous times, and people said our ancestor, Ọba Abiodun, had come back to life! And when he passed away, suddenly like that, your father, everybody, from the youngest toddler to the oldest man, paid him their fullest respects. All the drums celebrated for seven full days without stop. The revelry and the gun salutes went on for months, in memory of such a wondrous age. So why should he be angry with us? What could we have done wrong?

Létò Did you try to find out?

Ìyámọdẹ You still ask! Of course we sent for other diviners, after all our powers had failed. Irula, diviner from Shaki; Morepe from Oke Itase;

Ogungunmoga from the dreaded town of Agua—the day that one came, even the moon came to watch! So bright was it that all the cocks were crowing in confusion! The very best, my son, of diviners, not sparing expenses! But none of them could solve the mystery.

Létò Strange! But that time, long ago, when it first happened, what did the people do, do you remember?

Ìyámọdẹ That's the problem. No one remembers any more.

Létò So why have you brought me here?

Ìyámọdẹ Because ... well, it's just an intuition, I confess. Maybe it will work, maybe it won't, I can't say for sure. But your father left while you were away, and something tells me he wouldn't have wanted to go like that, without first talking to you. So you see? Perhaps it's you he's waiting for, to answer us.

Létò They said so too, Hamlet and his girl.

Ìyámọdẹ Who?

Létò Oh sorry, forget that. Well, what do I need to do?

Ìyámọdẹ Nothing really. Just your presence is all I need. But I must also warn you however that it could be dangerous.

Létò Dangerous?

Ìyámọdẹ The spirits of the dead can not always be predicted.

Létò He's my father. I can not be afraid of him.

Ìyámọdẹ Not him, that's the point. The danger is that, when we begin, not even I can say which exactly of the dead will be speaking.

Létò Well, I'll take my chances. After all, as you know, he trained me in the ritual. Already indeed, even as you speak I am beginning to feel my father's presence. Go on, Yeye, let's call him out.

Ìyámọdẹ Then, let's proceed.

[*Ìyámọdẹ changes her clothes, throwing off the upper buba to reveal an under-garment sewn all over with charms.*

With **Létò** *accompanying her, she begins to chant. After a while, we hear a noise, as if of some wind, rising from afar but coming closer. It sends the two of them reeling back.*

Light changes occur rapidly. Then out of the dark, a **Mask** *begins to emerge.*

When it speaks, its voice is a thin falsetto, distinct but not recognisably human.

   Ìyámọdẹ falls on her face in respect]

Ìyámọdẹ Ka-a-a-biyesi, our father!

Mask Leave us, Ìyámọdẹ.

Ìyámọdẹ But, Kabiyesi—

Mask I wish to speak to my son alone.

[*She turns to* **Létò***, hesitating*]

Létò Go, Yeye. I'll be all right.

Ìyámọdẹ Right, I'll be just out there [*Ìyámọdẹ goes*]

Mask Létò! Létò! Létò! How many times did I call you?

Létò Three times, father.

Mask Listen to me. And listen well. I did not die a natural death as my people have been made to believe. I did not finish the time Obàtálá allotted me on earth.

Létò What, father?

Mask A usurper, a callous murderer, sits on your father's throne.

Létò Your brother.

Mask A murderer! A greedy man, and most cunning. He it was that poisoned me.

Létò *Èèwò! Ká má rì!*[11] Uncle a murderer?

Mask Hard to believe, I know. A man I lavished my love and affection on! Who knew all my secrets, shared my table, and entered my bedroom any time of day or night! How could I have known he would betray me?

Létò What happened father?

Mask Here, see with your own eyes.

[*Flashback scene follows as the* **Mask** *transforms to his human self as* **Qba Sayedero**. *We are in a room in the palace.* **Ayíbí,** *in 3-piece suit, storms in*]

Ayíbí What's this you sent to me? [*Shows arókò*[12]]

Qba Sáyédèrò You can read, can't you?

Ayíbí I've read it! [*Undoing the package one by one, and translating*] Tortoise head, ah! 'The journey of the tortoise ends in disgrace'. A carapace! 'The refusal to heed the warning of others is what made the tortoise follow the carapace into the supplicant's fire!' Then, skin of a python! 'The most poisonous snake wears the most beautiful colours'! Thank you, Kabiyesi! I thank you indeed! All this because of the proposed factory for the tobacco project, isn't it?

Qba Sáyédèrò Yes, of course.

Ayíbí You're changing your mind, is that it?

Qba Sáyédèrò Calm down first and listen. You see, a number of chiefs came to see me last night. They say they've talked with their subjects. All the educated people, except a few, are against it.

Ayíbí And you?

Qba Sáyédèrò I've also thought a lot about it since they left. That's why I sent you the message. I don't think it's a good idea after all. I think we should scrap it.

Ayíbí Scrap it! You remember how much I've already sunk on the project?

Qba Sáyédèrò I know but—

Ayíbí Scrap it! Over 25 million, remember, just to clear the site. And more than triple that for the equipment!

Qba Sáyédèrò I've considered all that. But we have no choice. For the sake of our people—

Ayíbí Which people? A few agitators, whom the police can deal with if they dare raise their voice! Because of a few rabble, all that money I've inves—

---

[11] Abomination! May it not be!

[12] An *arókò* is a message or letter consisting of symbols which the recipient is expected to decipher. It was the traditional Yoruba method of communicating, especially during negotiations involving a lot of diplomacy.

Ọba Sáyédèrò We'll find a way to compensate you and the other investors, I assure you. Though it's chicken feed to someone like you anyway—

Ayíbí So what if it's chicken feed! Does one just pick it from some dungheap or from some tree that grows money along the street? Every bloody kobo of the 'chicken feed' was earned through sweat! And I'm investing it to help bring jobs to the community, during your reign—

Ọba Sáyédèrò Yes thank you, Ayibi, but I'll find some other project for you. A safe one that will not harm the health of our people. Look, I'm really sorry...

Ayíbí Sorry! I could have gone elsewhere you know, to invest the money. But I said, no, it's no good leaving your own nose dripping, while you go to wipe the mucus off your neighbour's. I said it's my own town and my own people. It's also my brother. on the throne here. If I am going to start a project that will bring employment to so many, attract modern amenities to the place, and generally help improve the lives of the people, why should it be somewhere else and not here, in my own birthplace? I came to discuss it with you, didn't I, Kabiyesi? Not just once, but several times! And you not only endorsed it, Kabiyesi, but you were jubilant! Kabiyesi, you called the chiefs to thank me, these same chiefs you are talking about! And more, you even wanted to put in some of your own money. And now, just as we're about to start on the foundations, you're telling me we can't go on!

Ọba Sáyédèrò I know how you must feel, believe me. I spent the whole night agonizing over it, before sending you the message. But it's not me, can't you see? Everywhere there are growing complaints—

Ayíbí Rubbish, Deoye...er, sorry, Kabiyesi. But it's absolute nonsense. Complaints indeed! Is that what will stop me! When have we ever attempted anything new in this town without someone or other stirring up some agitation against it?

Ọba Sáyédèrò This time, especially after the visit of the chiefs, I could not disregard what the people are saying. And this morning again, when I called the Ilumesi—

Ayíbí The traditional Council, without me?

Ọba Sáyédèrò It had to be without you, Ayíbí, since you were to be the subject of discussion.

Ayíbí I see! So what did they say?

Ọba Sáyédèrò You can guess I'm sure. Tobacco is dangerous to human health. All over the world now, except in the non-Western and developing countries, smoking is being banned, because it leads to cancer. In the US, where your partners are coming from, major tobacco companies are closing down, because of the cost of litigation they are facing from tobacco victims...

Ayíbí Enough, it's the familiar, old story. What did you tell them?

Ọba Sáyédèrò What could I say? It's the truth, isn't it?

Ayíbí You see why I should have been at the meeting! Paranoia and propaganda, the white man's disease! That's all it is! Is it not in their nature to panic and exaggerate every little thing into apocalypse? Let someone sneeze, and the white man immediately sees a brewing flu epidemic! Cough, and every one in the neighbourhood rushes to the hospital to take a polio shot! That's their nature, to live in permanent hysteria, they can afford it. But are we, who are still developing, who need all the resources we can find, are we to start imitating this kind of obsession, and start discriminating about the investments we can get? Can a starving beggar afford to turn his nose at cash however dirty! Listen, let me remind you our grandparents have been using tobacco for ages, without dying of it! Grandma, our own grandmother, you remember how she could not let a day pass without that bit of tobacco powder under her tongue. But she lived for well over a hundred years, didn't she!

Ọba Sáyédèrò Yes, I know, she did. But suppose she was just lucky? What of the numerous others who never made it, who used to die prematurely? Suppose it was tobacco poisoning that killed them? How do we know, especially as, in those days, we didn't have these scientific ways of finding out?

Ayíbí Science! I'm talking of evidence you lived with, that you saw with your own eyes! And I'm talking of employment, of jobs—

Ọba Sáyédèrò Many of our people don't believe that, I'm afraid. They think you're only talking of profit, the money you're going to make—

Ayíbí Oh is that it? Even if it's so, it'll be profit for everybody, isn't it? Think of the difference an injection of so many dollars of investment will mean for the town.

Ọba Sáyédèrò And the pollution that will follow, how many dollars will it cost to deal with it? What price shall we have to pay for the potential invalids? Listen, my dear brother, I know how painful it all must be, this decision that I've taken. But we cannot always put money before everything. We must think of the future of our people.

Ayíbí Ah, sweet words! Just since when did that start being your headache, Kabiyesi?

Ọba Sáyédèrò All my life, and you know it! Even before I ascended the throne, the well-being and future of our people have always been my topmost concern! Look, my dear brother, forgive me, but—

Ayíbí It's really you, isn't it, Deoye? It's you who are against the project? Not some fictive conclave of chiefs or anything. But you! You!

Ọba Sáyédèrò I don't know what you mean—

Ayíbí Confess, Deoye! You've never been happy about my success, have you? Ever since I went into business, and grew rich, you've never been at ease, have you? Confess! Yet it's not as if I've not tried to help you against your indolence! I've given you shares here and there, all free of charge, without your having to pay a single kobo! But that has not helped kill your envy! Even when kingmakers approached me to offer me the crown yes, it's the truth, go and ask them! When they came to ask me to mount the throne, I declined, and deferred to you, because you're the older and by custom the throne belonged to you. But all that is still not enough to satisfy you. You'll not be happy till I'm reduced to zero, to a beggar grovelling in the sand!

Ọba Sáyẹ́dẹ̀rọ̀ You're angry, so you don't know what you're saying. I'll let you leave now and—

Ayíbí No, just listen! For it's finished, you hear? Finished, all that pretence between us! All that trying to appease you and make friends with you! War! That's what you want, and I'm going to give it to you! And I'll tell you right now, whether you approve it or not, that factory is going to be built!

Ọba Sáyẹ́dẹ̀rọ̀ Is it? Well, listen to me too, it's not only you that can shout and foam! So I'm indolent and jealous of your wealth! Thank you! So you made money and are rich! Thank you again! Congratulations! But let me tell you, I'd rather be poor, poorer even than a rat, than make money the way you do, on the blood of your own people! Oh I know it does not matter to you how many people die, or what the rest have to endure, as long as your profit swells in the bank. It doesn't matter the number of roads you abandon, after you've collected your money upfront! Or the hospitals not built, the housing projects uncompleted. It's all the same to you, as long you make your own loot out of it. That's what you boast about, that's how you grow rich! And you think that, but for my position here, as king, able to protect you, you think the people would not have found a way of dealing with you by now—

Ayíbí Ah-ha! So that's your plan! You're threatening violence, to send assassins after me perhaps—!

Ọba Sáyẹ́dẹ̀rọ̀ Who talked about assassins? You see how your mind works! But you just go on about that factory, and you'll see! You'll learn that an Ọba also has many means at his disposal to protect his people.

Ayíbí I am not a child, Deoye, to be frightened by such words.

Ọba Sáyẹ́dẹ̀rọ̀ Go now. But just remember that it's going to be over my dead body, you hear. That factory will be built here only over my dead body!

Ayíbí All right. So be it then!

[*As he storms out, end of flashback. The* **Mask** *returns to face* **Létò**]

Mask That was the quarrel, Létò. After that, your father should have been vigilant. But somehow I still believed my brother incapable of going beyond certain limits to get what he wanted…and so one day, while I was drinking at the palace, some potent poison was poured into my glass. That was how my life was cut short! And the murderer played his game well, married your mother and built his factory. I've not been at peace since…

Létò Poor father…

Mask I cannot be at peace, till I can rightly join the ancestors I've been placed now only in the corner reserved for potsherds! I won't leave there to rightly join the ancestors until my death has been properly avenged. Létò, you're my only salvation now! Avenge me! [*Beginning to go*] Avenge me! Avenge me!...

Létò Father, wait! Wait!

[*His shout brings* **Ìyámọdẹ** *running in.*]

Ìyámọdẹ Prince! Prince! What happened? You look dazed.

Létò Avenge me, he said! Ah!

Ìyámọdẹ Who?

Létò My father!... What a story! And what a task he's given me! Ìyámọdẹ, I am dazed! I beg you, promise not to mention this meeting to anybody. At least till I say so. You promise me, don't you?

Ìyámọdẹ *(Doubtfully)* Well

[**Mask** *reappears, but apparently invisible to* **Ìyámọdẹ**]

Mask Make her swear!

Létò Swear!

Ìyámọdẹ Swear?

Mask She's faithful, but still, let her swear by Ogun, or you'll never trust her word. The murderer has his ears everywhere.

Létò Well, if that's what you wish—

Mask No one is to be trusted, son!

Létò All right father. It shall be done as you wish.

Ìyámọdẹ Whom are you talking to? Are you all right, Prince? What did the mask tell you?

Létò Swear, Ìyámọdẹ. By Ogun!!

Ìyámọdẹ Swear what?

Létò Never to reveal what you saw here! [*Seizes some piece of iron and holds it to her mouth*] Swear!

Ìyámọdẹ All right, all right, Ọmọba, I swear!

[**Ìyámọdẹ** *swears. Enter* **Túndùn**]

Túndùn Létò! Oh my dear Létò!

Létò You! What are you doing here?

Túndùn I was told you're back and—

Létò Go Túndùn, quickly. We'll talk later.

Túndùn I've been searching for you everywhere!

Létò Please, Túndùn. Not here, not now!

Túndùn But—

Létò Look, if you won't go, I will. See you later!

[*Goes.* **Túndùn**, *puzzled and hurt, moves to follow, but is stopped by* **Ìyámọdẹ**.]

Ìyámọdẹ What recklessness drove you, girl? You were born here, you know the rules about this place!

Túndùn [*Falling on her knees*] Please forgive me, Yeye. You know, it's the very first time I'll see him since his return!

Ìyámọdẹ And so?

Túndùn I was desperate, I just couldn't wait any more!

Ìyámọdẹ And so you chose to defile the sleep of the dead?

Túndùn I am sorry, Iyámode, please beg the dead for me!

Ìyámọdẹ As easy as that, eh? You fool! Because you 'couldn't wait any more' you decided to contaminate yourself and put a curse on your head?

Túndùn I'm really sorry—

Ìyámọdẹ Now you may never live long enough to be married, don't you know? Or if you marry, you'll never have an offspring! Which do you choose? An early death, or the pain of barrenness?

Túndùn Neither, Yeye! Neither! I am on my knees! Please take that curse off my head! You're a woman too, you should understand! How I've missed him!

Ìyámọdẹ Is it me you need to beg, or the ancestors whose heads you have turned into your footmat?

Túndùn Please intercede on my behalf! Please, Yeye, I'm your daughter...

Ìyámọdẹ Oh what have you done! You of all people! Go now, run! I need to be alone with the dead, before their anger swallows us all. Go. But you must return soon for the rites of cleansing! Go!

[*Lights*]

SIX

[*Enter* **Ophelia**, *half-clad, her eyes wild, and with flowers, preferably hyacinths, in her hair. She is singing:*
'*How should I your true love know*
From another one?
By his cockle and staff
and his sandal...'
Hamlet *appears*]

Hamlet You're not ... going to start that again?

Ophelia Are you scared?

Hamlet It was not a pleasant experience, you know, watching you drown.

Ophelia So don't watch it.

Hamlet But why must you go through it again? Is it necessary at all?

Ophelia Not to you perhaps. But to her.

Hamlet Túndùn?

Ophelia Yes, I need to warn her. She too is about to be ruined by love.

Hamlet What of Létò himself then? Do you consider what he too much be going through?

Ophelia That's his business, not mine. Or maybe yours. So, if you'll please excuse me? I have an important meeting coming up.

[*Hamlet hesitates, but then agrees to withdraw as* **Túndùn** *enters*]

Túndùn He wouldn't talk to me!

Ophelia Yes I know.

Túndùn I waited, oh how I waited! Dreaming of him. Denying myself. And now I have gone and damned myself, entering the forbidden shrine.

But he still won't speak to me.

Ophelia He's off to see his mother.

Túndùn That slut! Excuse me.

Ophelia I understand. That's what people thought too, of Hamlet's mother. But she's still his mother.

Túndùn Eh, do you think… do you think that's why he won't see me?

Ophelia I don't understand.

Túndùn Suppose that's why? That he thinks that we, women are all like her? That, we too, we have no fidelity? Ah, Ophelia, suppose that's why he doesn't wish to see me?

Ophelia Then it's your duty to show him you're different, isn't it?

Túndùn He won't give me a chance!

Ophelia He has a great burden on his mind.

Túndùn He can share it with me! If he still loves me, why won't he share his problems with me?

Ophelia Just be careful, Túndùn. Look at me, and learn from my plight! Whatever happens, don't let them make you lose your mind! Please.

Túndùn I'll try. Thank you. I'll be strong.

Ophelia And don't forget, you must go back soon to Ìyámọdẹ for the rites of purgation.

Túndùn I promise, I will.

Ophelia Here comes the queen.

Túndùn [*curtseying*] Ẹ wẹ́sóo, Olorì.

Olorì My son! Where's my son?

Túndùn I thought … I thought he'd gone to see you.

Olorì Me?

Túndùn He walked off just now in the direction of the palace.

Olorì Did he… did he say anything?

Túndùn No, ma. He wouldn't talk to me.

Olorì Nor to me either. What could be troubling him?

[*Létò re-appears*]

Létò You know, mother!

Olorì Ah Létò!

Létò How could you, with my father's body still fresh in the grave?

Olorì [*To* **Túndùn** *and* **Ophelia**] Excuse us.

Túndùn Létò, you still won't talk to me?

Létò [*Impatiently*] Later, Túndùn! I've told you, later.

Túndùn When? We haven't talked even once since you returned.

Létò Yes, I know, and I'm sorry. But, it can't be now.

Túndùn When then? Give me a definite time and I'll come to.

Létò You heard the Queen, Túndùn. Excuse us!

Túndùn Is it something I've done? Something they told you?

Létò Why not just wait? Go away now.

Ophelia Come. Come with me.

[*Túndùn collapses on the shoulders of* **Ophelia**. *They go out*]

Olorì So that's the problem then?

Létò I need an explanation. Surely, at your age, it can't be love or passion!

Olorì And why not, young man? What do you know about age, or passion?

Létò Was it all pretence then, all that show you put up with my father while he was alive, only to rush so disgracefully into his brother's arms?

Olorì Rush! Disgrace! Are you forgetting then, Létò, that it's our tradition? When a king dies, all the wives, automatically, pass on to his successor.

Létò Not you! You could have refused.

Olorì And where would that have left me? Or you?

Létò What do you mean by that?

Olorì Your mother had no choice, Létò.

Létò Everyone always has a choice

Olorì Not if one has been foolish, like your mother.

Létò Foolish?

Olorì Yes, foolishness! That's what it turns out to be in the end, unfortunately. I've learnt that now. When you have allowed love to grow like a noose around your neck, you pay dearly for it afterwards.

Létò You're still talking in riddles, Olorì.

Olorì Ah, my son, do you think it has been easy? I spent all my married life doting on your father as you said. Caring for him. Helping him to be a good king. I didn't think of anything else but only of him, and him alone! Who could see the future then? I spent every moment with him, and on him. I never thought of myself, or of my personal needs. And then, one afternoon, after he'd been drinking with his friends, he came back home, and collapsed in my arms! Just like that, one moment talking, and the next moment silence! A deep and cold silence, where he was sitting by me. No noise, no cry of pain, he was just suddenly still dead! Dead! Dead! With no consideration for me, or for you, just dead! And I, just sitting there, alone…

Létò Yes? Then what happened?

Olorì In the days that followed, I came to know the terrible price of love! Oh they made me pay for it, all the women of the palace! All the men who used to depend on us, his brothers, the men he called his friends and kinsmen! Now their words, their actions, were like whips lashing at me, lashing me out of my dreams! Létò, I came to know with great shock that, not only does a dead man have no friends, but his widow too inherits nothing but a battle with parasites!

Létò Go on, I'm listening.

Olorì I was not the only widow, of course, as you know. But I was the closest to him, the one he loved most, and did they punish me for it! But to cut the story short, I found, to my bitter surprise, that I was the only wife who had not thought of providing for myself, while he was alive. Now that he was dead, and all the vultures came clawing at us, I was the only wife who had nothing! Absolutely nothing of my own to protect myself! Not even a separate bank account, no property anywhere, no house of my own. Love had so blinded me, I'd not made provision at all for myself—or even for you! Ah, I was not thinking of death! Whereas the other wives had been more calculating, less reckless and less foolish! Each had all regularly, secretly, put something aside for herself, had not trusted her life or her future so blindly to love. But I alone, I'd wanted nothing for myself, even though, to be fair to your father, he did ask me, many times. But I always said no, that he should not speak of such things. That it was not for his property that I loved him! But now, he was gone, suddenly, and I was left, naked on the deck, the storm rising around me! Létò, I was going to be driven away from the palace with only my empty hands!

Létò His will? He made no will?

Olorì Not him! You should know your father. His faith in life was so robust that he never had time for such things! He was going to write his will of course. But tomorrow, always tomorrow! He was strong, he was in his prime, and he glowed with energy like one of our bronze carvings! How could we have known that death was stalking so close, waiting in ambush for him?

Létò And so you agreed to be passed on to his successor! Like a shirt or a piece of rag.

Olorì Yes, a rag! That's truly what I'd become! Torn, tattered and desperate! Broken by grief, and all alone, I was scared to my bones about the days that would follow.

Létò You could not have waited for me?

Olorì What could you have done, my poor son? What can you do? Besides, there was no time to wait When the family met to decide, you were far away in England, your address unknown. I had to choose on the spot. Son, maybe I am not strong, but I opted to have a shelter on my head, to keep these clothes on my back, and to give you a home.

Létò Still he made you his Olorì, and you agreed!

Olorì Yes. It's never happened before! The same woman, to be Olorì to two successive kings! One day in total desperation, and the next, the favourite of the palace, again! It was a generosity I never dreamt possible! Kabiyesi has been kind to me, and I've kept a good place for you! It would be remarkably ungrateful of me not to respond.

Létò But what if I told you now that he killed my father?

Olorì What nonsense are you talking, Létò?

Létò Your husband, mother, he killed my father! All that gushing kindness, it's just a ploy to salvage his conscience!

Olorì Careful, Létò! Ssssh! That's not a joke, you know!

Létò I tell you, he's a murderer, mother! He was the one who put poison in my father's drink!

Olorì Softly, I said! Poison! Where on earth did you hear that?

Létò It's true, mother! Ask him!

Olorì Ask him! Are you out of your mind?

Létò I mean it! Let's ask him together!

Olorì No, say no more! Look, my son, such talk is dangerous, I'm telling you!

Létò I have the proof!

Olorì You do!

Létò My father himself came and spoke to me!

Olorì Your father!

Létò Yes, last night in the bàrà.

Olorì You went into the bàrà.

Létò Ìyámọdẹ agreed to take me there.

Olorì And your father spoke to you! He himself!

Létò His spirit. Ìyámọdẹ invoked his spirit.

Olorì Ah! [*Sighs*] Létò, my son, be careful. Be very careful. I know about the politics here, and I know about these invocations by Ìyámọdẹ! We women are not allowed into the bàrà, it's true, but your father used to tell me about what goes on at these rituals. I know how voices are planted behind mats, and made to speak through bamboo pipes…

Létò Mother! You don't believe? Or you just don't want to believe?

Olorì My poor son! You need a rest very badly, I can see. The grief has obviously affected you far more than I imagined. Now I fear for your life. You need protection very urgently. I'll send for the babalawo immediately—

Létò Wait, mother—

Olorì No, let Baba Aṣípa attend to you first. Come with me—

Létò No!

Olorì It's urgent, don't you understand? He must—

Létò No, I said! Leave me alone!

Olorì You won't come? Then I'll go straightaway to fetch him. Afterwards we'll see.

[*She rushes out. **Létò** is now torn by doubt.*]

Létò Can she be right? But I saw him, heard him! And he showed me their bitter argument! Could all that have been faked? Oh what is the truth?

[***Hamlet** appears*]

Hamlet Wèsóo, Létò.

Létò Wèsóo, Hamlet.

Hamlet You know, it was the same doubts I had.

Létò 'To be or not to be?'

Hamlet 'To be or not to be?'

Létò No, that is not the question, Hamlet. That is an evasion.

Hamlet Still, you ask yourself was it all a hallucination?

Létò Yes, suppose the whole show was a set-up? Suppose Ìyámọdẹ is only an agent after all of some forces I am yet to discover?

Hamlet Doubt, that's what paralyses action. The need to be sure, and be just.

Létò Yes. Oh God!

Hamlet Just the same dilemma I faced. But it's no use calling on God.

Létò So what did you do? Don't tell me, I know.

Hamlet I arranged a play to find out.

Létò Just what I am going to do too. Come with me.

[*Lights*]

SEVEN

[**Ophelia,** *singing, leads* **Túndùn** *across*]

Túndùn This was where you drowned.

Ophelia In a river, like this.

Túndùn For the love of a man!

[**Ophelia** *does not answer*]

Túndùn On our continent, we do not die because of a heartbreak. We just weather the storm, till the climate changes.

Ophelia On your continent! You are sure?

Túndùn And the climate always changes. With time one heals.

Ophelia Perhaps you women here are stronger than us.

Túndùn Or perhaps it's just that our passion is weaker. We don't believe in the absolute.

Ophelia But God? You believe in God?

Túndùn God is much too distant, you see. To reach him, our priests must go through his servants, the lesser deities. That helps to cushion the shock.

Ophelia And kill the passion? Tone it down?

Túndùn Perhaps. But not the passion alone. It also helps to weaken despair.

Ophelia How lucky! I remember my father. Always be true to yourself, he said. Truth is neither black nor white. If you love, be pure.

Túndùn But surely, truth wears many colours!

Ophelia Not in the house of my father.

Túndùn He was a saint?

Ophelia No. Just a simple, honest man.

Túndùn My father didn't talk much to me. But one day, I remember, he took me to the forest. It was shortly after a big storm, and many trees had fallen. See, said my father, they were the ones which resisted the wind. Then he pointed to the reeds standing and dancing in the sun. Those, he said, were the ones which learnt to bend to the season. In life, one always has a choice.

Ophelia So we all like to believe, isn't it? But what will you do now?

Túndùn How do I know? I am frightened, Ophelia!

Ophelia Frightened?

Túndùn Because... [*She breaks down, sobbing*]. Because I cannot be like my father, you see. I cannot bend like the reeds to survive.

Ophelia You love Létò that much?

Túndùn I can't help it.

Ophelia　Then, you're doomed, my friend. Like me.

Túndùn　I'm going to drown too?

Ophelia　Men have no kindness. They use us and dump us. But without them, we'll shrivel, and die. Wipe your tears.

Túndùn　Do you have a cigarette?

Ophelia　You smoke?

Túndùn　Only when I need to calm my nerves.

Ophelia　And your health? Tobacco is dangerous, or don't you know?

Túndùn　So is love. And I don't know which is worse! [*Both laugh, briefly*]. See, he has no time to talk to me. But he's rehearsing a play! With Àdùkẹ́!

Ophelia　Do you trust him?

Túndùn　I did once. Now I don't know. He's turned strange.

Ophelia　Come with me. Let's go to the play. You won't drown, I promise. Not if I can help it.

[*They go. Lights.*]

EIGHT

[*Létò is giving final instructions to his actors.*]

Létò　Baba Ọ̀jẹ̀ and you Àdùkẹ́! Here's where you'll do your dance. And Hamlet, you enter from that side. You all know what to do.

All　Yes.

Létò　All right, to your places. Our royal guests will soon be arriving. Good luck!

[*Enter **Túndùn**, with **Ophelia**.*]

Túndùn　Létò!

Létò　Ah, you've come too! Well, we'll talk, after the play. I promise!

[*Túndùn makes to protest, but **Ophelia** pulls her to a seat. Enter **Ọba Ayíbí**, and some chiefs*].

Ọba Ayíbí　Létò, our son. Your actors are set?

Létò　All ready to go, Kabiyesi! Now you're here. I'll give the word for them to start. [*Goes*]

Ọba Ayíbí　I don't quite see the purpose of this play, Olorì. But well, I hope it will be entertaining. And since you say it will help restore his spirits, we are ready to play along.

Olorì　Thank you, Kabiyesi, for coming. I know you'll do anything for me. As for entertainment, I am sure there will be plenty of it.

Ọba Ayíbí　You've seen the play?

Olorì　No. But I'm willing to put my bet on it. Remember the prince was not only once the best dancer here but his troupe also won our championships!

Ọba Ayíbí　Yes, you're right! Quite a remarkable talent in those days!

Olorì　In fact, to confess, he was actually the one who came to me with the idea. And I was so astonished that I accepted at once! I mean, after all the days of brooding and acrimony! I was so pleased that he was now ready to amuse himself at last that I accepted to bring his invitation to your majesty.

Ọba Ayíbí Well here he comes. It seems the play's about to begin.

[**Létò**, *costumed as a theatre impresario, appears and takes a bow*]

Létò Your majesty, chiefs, dear brothers and sisters, we are honoured to present this dance drama to you! It is, we admit, the fruit of only a few days' rehearsals and is still full of imperfections. But we hope you will forgive us, for, we promise, we'll do our best to entertain you. So please sit back, relax now, and enjoy yourselves…

[*He stands aside, to join the company of* **Ophelia** *and* **Túndùn**.]

Túndùn What's the story about? Or we are not allowed to ask?

Hamlet It's the story of two friends and a woman, wife of one of them. The husband dies, poisoned, and then the second man comes to propose to the widow. Watch what follows.

Now Follows THE MASQUE OF BETRAYED LOVE

The three actors **Ọ̀jẹ̀**, **Àdùkẹ́** *and* **Hamlet** *dance in, bow and go out, amidst applause. Then two of them* **Ọ̀jẹ̀** *and* **Àdùkẹ́** *dance in, in full costume, with* **Ọ̀jẹ̀** *wearing a crown of feathers. It is a dance of courtship, and the two are obviously lovers.*

They sing, to the tune of 'Ẹ má tori mí, rèé jàajà kú…'][13]

Àdùkẹ́	Emi ti ṛokọ
	Maa sin kalẹ
	E wa ba mi yo
	Emi ti ṛokọ
	Maa sin kalẹ o!
Ọ̀jẹ̀	Eli ti raya
	Iyawo lọsingin
	Emi ti raya
	Emi ti raya
	Iyawo ododo o!
Àdùkẹ́	Ẹni o mọ
	Baye ti ndune
	Ko wọkọ lọ /2ce
	Emi ti ṛokọ
	Emi ti ṛokọ
	Ife dun joyin o.
Ọ̀jẹ̀	Aya mi ṣọra
	Ifẹ ndoṣuka o
	Ifẹ o lokun
	Ifẹ o lokun
	Ọta pọ laye o / 2ce
Both	Gbogbo iji
	To ba wu ko ja

---

[13] Please don't kill each other fighting over me.

> *Lalakoro / 2ce*
> *Ko s'ohunkohun*
> *Ko s'ohunkohun*
> *To le ya wa se ọ!*[14]

[*He sits down, exhausted. She signals that she will go and fetch him something to drink. He lies down, sleeps. Music changes. Now* **Hamlet,** *in a jacket draped with the labels of different cigarette and tobacco companies, dances in, a large cigar in his mouth. He carries a crown of lit cigars. Taking the feather crown off the head of the sleeping* **Ọ̀jẹ̀,** *he replaces it with a cigar crown, and holds* **Ọ̀jẹ̀** *down forcefully as the latter begins to cough and struggle. The struggle is marked by a grotesque dance, as* **Ọ̀jẹ̀** *fights to throw off the crown, is finally defeated, falls and expires.*

Àdùkẹ́ *returns, and sees what has happened. She runs to* **Ọ̀jẹ̀,** *but is held back by Hamlet. As she begins to mourn, Hamlet brings out a chain of glittering glass beads, drapes it round her neck. She marvels, begins to show interest.*

Smiling, he brings out a sheaf of dollar bills, shows her, then retreats from her. He signals for her to come and take it. She approaches, at first hesitantly, then more certain, and dances towards him. He gives her the dollars, she springs into his arms.

In the audience, the Ọba *rises abruptly, and leaves, followed hastily by attendants, etc.*]

Voices The king! Kabiyesi! Kabiyesi!

[*Lights return to normal*]

Túndùn Létò, what have you done?

[**Létò,** *still in a state of shock, does not answer.*]

Ophelia [*Pulling her away*]. Come, Túndùn! Come quickly now!

[*They go, leaving* **Hamlet** *and* **Létò** *alone on stage*].

Hamlet Will you kill him now?

Létò Hamlet, there's no doubt any more, he's the murderer!

Hamlet You will kill him?

Létò I must. Will you help me?

Hamlet Me!

Létò I've never killed before.

Hamlet But must you?

Létò My father—

Hamlet Is dead. The obligations he's demanding, should they be stronger than those you owe the living?

Létò That was your problem, wasn't it? Your cowardice?

Hamlet Conscience sometimes looks like cowardice.

Létò You're trying to weaken my will, you my friend?

Hamlet History doesn't always have to follow the same pattern.

Létò You're asking me to abandon my father then? To let him continue to suffer like that, in the purgatory of potsherds?

Hamlet He doesn't have to.

---

[14] See glossary on pp. 183–4 for the English version of the songs.

Létò No?

Hamlet No. He can also be rescued by your generosity.

Létò But what are you saying! That I should just turn my back on his murder?

Hamlet I mean that restitution can come in other forms than that of vengeance. The future does not have to be built on the crimes of the past, if there is a genuine repentance.

Létò You've seen signs of that?

Hamlet Speak to him first.

Létò About what? It's death everywhere, can't you see, from him and people like him? Not only my father, or the numerous casualties that will follow. Even our forests! Look at the farmlands they've had to tear down with their bulldozers, the plants that have died and are dying, the animals driven from their homes! Our land is dying because of tobacco and similar projects that our rich men are bringing from abroad in the name of modernisation!

Hamlet The world does not stand still. Nor can you—

[*Suddenly, they are surrounded by guards, led by **Aṣípa**.*]

Aṣípa The Kabiyesi. He wants an audience with you, Létò.

Létò He sent you?

Aṣípa Yes. He said so you won't think it's a trap.

Létò [*Looks at **Hamlet**, who nods*]. All right, I'll come with you, Baba Aṣípa. [*Lights.*]

NINE

[*Palace courtyard. **Létò** is brought to **Ọba Ayíbí**.*]

Létò You sent for me, Kabiyesi?

Ọba Ayíbí Yes, I think we should talk.

Létò I'm listening.

Ọba Ayíbí [*Nods for **Aṣípa** to go*]. Thank you, Baba Aṣípa.

Létò [*Mock salute*]. Kabiyesi!

Ọba Ayíbí This childish game you're playing, Létò, what's it for?

Létò You should tell me, Kabiyesi. What game you played to win your crown.

Ọba Ayíbí Ah, so it's true then. You do believe I killed your father, that was why you put up the ridiculous show!

Létò Deny it.

Ọba Ayíbí [*After a pause.*] Here, take this. [*Offers a pistol.*]

Létò What for?

Ọba Ayíbí Me and you, we're going to talk. And afterwards, if you still believe I killed your father, use it.

Létò I won't need it.

Ọba Ayíbí I'll place it here, where you can reach it. So, my own brother, why do you believe I would kill him?

Létò You tell me, Kabiyesi.

Ọba Ayíbí For the crown? Or for your mother?

Létò We know you won't kill for a woman, Kabiyesi.

Ọba Ayíbí For the crown then? Listen, I'll tell you something you don't know. When our father died, I was the one the kingmakers first asked to ascend the throne.

Létò I'm shocked, but not surprised.

Ọba Ayíbí You know why? Because of my wealth. Yes! Because of my money, they were ready to damn the tradition, and by-pass the eldest son. Their argument? That the town requires modernisation, and only a rich and daring businessman like me could help accomplish that. My brother was only a civil servant, they said. He knew nothing about business, or investments, or politics. He was a good man, they admitted, but too timid! He would not know how to kick awake the stagnant life of our community. And that even if he did, he would not have the means. So they came and pleaded with me to mount the throne—

Létò And you said no—

Ọba Ayíbí I said no. I said I could not do that as long as my brother was alive. I said he had to be king, because he was older than me, and that's what our tradition demanded. But I made them a promise however. I said I would stand by him and assist as best as I could. I gave my word that I would help him fulfil their wishes for modernisation and industrialisation. All the time your father reigned, I swear to you, I kept that promise. You were away, but ask anyone you know. Ask your mother. I stood by both of them, all through to the end. I wanted him to succeed because, for me, his success or failure would not be his alone, but that of our whole family, of all of us! So how could I have killed him?

Létò You talk well, Kabiyesi. You speak so persuasively of your allegiance to my father. But what about your other allegiance?

Ọba Ayíbí What do you mean?

Létò I mean your allegiance to wealth? Given the choice between making profit, and loving your brother, what side would you take, Kabiyesi?

Ọba Ayíbí [*Stung*].That question's an insult, Létò. Words too big for your mouth.

Létò You were the one who brought me here to talk.

Ọba Ayíbí Yes, but talk like a well-bred young man! I'm your uncle, and I'm also the Kabiyesi. You were taught in this very house how to show respect.

Létò Not to murderers!

Ọba Ayíbí That dirty mouth of yours! I can have it shut for ever, you know! You ant, you dare to call me names!

Létò Oh! I don't doubt your powers. But I don't fear you, Kabiyesi. I call you the names you deserve! I'm not afraid of you! If it wasn't because of money, and if you loved my father that much, why would you disagree so violently with him over the tobacco factory you've brought here?

Ọba Ayíbí Ah there it is at last! You've obviously been listening to rumours, and allowed your mind to be poisoned by mischief makers. Yes, your father did not agree with me over the siting of the tobacco factory here. But how would that be sufficient reason to kill him?

Létò Money, Kabiyesi! It's always been your single creed, the only god you worship! Ever since I was growing up! Yes! With that kind of obsession you can do anything! Whatever stands in the way of your making another pile is to be wiped out! Whoever threatens your investments! All these sanctimonious words won't wash, Kabiyesi! You're a murderer!

Ọba Ayíbí Something's definitely gone wrong with you, Létò! To dare to talk to me in those tones! I don't know what happened to you in that place you're coming from, but see the way you're talking! Clearly it's affected your mind! I don't think you can be left to roam around by yourself any more. You've become dangerous even to yourself ...

Létò Just say you're afraid, that's all! You're frightened I will expose you and let the people see your smelling backside ...

Ọba Ayíbí My—! You have really lost your mind then—

Létò Murderer! You should be facing the hangman, not sitting on the throne!

Ọba Ayíbí Me! [*Incensed*]. Take then, you lunatic! Take it! [*Forces the gun into his hand*]. Take it and shoot, madman! Shoot, I command you! Avenge your father! What are you waiting for! Dog! [*Hits him*]. If you have the courage, shoot! Shoot now!

Létò [*Fighting back, but cowed*]. Leave me! Leave me alone, you killer!

Ọba Ayíbí [*Hitting him*]. Afraid? Answer me! [*Forces the gun against his own chest*.] Why are you afraid, fool? Shoot, I say! Sho-o-o-t! I am your father's killer! Kill me, if you dare! Sho-o-o-o-t!

[*The gun goes off. Confused, out of his mind, Létò keeps shooting till the gun stops, bullets spent. Guards have run in.*]

Ọba Ayíbí You see? [*Taking the gun from him*]. I knew I couldn't trust you. That's why I filled it with blanks. [*To guards*]. Arrest him! He tried to kill the king.

[*Lights*]. [*Intermission suggested here.*]

TEN

[*Palace courtyard, near the palace cell. **Túndùn** and **Guard**.*]

Guard Wait here, I'll bring him out.

[***Túndùn** begins to wander about, obviously anxious. Suddenly, the sound of drums and festivity. She clutches her head, screaming and reeling.*]

Túndùn No, no! I don't want to remember! He-e-l-p!

[*But all the same, lights change swiftly, into a flashback: The figure of **Létò**, somewhat younger, appears, in dancing mask, as he was many years before, on one of the community's Nights of Courtship. This is a ceremony arranged every three years for young men and women, presumed to be virgins, who have reached the age of puberty. He sees **Túndùn**, also masked.*]

Létò [*Stopping short*]. What, you here?

Túndùn Yes. I came to see you.

Létò But you left here only a short while ago!

Túndùn I know.

Létò The other girls must be at the square already. You can hear the drums.

Túndùn Yes. And the boys too.

Létò So we're late and—?

Túndùn I won't be going again.

Létò You won't be going to the dance!

Túndùn No, I'm no longer dancing.

Létò But... it's our Night of Courtship! You can't stay away!

Túndùn I can, if I don't have a lover.

Létò If you don't have a—! Come, what's this about? What about me?

Túndùn Yes, tell me, what about you?

Létò Look, what kind of question is this?

Túndùn You've been lying to me, Létò. All the time promising to marry me, leading me on. Whereas you're going away.

Létò Oh is that it!

Túndùn Tomorrow at dawn. Mother told me, just now. You're going away to England.

Létò All right, Túndùn, just calm down and listen to me—

Túndùn Is it a lie?

Létò Let me exp—

Túndùn Is it a lie? Answer me!

Létò No. It's not a lie.

Túndùn You see!

Létò But, believe me, I was going to tell you myself.

Túndùn When?

Létò After the dance.

Túndùn You see! Thank you!

Létò Please, listen—

Túndùn After the dance! Thank you very much! After I would have committed myself, and got engaged to you. Then you will disappear. And what happens to me? I become the laughing stock of the entire community!

Létò No, Túndùn, that's not how—

Túndùn I thank you very much, I said! It's the fruit of my own indiscretion, so I'll bear it. They warned me, many times, you know. Different people came to me on various occasions to warn me about you. They said you're a prince, and I am only a poor common girl. They said we're oil and water, and can never mix. They reminded me that it is the habit of princes to use girls like me and then dump us. But I did not listen. Because my heart was beating wildly every time I saw you. Fluttering foolishly like a butterfly every time I heard your voice, felt your touch. Poor me, all my fences fell down, and... ah, you just walked over me. But... but it's all right, prince. [*She is crying*]. I am young, and I will heal… So goodbye to you…

[*She begins to go. He runs to stop her.*]

Létò Túndùn! Will you at least listen to me?

Túndùn No. Let me go! The earlier I begin to put my life together—

Létò I love you!

Túndùn Yes, the very words that led me astray.

Létò I don't want to lose you. Please believe me.

Túndùn Believe you, when you are going away?

Létò I'll come back, I swear!

Túndùn When?

Létò I… I don't know.

Túndùn You see!

Létò It won't be long, I promise.

Túndùn You will take me along then?

Létò I wish I could. But… it's a road I must travel alone.

Túndùn Go then. You don't need a wife.

Létò Not for this journey, no. But I will need you for my life afterwards. If you can wait.

Túndùn And suppose you never come back?

Létò I will, trust me. Because… Listen, what I am going for is precisely that kind of assurance. The assurance that henceforth, when we say we are happy, we will also be able to guarantee that our happiness will last.

Túndùn Now I'm totally confused. I don't understand.

Létò Words fail me, I confess. But, you see, it's like this… My father, as you know, is a just king. Everyone admits that he has ruled the land with wisdom and fairness. But still, with all that, we have not become a prosperous people, have we? So much poverty, so much unhappiness still everywhere! Not even my father has been able to purge his chiefs of corruption and greed. And as for our people, see, too many superstitions hold us down. Too many little rifts divide us. We are like a river that has spread into a lake and then grown stagnant. Soon, Túndùn, if we do nothing about it, we will decay, and die.

Túndùn Yes, you've said all this before.

Létò The signs of rot are already there, already spreading! Look at the misguided life our youths live, the rise of mindless violence on our streets, our gradual loss of faith in ourselves… Something has to be done! But what? Túndùn, we must discover new tributaries, new outlets of renewal. We must feed from fresh waters … but how?

Túndùn I don't know…

Létò Túndùn, the challenge is for us, for the youths of my generation, but unfortunately, we do not have the answers here. To find them, we must travel out to learn from others, from those who started earlier than us. You understand? That's why I am going away for now, before I settle down. Before the honey of marriage sucks me in too like a swamp. If I don't go now, I'll never make the journey again. Do you understand?

Túndùn So what are you saying... about us?

Létò Can you wait? Is your commitment strong enough?

Túndùn Prince, it was you came fishing in the muddy pond where I sat like a toad among my people, pulled me into strange waters, and gave me fins. Since that moment I first met you, my life has been like a dream. Tonight, if I go to the dance of courtship, and you dance towards me and place your garlands round my neck, I know I will never be able to say no. So tell me now, when I am still able to hold myself in check, should I go to the dance or not?

Létò Go, because of our future, my Olorì. Go and I will meet you there.

Túndùn Listen, the drums and the gongs are already calling! Do you say I should go and dance for you?

Létò Go and answer the drums! I am coming to join you. Yes, as soon as I finish my preparations, I am coming to catch the town's most beautiful maiden tonight! [*He runs out.*]

Túndùn [*Dancing*]. I'll wait for you! [*Excitedly, addressing her mother as if she is present*]. Mother, you're wrong! The Prince is mine, mine! He's not lying, he's going to marry me! Come, mother, make me up as you've always dreamt of doing, I must be the prettiest girl on the square tonight! Even the moon must be jealous! Ah, mother, see, my heart is dancing!...

[*She does another jig, as the music cuts off abruptly, to be replaced by the sound of chains. It takes a while for* **Túndùn** *to shake off the memory. And then she turns, to see* **Létò**, *in chains, being brought in by the* **Guard**. *The sight jolts her back to reality.*]

Túndùn Létò!

Létò They allowed you here?

Túndùn It took some arranging, yes. But here I am.

Létò Well?

Túndùn What's happening, Létò? What's the matter between you and the king?

Létò [*Showing chains*]. Do you still ask?

Túndùn But... what did you do?

Létò Not what I did, Túndùn, but what he knows I will do.

Túndùn I don't understand?

Létò I am going to kill him.

Túndùn Ehn? You are going to—what?

Létò That's why he chose to strike fast.

Túndùn You said—you're going to... to kill him, Létò!

Létò That man you see, Túndùn, don't trust his smiles! He's a most devious, most ruthless man. He killed my father!

Túndùn You mean, Ọba Sayédèrọ̀?

Létò Ayibi killed him and seized the throne. Then, to hide his crime, he tricked my mother to be his Olorì.

Túndùn What's all this story? What of...us? I've missed you, Létò!

Létò My father—

Túndùn Did you hear me? I said I've missed you. Terribly.

Létò I know. But you see—

Túndùn It was hard, waiting for you. All those long years. And you never wrote, even once!

Létò There'll be time for all that, Túndùn. Later, when I've settled this matter of my father. I'll be able to explain to you.

Túndùn Do you still love me?

Létò What a question!

Túndùn Answer me!

Létò Will the answer take these chains from my hands?

Túndùn In my heart, I've been bearing my own chains.

Létò It won't be for much longer, trust me. But frankly I am not in the mood now for that, Túndùn. A man has killed my father, and married my mother. And for what? Money! Just so he and his white friends could bring their tobacco company to our land. As long as my father was on the throne, they knew they could never have their way, because he was solidly opposed to starting such a venture here. They offered him all sorts of inducements, but he would not budge. So they put poison in his drink and got him out of the way. That's why my father died, Túndùn! Because of this tobacco business! Because his greedy brother could not resist the lure of a few more dollars in his pocket! And now he's got me too in chains!

Túndùn Does the Olorì know about all this?

Létò She doesn't believe. She is in love with him.

Túndùn Yes, I can understand that.

Létò At her age!

Túndùn There's no age, Létò, when it comes to the matter of love.

Létò You forget that I grew up knowing her with another man. And she swore she loved him too!

Túndùn Your voice, Létò! It frightens me!

Létò I must get out of here, to do what I must do! Will you help me.

Túndùn Tell me first, because I need to understand. Is this the reason then? Is this why you don't want me again?

Létò Oh Túndùn!

Túndùn I must know! The way you've been behaving, since you came back!

Létò I came back, and that very day, the truth came and hit me in the face! Like a brick! It shattered all my dreams, tore me into a chaos of different persons. I've been adrift since…

Túndùn I'll get you out of here, out of these chains.

Létò How?

Túndùn You'll see. Only, I need to be sure first. I've waited so long.

Létò I'm sorry. It should have been a sweet home-coming. That's what I was yearning for, but the scavengers had got here before me, and—

Túndùn I remember your words, when you were leaving. I remember your dreams. They were the companions that kept me sane all those years of your absence. Do you still love me? Say you still love me!

Lètò Túndùn, do I still deserve your love, the way I am now? A coward and—

Túndùn No, don't talk about yourself in such tones! Only say you're still mine, and I'll get you out of these chains, whatever it takes! I swear it to you! You're going to dance with me again, as before!

ELEVEN

[*A room in the palace.* **Ìyámǫdę** *and* **Aṣípa** *are having an audience with* **Ǫba Ayíbí**, *and have just presented him with an aróko.*]

Ǫba Ayíbí What's this?

Aṣípa It's from the town's chiefs and elders, Kabiyesi. They asked us to bring it to you.

Ǫba Ayíbí Well, what does it say?

Aṣípa Read it yourself, Kabiyesi.

Ǫba Ayíbí But you can tell us.

Ìyámǫdę Me! Kabiyesi, it's not the small rat that will show the vulture the tasty parts of meat.

Ǫba Ayíbí [*Amused*]. Ah but who's the small rat now? You, Aṣípa? Or you, Yeye?

Aṣípa Both of us, of course! And very small rats we are too, Kabiyesi, where you stand! It is true that the snail has horns, but can it perform the tasks of a cow!

Ìyámǫdę Your single wisdom, the whole world knows, can unravel the message much quicker than either of us. Read it yourself, Kabiyesi.

Ǫba Ayíbí All right, give it to me. [*Reads, as he unwinds the aróko*]: What's this? Ah, burnt thatch. Snake skin. Bone of a dog. Meaning, 'We do not set a fire to the house to catch a rat.' I see! [*Thinks*] Snakes. 'The snake dies because of the sins of his father, but it is the memory of his father's services that saves the dog.' Hm, what else? Two elephant carvings: 'When the animals bow to a young elephant, it is not because of his exploits, but those of his forebears.' Same thing. Thank you! This is what the elders sent to me?

Asípa Yes, Kabiyesi.

Ǫba Ayíbí Then go and tell them — We got the message. And we greet them.

Ìyámǫdę But your reply, Kabiyesi?

Ǫba Ayíbí We say we greet them. Is that not enough?

Aṣípa With all due respect, Kabiyesi, the chiefs and the elders, they did not send the two of us here to come and collect greetings.

Ǫba Ayíbí They didn't? You're sure you want to hear more?

Ìyámǫdę Of course, Kabiyesi.

Ǫba Ayíbí Then tell them — they don't know what they are saying! Tell them — their words are *isokuso!*

Ìyámọdẹ What, Kabiyesi!

Ọba Ayíbí Rubbish, yes! That is our response to their message!

Aṣípa With all due respects, Kabiyesi, who's to take that kind of answer to them?

Ọba Ayíbí Who brought that kind of message to us?

Ìyámọdẹ Kabiyesi, if only you'll be a bit patient—

Ọba Ayíbí No, we're not patient! Someone who tried to kill us! Three times too, or have you so quickly forgotten? He shot at us three times! But you tell me— 'We do not set fire to kill a rat!'

Ìyámọdẹ Yes, but—

Ọba Ayíbí He should not be punished, that's what your chiefs and elders are saying!

Aṣípa He's just a boy, that's what they are asking you to take into consideration. It's just an appeal.

Ìyámọdẹ Forgiveness, Kabiyesi, is always a higher virtue than vengeance.

Ọba Ayíbí Three times! But — snake skin! Elephant carvings! 'It's the memory of his father that saves the dog!'

Ìyámọdẹ As I said, if you'll just calm down for a moment, maybe—

Ọba Ayíbí You! Has any of you ever been at the end of an angry gun?

Ìyámọdẹ The gods forbid! *Kó ṣépè ré yẹ̀n wà, é ma ṣẹ!*[15] I hope never to be at—

Aṣípa I've been to war myself, Kabiyesi, so I know. It's not a pleasant experience at all, to have a gun, however small, shooting at you. But still, this particular gun, we heard, was filled with blanks.

Ọba Ayíbí But he didn't know that, did he! Nor has he ever denied that his intention was to kill!

Ìyámọdẹ No, Kabiyesi. And because of that, all of us share your anger and indignation. Still, all we are saying is that he is Ọba Sayédẹ̀rọ̀'s son, and so—

Ọba Ayíbí And so, licensed to kill?

Ìyámọdẹ No, of course that's not what I mean—

Ọba Ayíbí A prince, and he does not know what it means to attempt the life of his king! Tell us, if it was Sayédẹ̀rọ̀, here on the throne, and someone tried to assassinate him, what would the elders say?

Aṣípa They would of course have—

Ọba Ayíbí Done what? Allowed him to go, with perhaps a gentle pat on his back?

Aṣípa No, no. But all the same, we still plead with you, Kabiyesi.

Ìyámọdẹ He's Ọba Sayédẹ̀rọ̀'s son; your son too.

Ọba Ayíbí And a citizen, like others! Subject to the laws of the land.

Ìyámọdẹ Anger, Kabiyesi! You're saying all this out of anger. And what we're begging you to do is cool down and climb above it.

Aṣípa You have to agree that all trees stand in the sun, but they're not all the

---

[15] If that is a curse, it will not take effect!

same height.

Ọba Ayíbí Ah-ha? But it's the same rain that beats them, not so?

Ìyámọdẹ Even if it's the same rain that falls on all of us, some still remain standing after a storm, where some are squashed.

Aṣípa Our duty is to advise you well. The young man has done wrong, no one can deny it. But if we destroy a fowl for crowing in daylight, what will we do to the dog that barks in the moonlight?

Ìyámọdẹ A slave can be banished forever from the household for a bad offence, but with a trueborn, we do not go further than a reprimand. As we flog him with one hand, we must caress him with the other. Otherwise the entire household will be scattered one day. So—

Ọba Ayíbí Enough! We've heard enough of all that! You can go now!

Ìyámọdẹ Kabiyesi—

Ọba Ayíbí We said, go!

Aṣípa And what answer shall we take back?

Ọba Ayíbí Just what we told you!

Aṣípa Which is?

Ọba Ayíbí Go and tell the elders. There'll be no exception to the laws of our tradition! While these royal sandals adorn our feet, and the crown our head, the law shall be the law! Both for the high and the low, the rich and the poor! Tell them we swore to bring order here, and nothing will stop us from doing that! Now, go!

Aṣípa [*Displeased*] You don't mean that that's your last word, Deoye?

Ọba Ayíbí What! Did I hear you say—did you, I mean, dare to call your Ọba by name!

Aṣípa I'm sorry, Kabiyesi. But remember: there's ruling well, and there's ruling long. No king can last without the wisdom of others to hold him up.

Ìyámọdẹ Yes, Kabiyesi. If a roof seems solid and formidable, it is because it rests on strong pillars.

Ọba Ayíbí Thank you, both of you! But we have not heard yet of two crabs living successfully in the same pot! Or of any ship that sails safely to harbour with two commanding captains on board. We are the Ọba here, we alone, and we intend to rule! Go now, you've said enough, in fact more than enough to strain our temper. Go, and if you have any respect for yourselves, make sure you do not come back here with such a message again! Good day!

[*They go, while he fumes. Enter* **Claudius**.]

Ọba Ayíbí You too, here again?

Claudius Yes. It seems you are about to do a foolish thing.

Ọba Ayíbí And what is that, if I may ask your majesty?

Claudius You want to have the young man hanged.

Ọba Ayíbí Prince Létò?

Claudius Who else are we talking about?

Ọba Ayíbí [*Chuckles*]. Wrong there, Claudius. So you too were fooled! I was only bluffing with the chiefs just now. To frighten them, so they'll take me more seriously. But Létò won't be hanged.

Claudius No?

Ọba Ayíbí No. But jailed, yes — for a long time.

Claudius I'm relieved then. Still it would not be the wisest thing to do.

Ọba Ayíbí What do you mean? Look, let me explain it to you. Tomorrow, the court will sentence him to death for trying to kill the king. But then I intervene, change his sentence from death to life imprisonment. And I'll have him out of the way for years. What could be cleverer than that?

Claudius Yes, that sounds clever enough. But I still don't like it.

Ọba Ayíbí Why not?

Claudius It will only work in your favour for a while, I'm afraid. Soon there'll be delegations upon delegations. Like the one that came just now. Human rights groups. His townspeople. And in particular, his mother and the chiefs. All bringing appeals for his release.

Ọba Ayíbí Yes, that's true. But so what?

Claudius Sooner or later, you'll have to yield. And then he'll come out, more bitter, even more determined to harm you and get rid of you. So where will you run? At the twilight of your life, when you'll want to rest, you will be fighting a new battle for survival!

Ọba Ayíbí You have a better idea then, what I should do?

Claudius I think so. Something much simpler in fact.

Ọba Ayíbí What's that?

Claudius You have no son of your own yet. And you have married Létò's mother, promoted her your Olorì. I believe you can tie these two things together to strengthen yourself.

Ọba Ayíbí Yes, I'm listening.

Claudius Make Létò your Arẹmọ!

Ọba Ayíbí What!

Claudius Don't shout, just listen. Stop the trial, and summon your chiefs and kingmakers. Tell them that you have decided to take their advice, and forgive your step son. Say you agree that it was all youthful exuberance, for which you've now agreed to pardon him. Announce then that, instead of having him punished, you've decided instead to re-channel his youthful energy to some useful work. Say you will be investing him with some political responsibility straightaway, by making him the Arẹmọ.

Ọba Ayíbí The Arẹmọ! My official heir and successor!

Claudius Yes, Kabiyesi.

Ọba Ayíbí I have gone insane then? Is that it? Lost my senses completely?

Claudius Nothing could be more sane, believe me, Kabiyesi.

Ọba Ayíbí Someone who wants to kill me, who accuses me of murdering his father! Pronounce him my immediate successor! That sounds like sanity to you!

Claudius Examine it, quietly. Then you'll see the sense in it.

Ọba Ayíbí By our customs, as you must know, the Arẹmọ is taken as a parallel Ọba. When installed, Létò will have the right henceforth to be treated the same manner I am treated—

Claudius Exactly! He'll enjoy all your privileges—

Ọba Ayíbí Wear a beaded crown, like I do! Sandals of coral! Obtain tributes—

Claudius But with one very important proviso, Kabiyesi. Or have you forgotten? The Arẹmọ, with all his privileges, must never again be seen in the same place as the reigning Ọba! As long as you live, Kabiyesi, your laws forbid that both of you should ever meet again, face to face.

Ọba Ayíbí Yes, that's true, but—

Claudius That's it, Kabiyesi! That's your salvation, can't you see? You make him the Arẹmọ, and naturally you have to send him away. He will go to rule over some other part of your territory. Somewhere very far from here of course. And so, without jailing him, or spilling his blood, you get rid of him till the gods decide that you leave the throne!

Ọba Ayíbí Oh yes, Claudius! Absolutely brilliant! Why didn't I think of this before?

Claudius Grant him this amnesty, and watch everybody hail you for your kindness, your magnanimity. Then you announce that, out of love for his mother and your departed brother, you pronounce him your Aremo, and crown him. Then you send him away!

Ọba Ayíbí Sango o! No wonder Hamlet had such little chance against you!

Claudius When you're a king, you do what you have to do, that's all!

Ọba Ayíbí Oh of course! I forget it was under you that those adventurers came here, tricked our people, and negotiated the treaties that turned us into slaves in our own homeland.

Claudius Are you complaining? The tobacco company that's keeping your cheeks fat and gleaming, Kabiyesi, what difference is there between that, and the slave ships we used to send here? We take what we have to take, even if some people call that exploitation. And we pay those among you willing to co-operate!

Ọba Ayíbí Oh come, you know it's different now! Now we make these sacrifices for progress!

Claudius Sacrifices! Is that what you call your bank account in Switzerland! Those slave dealers of old, what else do you think they called the mirrors and beads and guns and whisky that we brought them? Yes, those second-hand shirts and waistcoats? Were they not 'items of civilisation', just like your tobacco factory!

Ọba Ayíbí Nonsense! We're going to modernise the town, you'll see!

Claudius Ah, yes, you are, aren't you? The old agenda of 'civilising the natives'!

Ọba Ayíbí Be cynical if you wish. But in this reign, we will build roads, houses, bridges, water works, hospitals—

Claudius Yes, hospitals! And I hope you'll build many of them, for the numerous cases of lung cancer and other diseases that you will soon have to deal with! Look, why are we arguing? The beast of power never changes its aims, only its tactics. Fortunately, you and I, we are rulers, and our business is to survive.

Ọba Ayíbí By any means, I agree! But can we ever fathom the depth of your cunning, however, you of the white race? You've had such a long start over us!

Claudius Not in the strategies of survival. In that, we are brothers. This Aremo solution was all invented by your predecessors, don't forget, to get rid of impatient sons!

Ọba Ayíbí Well, I am glad they did. I am going to give orders right away for the young man to be freed. And then I will — wait! Oh no! No...it won't work, Claudius.

Claudius Why won't it?

Ọba Ayíbí Létò... Létò will not accept.

Claudius He won't?

Ọba Ayíbí He's not stupid, you see. He'll see through the whole scheme at once, and suspect a ruse. Or his friends will alert him.

Claudius In that case, don't tell him yourself. Go through someone else — his mother.

Ọba Ayíbí His mother? You mean the old game of 'divide and rule'?

Claudius In the night, when she is lying dazed there in your arms, sell the idea to her. Tell her it's a reward for her devotion, something you've just thought about. Then let her take it to him.

Ọba Ayíbí Great, that's the idea of course! He'll be less suspicious if the offer comes through his mother. Claudius, how can I ever repay you for this?

[*Lights*]

TWELVE

[*Palace courtyard. **Létò**, in chains, is brought to the **Olorì**.*]

Olorì [*To **Guard**]. Take off the chains.

Létò No need, Olorì. I'll keep them.

Olorì Take them off. [***Guard** does so*]. Leave us. [***Guard** goes*].

Létò Your husband, he agrees to this?

Olorì What does that matter? Just come with me.

Létò I need to know, Olorì!

Olorì You're free, aren't you? That means he must have agreed.

Létò Ah! Then it's bound to be a trap.

Olorì Please don't talk like that, Létò.

Létò Did he tell you how he tricked me into this?

Olorì He said the two of you had an argument, and you tried to kill him.

Létò And did he say what he did to provoke me?

Olorì Whatever it was, I want you to forget it now. I've talked to him, he's forgiven you.

Létò Forgiven me! How generous of him!

Olorì Are you ready to listen to me, or not?

Létò I'm ready to listen to my mother. But not to the Olorì.

Olorì Son, your mother is the Olorì, and the Olorì is your mother. We can't revise that any more. Even if I leave the palace today, I'll still remain his wife. So what do you want me to do? I can't deny that he's been good to me.

Létò Because he has to salvage his conscience, don't you understand?

Olorì Are we still on that?

Létò You wanted proof. I gave it to you!

Olorì What proof? That he walked out of your play?

Létò You saw it with your own eyes! He ran out when he recognised his own guilt!

Olorì Don't be ridiculous, Létò! How can that be taken as a proof of something as grievous as murder?

Létò You still don't believe!

Olorì How can I? How can anyone? Look, I asked him, and he told me how angry you made him. You were trying to paint him dirty before his subjects.

Létò Of course he'll say that!

Olorì I would react the same way too, in his shoes. You were maligning him...

Létò If that's how you feel, Olorì, then there's no need any more for this conversation. My father—

Olorì Would not have approved of this way you're carrying on, I tell you! Not the man I lived with for so many years. Your father was never a man of spite or malignity. He would not have been pleased by all this bitterness you're carrying around.—

Létò So why did you think he came back to ask me to avenge him?

Olorì I'm telling you it could not have been him! The late Ọba was a man of compassion! Indeed vengefulness was one of the things he preached often against! Death could not have altered him so completely? Listen, even if it was true, that his brother killed him, I am certain that he would not have ordered you on the road of vengeance. The kind of man he was, he would have asked you instead to leave it all to the gods. Whatever the spirit that came to speak to you, son, it could not have been my husband, I swear to you.

Létò Mother, you don't know what you're saying! Because you live with an evil man, and have accepted him for husband!

Olorì An evil man! I'm asking you to be fair! In the name of all our gods! If he was that evil, why would he have sent me here to free you?

Létò He sent you!

Olorì Yes, and not only to free you, but also to give you an offer you would like.

Létò An offer! What is his game this time?

Olorì Listen to me patiently. He said he'd tried to talk to you, to bring you close to him, but that you rebuffed all his gestures. He says you don't trust him. But at last he's thought of something that he feels should convince you of his good will towards you. An offer of appeasement.

[*Pause*]. Son, he's asking you to become the Arẹmọ!

Létò What! What are you saying, mother?

Olorì As you know, he has no male child of his own. If he goes tomorrow, it will be one of your uncles that will ascend the throne. By rule, it will take another decade or so before it comes to our turn again, in this branch of the family. But all that will change, if he elects you his official Arẹmọ before he dies. So out of love for me, and out of love for your late father, he's proposing it to you—

Létò Me, Arẹmọ!

Olorì I know how happy I'll be, Létò, to see you mount the throne! The throne your father left with such honour! Afterwards, nothing will be left for me to accomplish in this life again, except to dance gracefully to my grave!

Létò Mother, stop dreaming. Arẹmọ! He can propose it, but what of the kingmakers? Or you have forgotten they have a say in it?

Olorì Do you take me for an infant, Létò? Naturally, they were the first I went to see. Baba Oluwo and the others. And they'll be thrilled to have the son of your father on the throne, that it will be like having Ọba Sayédẹ̀rọ̀ back on the throne again. They give their blessings.

Létò And the tobacco company then? Have you asked the white men of the tobacco company whether they'll want me on the throne?

Olorì What do they have to do with it?

Létò Mother, you know they very much come into it. You see their hands everywhere! Soon the company will be ruling our lives, don't say you don't know! Every one in the town will be eating from their palm. They will choose our rulers, choose our wives! They are the new conquerors of our land...

Olorì It still will not matter for you, even then! As the Ọba here, you automatically become the largest shareholder in the company, so—

Létò And the most important killer of our people? How can I be happy to own shares in a company that—

[*A scream. Shouts.* **Àdùkẹ́** *breaks in, carrying a near hysterical* **Túndùn**, *dishevelled, and burnt all over.*]

Létò What, Túndùn! What happened to her, Àdùkẹ́? Tell me!

Túndùn [*Laughing hysterically*]. The Ọba's fac... fac... tobacco factory ... ha...ha... the tobacco factory, we have... hahaha!...

Létò What? What's she saying?

Àdùkẹ́ It's the tobacco factory, Omoba. She—

Túndùn We've set it on fire!

Létò and Olorì What! No!

Túndùn Yes! Fire! Blaum! Blauum! Hahahaha!... Come and see!...fire!...

Létò Oh God!

Túndùn No more, Létò! You won't have to worry any more about the factory!

Létò Oh my God, Túndùn, what have you done!

Túndùn Come and see! The whole place...on fire! Blaum! Blauum!! Hahahaha! Oh Létò, come and see-ee-ee!... [*Collapses.*]

Létò Túndùn!

Olorì No, leave her to me. Àdùkẹ́, help me. Let's carry her to Ìyámọdẹ at once. The bàrà, that's the only place she can be healed now!

[*She and Àdùkẹ́ carry her out.*]

Létò Oh Túndùn, Túndùn! See, the prince drools and dawdles, argues and debates and finds a thousand reasons to stay from action! And yet she, with one bold and daring decision, went and... Oh coward! Coward! Too scared to act? A liar and a murderer, a most brazen and self-centred cheat, a mindless parasite and plunderer of our people and our resources, this villain sits on the throne of my father! He sleeps in the same bed as my mother! And I wander around, half asleep, seeking what? Proof?... Now, see how she has shamed me! Ah, Túndùn, Túndùn...! What's that? Fumes? The smell of smoke! Yes, a big fire out there! What am I waiting for? Time to go and—

[*As he makes to go, enter* **Ọba Ayíbí,** *with guard.*]

Ọba Ayíbí Where's she?

Létò Who, Kabiyesi?

Ọba Ayíbí Don't play games with me! Where's the crazy woman?

Létò If it's Túndùn—

Ọba Ayíbí You sent her, didn't you? Pushed her to it?

Létò Me?

Ọba Ayíbí No need to lie! You sent your woman to burn down our factory!

Létò But that's preposterous!

Ọba Ayíbí It is? Did you think, while you were sending her—did you think, even once, of the workers there? How they will feed afterwards, take care of their families, pay their children's fees? Or of those who invested their money, this money which most of them obtained only through years of hard labour and grinding work?

Létò If you'll let me talk, Kabi—

Ọba Ayíbí No, you listen to me! You, you are a prince, the son of our dear brother and our dear Olorì. So you cannot be touched, according to our traditions. But she is just a plain common girl, and has evidently allowed you to erode her senses! So let me assure you, wherever she may be hiding now, she will be hunted down! We'll find her! And we will punish her, without mercy, for this act of recklessness! Yes, she will serve as an example to all of you who want to impede our progress and cause chaos here!

[*He storms out, followed by guard. As* **Létò** *moves, to follow him, the lights cut into a blackout.*]

THIRTEEN

[*Hamlet/Ophelia.*]

Ophelia Will he find her?

Hamlet The king?

Ophelia Yes, will he find the girl? She's been taken to the bàrà by Ìyámọdẹ, as you know.

Hamlet Yes.

Ophelia His guards won't be able to go there.

Hamlet No, but there are ways.

Ophelia What do you mean?

Hamlet I mean—well, see for yourself!

Ophelia [*Putting on her mask to see*]. Oh God!

Hamlet Precisely. He's already found her.

Ophelia Let's go, let's go! Our mission has failed! I don't want to see the next scene!

[*They go, as she starts to sing her song again. Lights come up on the bàrà.* **Ophelia's** *song trails on in the background throughout the following scene.*]

Létò Yeye

Ìyámọdẹ Ah, I was just coming to see you.

Létò How's she?

Ìyámọdẹ Still unconscious, I'm afraid. Lost too much blood.

Létò Can I... see her?

Ìyámọdẹ She won't be able to talk to you.

Létò All the same—

Ìyámọdẹ How strong are you, Létò?

Létò What do you mean, Yeye?

Ìyámọdẹ I mean, how strong to bear pain?

Létò Pain? What are you trying to tell me?

Ìyámọdẹ You have to be strong, you see.

Létò You mean she's that bad?

Ìyámọdẹ You are a man now, remember that. And one of the marks of manhood is the strength to cope with pain and loss.

Létò Yes, I know that.

Ìyámọdẹ Sometimes, there are mistakes... Sometimes our herbs are not powerful enough. And sometimes...

Létò Tell me Yeye! Tell me the worst!

Ìyámọdẹ Yes, I will. But I want you to know that sometimes our enemies are more cunning, and more diabolical than we imagine.

Létò What's all this got to do with Túndùn?

Ìyámọdẹ Just be patient first. Last night, you see, I found these. [*Shows him.*] You recognise them?

Létò No.

Ìyámọdẹ Pieces of the tobacco plant. Someone had slipped in here, while I was away, and crushed tobacco leaves into my herbs!

Létò What!

Ìyámọdẹ And I found out only this morning, when it was too late!

Létò. Too — what are you saying Yeye?

Ìyámọdẹ I mean, my son, you have to be strong! I couldn't save her.

Létò No, Yeye! No!

Ìyámọdẹ I tried my best, Edumare is my witness! But the tobacco had formed into a poison too lethal for her heart, especially after all all the blood she lost.

Létò Túndùn! She's not...dead?

Ìyámọdẹ I am sorry, my son. Try and be a man.

Létò She's dead!

Ìyámọdẹ Her body's in there. You can go and see her. Your mother's with her.

Létò [*Going, stops*]. No! Not the Olorì! I don't want to see her here! Tell her to leave Túndùn's body alone! Tell her to go away!

Ìyámọdẹ All right, all right, son. Calm yourself. I'll go and tell her.

[*She goes in. Suddenly the lights change, and the stage is invaded by* **Masks**. *It is the* **Tobacco Procession**. **Masks**, *portraying various ailments related to tobacco, even as they stubbornly continue to smoke grotesquely huge cigarettes, cigars and pipes, march and dance to some popular tobacco advert music. Then the* **Ghost of Sayédẹ̀rọ̀**, *Létò's father, and one or two other Masks, come in, from the opposite direction, carrying equally large flit guns and some Red Cross and/or Red Cresent banners. They do not survive the confrontation, as the pro-tobacco masks quickly subdue them. They tie up Létò's father, paste dried tobacco leaves all over him. He bolts up, a phantom tobacco tree doing a weird dance, and then collapses. This is followed by a wild ovation from the tobacco lobby group. The scene ends with them carrying off his body in a triumphant procession.*]

Létò [*Running after them*] Father!

[*Lights return us to the* bàrà, *as before.*]

FOURTEEN

[*At* bàrà, *as before. Enter* **Olorì**, *with calabash of poison. She is crying. She looks round carefully.*]

Olorì Òrìṣà be praised, Yeye's not around! My dear husband! How can I explain?

[*Goes into his* orikí]:

'Ọba Sayédẹ̀rọ̀,
Ọkọ-ọ̀ mi Òrìṣà
Òlòlò
A báni-sọ̀rọ̀-má-tan-ni-je!
Rógun má tẹ́...'

Ah, Kabiyesi!

Will you forgive me? Every woman's joy is to be a good wife to her husband, and a worthy mother to her children. But I have failed in both. I have failed you, failed my only son, failed myself. How can I explain? After you left, I was so alone, so alone. I had nothing, I was afraid. I saw myself returning to the poverty you rescued me from, and I was scared. You had made me queen, brought me into the luxury of the palace! Sayedero, you taught me the life of ease. And then suddenly, you left like that, and I was totally unprepared. When your brother came and made me the offer, I grabbed at it with both hands, yes, with relief and joy! Because I saw it not only as a salvation, but also as a continuation of the nobility that your family has always been famous for. How could I have known that he is the crooked branch in the pile? How could I have known that he is evil, that he was only using me as a shield to cover his misdeeds? Now, see what he has done to our son! See what he has done to his woman, Túndùn! Léto̩ will no longer talk to me! I have failed him, I have not been a good mother, and I have failed you. There's nothing more to live for. So please make a place for me, over there, I'm coming. Perhaps, when we meet again at the feet of our ancestors, you will be able to forgive me.

[*Begins to drink potion as* **Ìyámo̩dẹ** *comes running, and pushes the calabash out of her hand.*]

Ìyámo̩dẹ Abomination! In the bàrà too! No, Olorì, don't do it!

Olorì [*Weakly*]. Let me go, Ìyámo̩dẹ.

Ìyámo̩dẹ But why, why? How did you slip in here?

Olorì Tell my son, Ìyámo̩dẹ, tell him I … I love him! That I'll always love him. Tell him to forgive me…

Ìyámo̩dẹ But he's already forgiven you.

Olorì He has?

Ìyámo̩dẹ Yes, Olorì. He left here just a couple of seconds ago to give you the news. himself. He understands now why you took the decisions you did. He has no anger any more against you.

Olorì Ah, O̩runmila be praised! I can go happily now…

Ìyámo̩dẹ Don't go anywhere, Olorì! Or you'll miss the best part of it all. Léto̩ wants you to be there when it happens!

Olorì What can that be?

Ìyámo̩dẹ Olorì, your son has not only forgiven you, but he's also accepted the offer that Kabiyesi sent to him earlier through you!

Olorì What are you saying, Ìyámo̩dẹ?

Ìyámo̩dẹ I mean that Léto̩ has agreed to be installed as Aremo̩ of the land!

Olorì No!… No! He should not! [*She's coughing badly, as the poison begins to take effect.*] It's… a trick! Tell him I say… tell him that…he…should… not…

[*She collapses, and dies.*]

Ìyámo̩dẹ Don't die, Olorì! Please, not now! Please…oh! Farewell then, [*Begins* **Olorì's** *oriki:*

'O̩mo̩ o̩ló̩ro̩, sùn re!
Alakẹ́ ti nmẹwa rode,
Agbe torí o̩mo̩ dáṣo̩ aró,
Àlùkò torí o̩mo̩ dáṣo osùn,
Àlàkẹ́, lekeleke torí o̩mo̩ rẹ̀ dẹ̀wù funfun…
SÙN RE O!…'

Chanting, tears falling down her face, she closes **Ìyámo̩dẹ's** *eyes. Lights die out.*]

FIFTEEN

[*Hamlet, with* **Ophelia**]

Hamlet Where's his royal highness?

Ophelia Not coming, I'm afraid.

Hamlet Claudius is not coming!

Ophelia I told him why you are asking for a meeting.

Hamlet That's why he's not coming.

Ophelia Yes.

Hamlet I am ashamed of him. See what he has been doing here.

Ophelia He'll have a lot to explain to Ọrunmila when we get back.

Hamlet He knows why we were sent here. Ọrunmila made himself very clear, that Olodumare wants to prevent a bloodbath.

Ophelia We have failed, I'm afraid. History's going to repeat its gruesome self. Just like in our story, the play's going to end with the palace littered with corpses.

Hamlet All because of King Claudius! Our mission's going to fail completely. Certainly we should not have come with him.

Ophelia Already Olorì has killed herself. And you know what will follow. Létò will want to kill the king, and then afterwards kill himself.

Hamlet Pity! Is there anything we can do?

Ophelia No. Létò is very bitter, and will have his revenge. At the coronation ceremony, when he's being crowned as the Arẹmọ, he'll kill the king. He's got it all worked out.

Hamlet How?

Ophelia Well, doesn't it surprise you that he accepted to be crowned as the Arẹmọ in the first place? And that he still decided go with it, even after the death of the two people he loved most?

Hamlet Yes.

Ophelia He's insisting too, that the installation be finished before either of them is buried.

Hamlet Very strange, I admit. Perhaps he needs the title for something else.

Ophelia For vengeance. You see, the coronation ceremony includes a sword fight in the bàrà, between the king and the Arẹmọ. All very symbolic, mind you, with wooden swords. But Létò has planned it that this time, they'll be real swords, and that the one he's using will also be tipped with poison!

Hamlet Ah!

Ophelia That's how he plans to kill the Ọba, and take his revenge. In the shrine, where no one will be present, except the priestess whose loyalty to his dead father has never wavered!

[**Claudius** *enters abruptly.*]

Claudius But he won't, you see!

Hamlet What?

Claudius He won't kill the Ọba as he plans.

Ophelia Why not?

Claudius Because I've warned Ayíbí.

Hamlet You did what!

Claudius I warned the Ọba. I told him what his nephew is planning to do. And he's made his own counter-plan.

Hamlet I hope it's all because of our mission here that you did that. To prevent bloodshed.

Claudius Well—

Ophelia Wait. I'd like to hear what the counter-plan is.

Claudius Simple. The Arẹmọ will fight the Ọba, as prescribed. And he will kill him with the poisoned sword.

Ophelia But I thought just now, you said—

Claudius But it won't be the Ọba, you see? Because they will both be masked, Ayíbí is going to ask Ìyámọdẹ to play the king's role in his stead, in the mock fight.

Ophelia Ìyámọdẹ!

Claudius Yes. It will be the disloyal Ìyámọdẹ under the mask. And when Létò kills her, he too will be killed by one of the guards! Thus with one stone, the Ọba disposes of two troublesome birds!

Ophelia Incredible! Who gave Ọba Ayíbí all these ideas?

Hamlet It wasn't you, by any chance, your majesty?

Claudius Well, I can't deny it. He got some tips!

Hamlet 'Some tips'! What game are you playing, King Claudius? Why are you doing all this?

Claudius I'll tell you. Because I too, I need to redeem myself. All these centuries that I have borne the opprobrium of men! How do you think I feel? Each time they told our story, who was always the villain, always the scoundrel, always the evil one! Claudius! Yes, me! Such a long and painful burden of shame! How do you think I've felt? But you were the heroes! Hamlet! Ophelia! You were the ones everyone sought to be! The ones remembered with affection! But Claudius? Claudius! Well, now, at last, all that's going to change! The history books will be re-written. The fable will reconstruct itself. This time, one person alone will be left standing, among all the corpses. And it'll be me! Me, my reincarnated self! Me to bury you all, and establish my own glory! At last!

Ophelia I can't believe this! How vile! You mean, all these centuries, death has not changed you a bit!

Hamlet What will you say, when we get back? How will you explain to Ọrunmila?

Claudius He knows. He must know the anguish of living in perpetual blemish among the ancestors.

Ophelia And that's why he gave us this chance to come back, isn't it? To allow us to redeem ourselves. But not by sowing further discord among our successors.

Claudius Say what you please. I am enjoying myself. And I am going now to watch the rest of the show! See you later! [*Goes.*]

Hamlet What shall we do? You know Ọrunmila will not intervene.

Ophelia I've tried my best, I know. If only men would not insist on repeating our errors!

Hamlet I will not give up yet. There must be something we can do to save the situation.

Ophelia Too late, I'm afraid, Hamlet. See, they've already gone into the bàrà, and the ceremony has reached its point of intoxication. We can no longer intervene.

Hamlet We'll see.

[*Rapid transfer of lights to the bàrà.*]

SIXTEEN

[*The bàrà: the installation ceremony in progress…*]

[*The drums are in their final, ecstatic mood now, with the songs and incantations filling the grove. In response, the dance of the masks has also climbed into a frenzied state.*

Abruptly the music changes, turns sober.

Solemn, one of the masks hands out two swords to the other two, who now confront each other, moving to the beats.

The talking drum alone speaks to them, calling out their ancestral names.

The antagonists circle each other warily, in a verbal duel:]

1st Mask *Ilá tiiri!*

2nd Mask *Ilá gbo! Awo!*

[*Then they bound forward and clash, briefly, bouncing back at once to resume their stalking. Then for a second time:*]

2nd Mask *Ogbón lẹnú mọ̀, ẹnu ò m'èrú!*

1st Mask *Bẹ́nbẹ́ ò dún gùdù, árábá ò wó jẹjẹ! Awo!*

[*They clash again and spring apart.*]

2nd Mask *Níjọ́ inú bá bígi, igi á ya lomi!*

1st Mask *Níjọ́ ínú bá bómi, omi á gbégi lọ!*

2nd Mask *Gbogbogbo lọwọ́-ọ́ yọ jorí!*

1st Mask *Gbògbògbò lògọ́mò-ó yọ ju ígi ọpẹ!*

1st Mask *Tólógbò bá réku, dandan ni kó gbe mì! Eriwo-o-o!*

[*This third time, he strikes before the other **Mask** can respond. The latter falls back, wounded.*]

Ìyámọdẹ No! No! I'm wounded! You've cut me!

[*Throws off mask to grab at wounded hand.*]

Létò What, you, Ìyámọdẹ?

Ìyámọdẹ Yes.

Létò The Kabiyesi?

Ìyámọdẹ Is there. He asked me to carry the mask for him!

Ọba Ayíbí [*Shouting*]. Guards! Guards! Come in now! This is the moment!

Létò Oh is that your trick then? Die too! [*Stabs him*]

Ọba Ayíbí Guards! [*Guards rush in*]

Ọba Ayíbí Arrest him! Murder! He…he…

[*Dies. General pandemonium*]

Létò [*Laughing*]. On the other side now, Kabiyesi! When we meet again on the other side, with my father, we will continue our argument! [*To guards*]. Come, my friends, I'll go with you, willingly. I am eager to be put on trial, publicly. Then I can show the whole world what the vile king has been doing to our people! Let us go!

[*Enter **Àdùkẹ́, Baba Aṣípa, Hamlet,** and **Ophelia***]

Aṣípa Ah there you are, my son!

Hamlet Prince, you didn't kill yourself!

Létò No, of course not. What for? Who would tell the story of this villain?

Ophelia I'm so, so glad then!

Àdùkẹ́ And I. Congratulations! Here, have a drink to your victory!

[*Hands him a calabash, which he drains.*]

Létò Thank you! I needed that! How relieved you must feel at last, that the spirit of your friend is avenged!

Àdùkẹ́ Yes, truly avenged now, Prince! By that drink in your hand!

Létò What do you mean?

[*The calabash clatters down from his hand as he falls. General exclamations.*]

Àdùkẹ́ You saw the wreck you made of her life? Think you can get away with that? No, never! Now the poor woman can truly rest in her grave!

Aṣípa Arrest her!

Àdùkẹ́ Too late, Baba. We're all going! I too have already had my drink. Goodbye to this cruel world!

[*Falls, dead*]

Aṣípa What a sad day! What a story! Don't just stand there now. Help me, gather the corpses.

[*A dirge starts. Gradually the lights pick out the **Masks**, as they join the singing and dancing. Slow fade out.*]

END

GLOSSARY

Page 159 *Masque of Betrayed Love*

Àdùkẹ́: I have found the husband
I will worship till death
Come rejoice with me
I have found the man
I will adore till I die!

Òjẹ̀: I have found a wife
A woman to cherish
I have found a woman
I have found a woman
A wife like a flower!

Àdùké: Whoever does not know
How sweet life can be
Should go and find a husband! (2ce)
I have found a husband
I have found a husband
Love is sweeter than honey!

Òjè: My wife, beware
Love can turn to rags
For love is fragile
Love can be shredded
And many are its enemies (2ce)

Both Whatever storm so wishes
Can buffet us
Any time it chooses (2ce)
There is nothing at all
No power anywhere
That can separate us!

Page 178
Ọba Sayédèrọ
My husband like a god
He with a stammer
Whose counsel is never false
Who is never disgraced in war...
Ah, Kabiyesi!

Page 179
Daughter of the Wealthy, rest in peace!
Alake, whose beauty shone in public,
The agbe bird who, to nurse children, dyed her clothes in indigo,
The aluko bird who, instead, dyed hers in camwood,
Alake, the cattle egret whose own clothes were sparkling white,
REST WELL IN HEAVEN! ...

Page 182
1st Mask The okro stays too long unplucked!
2nd Mask It grows over-ripe! Cult secret!
[*Then they bounce forward and clash, briefly bouncing back at once to resume their stalking. Then for a second time:*]
2nd Mask Wisdom's what the mouth knows, never deceit!
1st Mask The sound of the Bénbé drum is not a whisper, the araba tree can never fall unnoticed!
[*They clash again and spring apart.*]
2nd Mask The day the tree gets angry, the day it crashes on the water!
1st Mask The day the water gets angry, that day it carries the tree away!
2nd Mask The arm always shows itself confidently above the head!
1st Mask Arrogantly does the palm frond display above the palm tree!
1st Mask If the cat sees a rat, it must swallow it!

Book Reviews

Natasha Distiller, *Shakespeare & the Coconuts: On Post-apartheid South African Culture*
Johannesburg: Wits University Press, 2012, 225pp.
ISBN 9781868145614, £25.95

Natasha Distiller writes with the urgency of a polemicist and, contradictorily, the coolness of a cultural theorist. 'Looking at Shakespeare in South African literary history', she argues, 'is one way to look afresh at our cultural politics, particularly in the current context where racial identities are being hardened and simplified' (143). She places Shakespeare at the heart of a fierce and far-from-resolved debate about 'English', 'Englishness' and 'English Literature' in a country bent on identifying itself afresh, but she keeps in focus South African writers (Plaatje, Themba, Modisane, Nkosi, Mphahlele) and politicians (Malema, Mbeki, Zuma). Given particular prominence are her references to Kapano Matlwa's novel, *Coconut* (2007).

The coconut – 'black outside and white inside' – is an easily maligned figure in post-colonial countries, and part of Distiller's project is to assert the viability of 'coconuttiness' in post-apartheid South Africa: 'the African coconut is both/and, both Englished and transforming of Englishness. And this is a legitimate South African identity' (45). Without a recognition of its complex history, South Africa will find itself a post-colonial victim of the 'toxic politics of the binary formation' (99). There is much more than this in the supple arguments deployed in this book, a painstakingly articulated essay on cultural politics. Or, to be more accurate, a collection of six related essays on the cultural politics of post-apartheid and post-Mbeki ('the coconut president' – [126]) South Africa.

The Introduction and the first essay (Chapter 1) chart the territory that subsequent essays explore: 'If, for Plaatje, Shakespeare was the embodiment of what English had to offer, in our times Shakespeare may be the embodiment of its empty promises' (47). Distiller's judgments are characteristically inflected and provisional. In Chapter 2, she mulls over various claims that South African violence echoes the violence of Shakespeare's England, touching on the Anthony Sher/Greg Doran production of *Titus Andronicus* (1995) which she blisteringly attacks in Chapter 3. The production at the Market Theatre was less warmly received than Sher, returning rich in reputation to his homeland, expected. With irresistible clarity, Distiller tells us why in terms that are chilling for well-meaning British readers: 'Sher's inability to see other than from his own centre of experience is more than the narcissism of the great actor; it is a typical element of liberalism' (91). It might be seen as ironic that this *Titus* fared much better in liberal England, which sees South Africa from its own centre of experience. In Chapter 4, Distiller looks for the traces of a distinctively South African Shakespeare in school editions of *Macbeth*, and finds little of comfort. In a hard-pressed educational system, the moribund 'universal' Shakespeare is aimlessly revived. That is in line, perhaps, with the subject of Chapter 5, the 'African Renaissance' trumpeted by Thabo Mbeki. In a broadly reflective Chapter 6, Distiller proposes that 'Mbeki's Shakespeare becomes emblematic of a fatal character flaw' (157), an alienation from his constituency that was expertly exploited by the populist, Jacob Zuma.

Shakespeare and the Coconuts is designedly provocative, but with the kind of provocation that cannot be easily ducked. Distiller's prose is finely chiselled, only occasionally overloaded with the professionally correct style of academics in discourse with each other. (Jarringly ugly Latinate buzz words – 'instantiate', 'imbricate' – are weapons of intimidation, aren't they?) And it is a curious quirk that whenever Shakespeare becomes 'he' or Shakespeare's 'his', 'he' and 'his' are quarantined in single inverted commas. I would like to ask Distiller why 'she' insists on this, because 'her' answers to the questions 'she' asks are so informative.

Peter Thomson
University of Exeter

Ashwin Desai, *Reading Revolution: Shakespeare on Robben Island*
Pretoria: Unisa Press, 2012
ISBN 978-1-86888-683-8 (hb) £34.95, (pb) £10.22

Much has been written about Shakespeare in the post-colonial context, including Christopher Balme's *Decolonizing the Stage: Theatrical Syncretism and Post-Colonial Drama* (1999), Thomas Cartelli's *Repositioning Shakespeare* (1999), Ania Loomba's *Shakespeare, Race, and Colonialism* (2002). More specific to the South African context there is Antony Sher and Gregory Doran's *Woza Shakespeare!: Titus Andronicus in South Africa* (1996), Ania Loomba and Martin Orkin's edited collection *Post-colonial Shakespeares* (1998), Natasha Distiller's *South Africa, Shakespeare, and Post-colonial Culture*

(2004) and her more recent *Shakespeare and the Coconuts* (2012), alongside articles published in the *Journal of the Shakespeare Society of Southern Africa*.

2012 was heralded 'A Year of Shakespeare', framing the London 2012 Olympic and Paralympic ceremonies, and the parallel 'Cultural Olympiad', which included almost 100 theatrical productions, television programmes, radio broadcasts, digital projects and museum exhibits that explored the work of Shakespeare. This has led to *African Theatre 12* focussing on the Globe to Globe festival, which staged 37 Shakespearean plays and a dramatic rendering of one of his narrative poems in as many languages by companies from around the globe; and a network of Shakespeare scholars, supported by a UK Arts and Humanities Research Council Grant, have created the www. yearofshakespeare.com web-site and will publish *A Year of Shakespeare: Reliving the World Shakespeare Festival* (2013).

Although many scholars have argued that Shakespeare is part of a Eurocentric canon that has marginalised black voices, this book provides a solid body of evidence that reveals the extent to which the Bard can be subversive in specific contemporary contexts and continues to speak to universal human experiences and emotions.

One truly universal human trait is the desire to know the thoughts and experiences of others. For me, one of the joys of a second-hand book is finding the notes of someone else written in small characters in the margins. One of the many strengths of this book is how Desai discovers the engagement of various prisoners with Shakespeare and other classic European texts, including Nelson Mandela, Thabo Mbeki, Govan Mbeki, Neville Alexander, Ahmed Kathrada, Strini Moodley and Walter Sisulu. Through unstructured interviews that cut across significant political divides, and the experiences of prisoners both in 'single' and 'general' sections of Robben Island, Desai movingly illustrates how the few texts that made it onto the Island not only relieved the tedium and stress of the mindless, soul-destroying work that defined prisoners' endless days, but also stimulated study, opened new worlds to long-term prisoners, and facilitated heated debate. Men who arrived unable to read or write were taught by others who were teachers, lecturers, doctors or lawyers on sand or slates spirited in from the quarry of hard labour. The individual narratives highlights why Robben Island has been termed the University of the Liberation in South Africa. It also highlights the ironies of apartheid, as the 'warders of the master race', who were often poorly educated and resistant to knowledge, censored the assignments of prisoners who were often engaged in post-graduate study.

The individual life-stories, or what Goodson calls 'life politics' (2006), suggests the complex roles that literature played in the prisoners' political debates, personal development and resistance to apartheid's attempts to render them 'kaffir[s] … a number … nothing' (Tshwete, quoted Desai, ix). The life stories include that of atheist Sony Venkatrathnam's (member of the African Peoples' Democratic Union of Southern Africa) story of how he recovered his confiscated copy of *The Complete Works of Shakespeare* by saying it was his Bible and he'd left it in the storeroom. He focusses on how the selections his comrades made and noted in the margins of the text 'made so many lines resonate with new meaning' (14). He analyses the themes running through these choices, including confronting time, love, tragedy and loneliness.

Mzwandile Mdingi (ANC, from a Unity Movement background) draws attention to the importance of an ethical education, and how this related to the two-sided education on the island: literacy and political education (35); and how both were aimed at preparing them for freedom.

Ahmed Kathrada (Indian Congress alliance with ANC) finished four degrees in prison, included a BA in Bibliography, because it would strengthen his position to be prison librarian. We perceive his delight in books, particularly in his ten-year correspondence with Zuleikha Mayat, who sent him an Urdu into English dictionary and a cook-book, *Indian Delights*; which were both rejected by the authorities.

Marcus Solomon (founder member of National Liberation Front) highlights the importance of reciprocal learning and teaching, and what might constitute 'an alternative education for liberation'. He continues to work closely with children, seeing education as important to creating the belief that people can be agents of change.

And yet, *Reading Revolution* goes beyond tracing untold stories of the struggle against apartheid. It asks: 'What then of the present? Are the new political leaders upholding the traditions that were so central to the struggle to defeat apartheid and build a new South Africa?' (9-10); and sadly the answer is negative. Desai ends his introduction by suggesting that remembering the stories of learning on Robben Island must be seen not only as an act of historical memory but also as a critical examination of the past as a means of responding to challenges in the present. Not to be imprisoned by history but to make it. (10)

This is a moving call for education of a high standard in (South) Africa. It also celebrates the power of literature, no matter its source, suggesting its implicit ability to access peoples' minds and hearts. *Reading Revolution* includes invaluable primary resource material, has a good bibliography and is visually powerful too.

I would recommend this book as an essential read both to specialist scholars of Shakespeare and anyone who love books.

Yvette Hutchison
School of Theatre, Performance and Cultural Policy Studies
University of Warwick

Mufunanji Magalasi, *Stage Drama in Independent Malawi: 1980 to 2002*

Zomba: Chancellor College Publications, 2012. Available at Chanco Publications MK4500.
ISBN 978-99960-23-20-0, (Malawi) US$22 (Africa) US$26 (Europe & World)

No substantial publication seeking to give an historically based overview of Malawian theatre has been produced since Chris Kamlongera's PhD in 1987. *Stage Drama in Independent Malawi* is also drawn from a PhD and continues roughly from where Kamlongera left off. Mufunanji Magalasi looks at two specific trajectories of Malawian drama: that produced by the hugely influential Chancellor College and its attendant Travelling Theatre, and popular theatre, in both Chichewa and English, produced in the area of the city of Blantyre. Magalasi is aware that this means not paying attention to increasingly important Theatre for Development initiatives or to the school drama competitions which draw many young people into the acting profession, but his repeated referencing of these theatrical areas ensures we are not unaware of the wider theatrical environment.

The period covered is dramatic in itself, dealing with the latter half of the dictatorship of President for Life Hastings Banda, through to the move to a multi-party state and subsequent elections ushering in a new leadership in 1994. While all the plays looked at from the earlier period, with the exception of Chichewa comedies, deal with coded critiques of the Banda state, Magalasi charts a subsequent rise in concern with a range of social issues dominating the theatre in more recent years.

Stage Drama in Independent Malawi devotes a section each to university and popular drama. For university drama this means four chapters, each devoted to a particular decade from 1970, with the final one just looking at 2000-2002. Popular theatre is dealt with in two chapters, one on Chichewa, and the other on English language productions, and the whole is framed by a rather over-PhD-ish, although contextually quite helpful Introduction, and a short Conclusion offering some thoughts on constructive ways forward for Malawian theatre. In each of his main chapters Magalasi follows a similar format. He offers an overview of the context of the time and the kind of theatre concerned and then gives detailed description and analysis of three or four key plays, which one presumes – it is not explicitly stated – are representative of the wider body of work at the time. This formula is a little ponderous and repetitive, but it does leave the reader with a clear sense of developing trajectories in theatrical performance.

The early parts of this book demonstrate just how oppressive and pervasive the Banda regime was in every area of Malawian life. They are also a testament to how the theatre, through necessarily coded stories and language, repeatedly sought to criticise and challenge the state, even when this led to a risk of imprisonment, summary violence and even death. All plays seeking permission to perform publicly under Banda had to submit to censorship and it becomes clear that censorship was not only of political criticism but extended to morality, so that swearing or discussion of the sexual could also become grounds for refusal and led to a particularly prudish performance tradition.

Magalasi charts a dynamic university theatre pioneered initially by a group of expatriates in the late 1960s, which began by putting on English language plays from around the world. However, encouragement for Malawian writing was present from early on, and particularly supported by the university Travelling Theatre movement which saw plays being toured around the country throughout the 1970s and 80s, and therefore responded to audience interest in topics that ordinary people perceived to be relevant to their lives. There are a number of key names in the Malawi university drama narrative: playwrights Lance Ngulube and Innocent Banda, and teachers James Gibbs and Chris Kamlongera among them, but the name which keeps recurring in the narrative of a university producing an extraordinary amount of theatre despite limited resources and very limited personnel, is that of David Kerr. Kerr worked in Malawi over a number of time periods but appears to have been most influential in the 1980s when his socialist sensibilities encouraged highly democratic processes in both play creation and organisation of the Travelling Theatre movement. He also joined many Malawians in pushing as far as he possibly could in allegorical critique of the government. Topics discussed in key plays include repeated allegories of abusive leadership, discussion of corruption and criticism of Banda's widely hated Official Government Hostess, Cecilia Kadzamira. Kerr also seems to have been important in promoting experimentation with form. Magalasi points to a number of plays of the 80s and 90s in which Kerr played a key role and which were influenced by Brechtian techniques. These included *They Call it Africa*, about aliens coming to earth and witnessing abuses of power throughout history, and *Refugees* which was based on Brecht's *Mother Courage*. By the early 90s, thankfully, the writing was on the wall for Banda, but only in his most recent example from the new millennium does Magalasi tell of a play, *Tippex*, by veteran playwright Lance Ngulube, which is finally able to openly analyse and condemn the Banda regime.

Both Chichewa and English language popular commercial theatre emerged from links with the university via travelling shows where entrepreneurs realised there was the potential to make money from the large crowds attending popular plays. Commercial English language theatre dates back to the 1970s and Magalasi refers to a number of more or less ephemeral groups before focussing the bulk of his analysis on the evidently charismatic if somewhat authoritarian actor/director/playwright Dunduzu Chisiza Jr and his Wakhumbata Theatre. The prolific Chisiza was US trained and appears to have dominated the commercial English language theatre scene with plays that dealt with serious social issues but retained their popularity with audiences by incorporating buffoonery and portrayals of glamorous high-life. This section also features the only mentioned woman director,

Gertrude Kamkwatira and an analysis of her play, *It's My Fault*, which looks at domestic violence and urges women to find the strength to resist sexual oppression. Chichewa drama apparently emerged only in the 1980s. Like its English language counterpart, actor/managers predominate and dominate their companies. All the commercial companies recruit actors with relatively low educational achievement and no prior actor training who are therefore substantially subordinate to those running the theatres. However, in the Chichewa theatre Magalasi describes how often illiterate actors are given a scenario rather than a play script and improvise around that, with plays being mounted after only two or three rehearsals. The commercial theatre also suffers from a severe lack of actresses. As in many African nations women on the commercial stage are often seen as 'loose', and in some cases men have to act the female parts for lack of volunteers. This theatre is apparently exclusively focussed on comedy, with many jokes addressed direct to the audience, and loosely constructed plays made up of a series of comic episodes.

Magalasi gives considerable space to Malawian debates about what many see as 'substandard' commercial performance. Critics apparently complain of staging in a simple straight line of chairs, of little actor interaction and of focus on comic language. Magalasi attempts to understand how these performance modes arose and contests claims that the comedy resides only in jokes and language rather than in more complex acting and plot construction.

Despite commercial theatre being inspired by university theatre there appears to be a great gulf between the two, with commercial performances being seen as of poor theatrical standard and university drama criticised as being 'elitist, inaccessible and obscure' (236-7). The conclusion argues for better support in the face of a government only interested in 'so-called presentation of the Malawian heritage' (237), and for a need for training and innovation in the commercial theatre.

Mufunanji Magalasi provides his reader with a clear picture of the major strands of national theatre in the genres and periods under consideration, with a particular emphasis on the political. It is a shame that information on dates and performances is patchy and that there is not more of the very interesting snippets on audience response and form in Malawian theatre. Some more substantial rewriting from the PhD form might have resulted in a less formulaic text, and certainly the book would have benefitted from editing of occasional lapses in English. However this is a valuable contribution to the project of recording Africa's theatre histories. The African theatre scholar is gradually being enabled to see not only the many parallels in national experiences of, for instance, how theatre has been used as an instrument of political dissent, and how so many African theatres struggle with the idea of women on stage, but also key national differences. I had never heard of a purely comic African language theatre tradition, and the Travelling Theatre phenomenon common to many Anglophone African nations appears to have been particularly influential in Malawi.

Jane Plastow
University of Leeds

Victor N. Gomia, *Mobilizing the Hordes: Radio Drama as Development Theatre in Sub-Saharan Africa*
Bamenda: Angaa Research & Publishing CIG, 2012. *Distributed by African Books Collective*
ISBN 9789956727544. £24.95

Mobilizing the Hordes is a difficult book to review. To my knowledge, nobody has written at length on this topic, so a reviewer needs to be somewhat protective of such innovation. Nonetheless, it is impossible to avoid pointing out that the book has problems of consistency, content and structure.

The core and most useful part of the book is a chapter (African Radio Drama and Theatre for Development) showing the results of a survey on radio listening in two Anglophone, Cameroonian regional capitals (Buea and Baganda). Gomia describes the research and provides a sensible analysis. Some of the significant findings are that entertainment programmes are more popular than news and current affairs, and that 58% of the respondents said they listened to radio drama.

A rather different piece of research is found in Chapters 5 and 6 in which the author summarises the plots of a 'corpus' of radio play texts (some never produced or broadcast); these were discovered in the archives of a sponsor for the radio drama competition, the Guinness Cameroon Radio Drama corpus. It allows the author to make a close textual analysis of the texts, chosen not on a random basis, but to illustrate the variety of attitudes to modernisation shown by their authors. Gomia also uses the corpus as the material for what he calls 'radio theatre aesthetics'. This is mostly a useful 'How-to' chapter on the basic techniques to be learned by a radio drama script-writer.

The main problem with *Mobilizing the Hordes* is that these empirically well-grounded sections do not significantly support each other, nor do they really grow out of the much more theoretical earlier chapters. Although sometimes referring to the origins of radio drama in Africa, Chapters 1, 2 and 3 are much more concerned with conventional Theatre for Development designed for the stage or street. This has some relevance to developmental drama in general (especially a useful discussion in Chapter 1 on the word 'popular'), but hardly requires three chapters when there are so many already published surveys of this material. More damaging still, the thrust of these three chapters is to valorise the role of the participant audience, which forces Gomia into some theoretical somersaults when it comes to showing the benefits to African development of radio drama, with its limited opportunities for participation.

There are other less obvious contradictions. The title of the book, with its pejoratively loaded word 'hordes' contradicts the positive role Gomia allocates to the 'masses'. Another contradiction is to do with language. Gomia endorses the need for development communication to use 'the languages spoken by the people' (232), but the language of the plays which provide the bulk of Gomia's evidence is English, owing to the rules of the Guinness competition.

A further issue which troubles me is that the book's subtitle is 'Radio drama as Development Theatre in Sub-Saharan Africa'. The first three chapters do range over most of the sub-continent, but the chapters on radio drama focus predominantly on Anglophone Cameroon and to a lesser extent on South Africa and Malawi. Admittedly, it is not easy to find information about radio drama in Africa, but the information does exist. Gomia flatters me when he suggests that I am the only scholar to have provided 'informed academic discourse on African Radio Theatre' (36). In truth, there are other contributions to this growing academic field. Gomia is unlucky in that two very useful texts by Manyozo and Gunner, Ligaga & Moyo were published in 2011, too late for Gomia to draw upon. All the same, Gomia misses older sources, such as the 2000 collection by Fardon & Furniss, which is a very valuable source of information about community and national radio in, among others, Burkina Faso, Mali, Niger, Zambia and Rwanda. Other information can easily be found on the internet by such authors as Dina Ligaga (Kenya), and Mirirai Moyo (Zimbabwe), while numerous articles on the developmental uses of radio drama can be found on the Drumbeat website.

Although Gomia is comfortable with the technique of radio script-writing, he neglects the changes in radio technology which have taken place during the last two decades. The switch from analogue to digital recording, editing and even receiving radio drama means that it is even cheaper to produce and easier for artists to learn the technology than in the analogue period (1940s to the early 1990s). The use of podcasting is at present only accessible to listeners with either computer or smart phone access to the internet. However, the spread of telephone technology on the continent is so rapid that it is likely to become a 'popular' medium in the next decade, thus opening not only new ways of recording and transmitting radio drama, but also of receiving it. Already, at the University of Botswana a popular stage theatre process called SCARS uses a computer podcasting radio show and a blog page in order for listeners to discuss the issues of gender-based violence raised in the plays. Thus the heated reactions of audiences to the live plays can be followed up by more measured reflections through written blogs or radio interviews.

This articulates with another issue that *Mobilising the Hordes* does not completely reflect, namely the changing industrial base of African radio drama. Gomia suggests that the two main funders are Government and the private sector (20). This ignores the rising role of NGOs in the funding of African radio drama in the last two decades. In the future, with the use of digital technology it is possible that community-based organisations with almost no funding but relying on voluntary work, would be able to run community stations.

Finally, there are numerous errors that the author or his editors should have attended to. ChiBemba, which is a Zambian language is allocated to Malawi (43). There are several long quotations which are not indented, thus making it unclear to the reader where the quotation ends (e.g. Harding, 246). Sometimes authors are confused, for example Martin Byram with Dale Byam. There are a distressing number of typos, and several authors who are quoted or referred to do not appear in the bibliography.

Although I am concluding that Gomia's attempt to identify radio drama as a 'viable alternative' to a theatre of conscientisation or 'Literature of combat' (xii) is not proven, there is enough informative material, especially on Cameroonian radio drama, to tempt the reader to buy the book as a founding block for further research on this potentially important field.

David Kerr
University of Botswana

Books Received

Bole Butake. *Dance of the Vampires and Six Other Plays.* Langaa Research and Publishing CIG, Mankon, Bamenda, 2013. ISBN 9956 790 39 7 (pb) £24.95. Distributed by African Books Collective, Oxford (A review of this collection will be carried in *African Theatre 13*)

Bereket Habte Selassie, *The Devil in God's Land. An Eritrean Play* Dar-Es-Salaam: Mkuki na Nyota Publishers Ltd, 2011, vii+117pp. ISBN 9789987081615, n. p.

Printed and bound by CPI Group (UK) Ltd, Croydon, CR0 4YY

13/04/2025

14656514-0002